MW00573238

A long time ago in a galaxy far, far away.....

PAUL DUNCAN

THE STAR WARS™ ARCHIVES

EPISODES I–III
1999–2005

TASCHEN

Contents

Foreword

By George Lucas

Movies are an illusion. Cinema is the art of the moving image; the moving image isn't any more truthful than are cave paintings, or hieroglyphics, or the Sistine Chapel. What the artist finds is the truth behind the "truth." Art portrays the aspirations of the society in which it is made.

Two of the most important things human beings do are expressing themselves and communicating with others. How they do that and how clever they are in doing that have always been some of humanity's major accomplishments. Children learn to scratch on rocks just as the cavemen did. And even though the technology is extremely simple — it's a stick and a rock — part of human nature is to innovate, to figure out better ways to do things.

I'm not that keen on technology. I'm a storyteller, but to enable me to tell my stories, I've had to develop the necessary technology. After all, to do a moving portrayal on a cave wall of a dying bison, early man had to invent red paint.

While doing *Star Wars*, I was very limited in what I could achieve in terms of the story's scope. I couldn't show large street scenes; I couldn't have alien characters that were not anthropomorphic walking around on the streets. I couldn't have them as characters. Throughout the making of the *Star Wars* films, I was struggling with such questions as, "How do I create Jabba the Hutt? How do I create a Yoda, who's only a foot and a half high, and have him believably play a scene?" I could imagine these characters, but I couldn't realize them. It took a lot of effort and talent on the part of many people to manipulate the puppets, latex, and remote-control systems that allowed us to create these creatures. Even then I was unable to move them around to any significant degree.

With the digital technology available today, I've finally reached a point where I can move such characters freely on a set, and I can get better, more dramatic performances out of them. That's been my challenge. It's the same with sets. In the past, I couldn't afford to go to a place in the story that would involve a very large set. Now I can expand the environments in which I'm able to place my stories, which is obviously very important in the fantasy genre.

I put the brakes on my imagination when I was writing the original *Star Wars* because I wanted to write only what I knew I could realize on film. And even then, I was writing things that I wasn't quite sure I could create

0.1 The Phantom Menace (1999) Teaser poster released November 10, 1998, designed by Ellen Lee. The long shadow of Darth Vader hangs over the film.
0.2 Revenge of the Sith (2005) Concept art by Erik Tiemens, dated January 16, 2003, showing Anakin Skywalker being rebuilt as Darth Vader.
0.3 Revenge of the Sith (2005) George Lucas poses with many of the computer-generated characters and objects that populate the prequel trilogy.

on-screen. And therein was a large risk. I have taken those risks on all the *Star Wars* movies, and I'm taking them on *Episode I: The Phantom Menace*. Can I pull this off? But the idea of being able to explore my imagination and make it literal is exciting: it moves me forward to try to get my visions onto the screen.

Art Is Technology

In the 20th century, cinema was celluloid; the cinema of the 21st century will be digital. Movie theaters are going to have better presentation, seating, and entertainment services. And the quality of the experience in terms of the sound and the images on-screen will increase — especially when theaters become all digital. You'll have a better, clearer, more realistic moviegoing experience.

Digital technology will bring down the cost of making movies. More people will have access to rendering epic or fantasy stories. It used to be that literary genres such as science fiction and fantasy couldn't be portrayed adequately on film because they had to be shown as opposed to suggested in words, as they are in books. The gap between those two media is going to close up.

Black-and-white silent movies will still be made, even in the digital era, because there are a million ways to tell a story. The creator's palette has been continually widened. It was the same with painters during the Renaissance, most of whom were technologists because of the huge emphasis on creating new colors and different ways of dealing with plaster and metal. Artists have always been coping with the limits of technology.

When French director Georges Méliès showed men on the moon in 1902's *A Trip to the Moon*, it was the first time anyone had tried to make the unreal real in a moving photographic medium. That magic trick was the start of an art form. *King Kong*, in 1933, was a landmark in stop-motion photography. The art of moving puppets was then perfected in the '60s and '70s with Ray Harryhausen's *Jason and the Argonauts* and *Sinbad* series. Stanley Kubrick's *2001: A Space Odyssey*, in 1968, represented the state of the art of special effects up to that point. In 1977, *Star Wars* shifted visual effects to a different medium by introducing the use of computers. The pivotal moment in the digital cinema was ILM's realistic dinosaurs in *Jurassic Park*. But this achievement was inspired by all those that came before, from *King Kong* to Harryhausen's puppets. In the animation medium, John Lasseter's *Toy Story* team delivered extraordinary acting in an entirely CG (Computer Graphics) feature. I believe the next milestone will be *Episode I*, because it will have photorealistic digital characters interacting with actors.

A Question of Limits

There will be limitations on what this new technology will be able to accomplish. As long as our minds have the capacity to imagine new possibilities, there will be difficulties in trying to realize them. At this point, the possibilities with digital technology seem almost limitless, but we have only started to imagine them, because we haven't really used the medium. As time goes by, our minds will open up, and we'll be able to imagine things that will hit up against the boundaries of the medium.

Computers are run by humans. It's science fiction to think that computers could make movies by themselves, or that digital characters aren't created by people. Because digital cinema is a much more sophisticated form of moviemaking, filmmakers need both sophisticated backgrounds and plenty of inspiration. And you'll still need actors to do the voices and to perform, and whether those actors are literally actors or an animator's creation — or

0.4 The Phantom Menace (1999) George Lucas filming on location in Tunisia. Despite the latest technology, the production was still subject to the whims of the weather — a storm ripped through and destroyed sets and props, just as one had done while filming Star Wars in 1976.

a combination of the two — it's still humans communicating with humans.

Film is a communications medium. And digital cinema is, essentially, the same communications medium: one human being is communicating ideas to a number of other human beings, most often through the depiction of human beings. Whether you do it digitally or photographically, it amounts to the same thing. People have said, "Gee, digital cinema isn't like real cinema. It's phony. It's not real." Well, that's one thing you can depend on: film is not real.

Nothing you see on a movie screen is real. It never has been, and it never will be. The images have been manipulated by some filmmakers to be what they want them to be. Cinema is a highly technical medium: by running celluloid through sprockets and exposing it to light, you have a chemical photographic process that is manipulated a million different ways. In movies, the characters are just actors playing parts, and the sets have been built by a crew. They're phony, they're backdrops. Nothing in a movie is real.

And a digital back lot is no different than a real back lot. You're just using numbers instead of two-by-fours. The stories are what you're trying to communicate: they have to have some insight into human behavior — the way we live and, most importantly, our intellectual and emotional ideas. These things — whether you're using a stage or music or words or paint on a cave wall — are always the same.

The Phantom Menace

Episode I: The Phantom Menace (1999)

Synopsis

Stranded on the desert planet Tatooine after rescuing young Queen Amidala from the impending invasion of Naboo, Jedi apprentice Obi-Wan Kenobi and his Jedi Master Qui-Gon Jinn discover nine-year-old Anakin Skywalker, a young slave unusually strong in the Force. Anakin wins a thrilling podrace and with it his freedom as he leaves his home to be trained as a Jedi. The heroes return to Naboo where Anakin and the queen face massive invasion forces while the two Jedi contend with a deadly foe named Darth Maul. Only then do they realize the invasion is merely the first step in a sinister scheme by the re-emergent forces of darkness known as the Sith.

RELEASE DATE May 16, 1999 (US)
RUNNING TIME 136 minutes

Cast

QUI-GON JINN LIAM NEESON
OBI-WAN KENOBI EWAN MCGREGOR
QUEEN AMIDALA / PADMÉ NATALIE PORTMAN
ANAKIN SKYWALKER JAKE LLOYD
SENATOR PALPATINE IAN MCDIARMID
SHMI SKYWALKER PERNILLA AUGUST
SIO BIBBLE OLIVER FORD DAVIES
CAPTAIN PANAKA HUGH QUARSHIE
JAR JAR BINKS AHMED BEST
C-3PO (VOICE) ANTHONY DANIELS
R2-D2 KENNY BAKER
YODA (VOICE) FRANK OZ

CHANCELLOR VALORUM TERENCE STAMP
BOSS NASS (VOICE) BRIAN BLESSED
WATTO (VOICE) ANDY SECOMBE
DARTH MAUL RAY PARK
SEBULBA (VOICE) LEWIS MACLEOD
WALD / PODRACE SPECTATOR /
   MOS ESPA CITIZEN WARWICK DAVIS

Crew
DIRECTOR GEORGE LUCAS
PRODUCER RICK MCCALLUM
SCREENPLAY GEORGE LUCAS
EXECUTIVE PRODUCER GEORGE LUCAS
PRODUCTION DESIGNER GAVIN BOCQUET
DIRECTOR OF PHOTOGRAPHY
   DAVID TATTERSALL

FILM EDITORS PAUL MARTIN SMITH, BEN BURTT
COSTUME DESIGNER TRISHA BIGGAR
DESIGN DIRECTOR DOUG CHIANG
VISUAL EFFECTS SUPERVISORS JOHN KNOLL,
   DENNIS MUREN, SCOTT SQUIRES
ANIMATION DIRECTOR ROB COLEMAN
SOUND DESIGN BEN BURTT
MUSIC JOHN WILLIAMS

1.1 *Drew Struzan's poster for*
The Phantom Menace was released
on March 11, 1999.

A Symbiont Circle

By Paul Duncan and Colin Odell & Michelle Le Blanc

George Lucas After I finished *Star Wars, The Empire Strikes Back,* and *Return of the Jedi* in 1983, financially and physically the prequels couldn't be done. I was recovering from a divorce, which was pretty consequential on the financial side of things, and I didn't have the technology. Yoda couldn't move more than six feet, and I couldn't show his legs, so I couldn't show him in a wide shot and I couldn't show him running, jumping, or walking any distance. Yoda couldn't fight. We could have tried to animate him with stop-motion but I couldn't really get him to do what I wanted him to do. So I said, "What the heck, I'll just spend my time developing the technology, and produce films."

Also, I was so tired and burned out that I needed to go and do other things for a while to replenish my creative juices. I said I would do the new *Star Wars* when my life was able to accommodate it.

I learned a lot of lessons in those years! One is that the only true route to happiness is through caring about other people. If all you care about is yourself and about your things and your stuff, you will be unhappy the rest of your life no matter how much you accumulate.

For 15 years I dealt with my family. The idea of taking five or six years to do the intense work that it would take to make the prequels is daunting, and it's also something I haven't

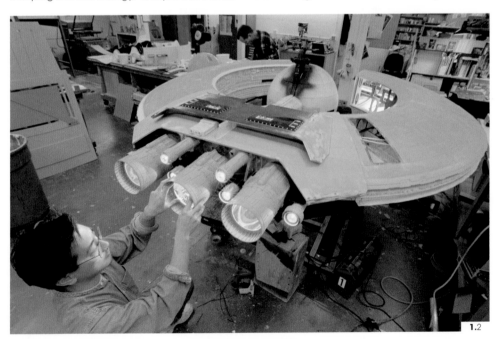

1.2

really had the mindset to get into. I'm going back and doing them now because I'm not getting any younger. We've also advanced the technology to the point that we can bring characters and environments to life on the screen, and I can tell stories that I couldn't tell before, that I've wanted to tell but I wouldn't dare attempt, and do it in a cost-effective way. I think I can push the envelope to tell stories that are fanciful in nature and fantastic in scope.

The Tragedy of Darth Vader

George Lucas For *Star Wars*, *The Empire Strikes Back*, and *Return of the Jedi*, I had to know where the Empire and Darth Vader came from to make the story of Luke Skywalker coherent.

In 1981, during a five-day story conference for Return of the Jedi, *Lucas gave details on how Anakin Skywalker, Luke's father, became Darth Vader.*

George Lucas / Story Conference / July 13 – 17, 1981

Anakin Skywalker began hanging out with the Emperor, who at that point nobody knew was that bad, because he was an elected official. He was a politician. Richard M. Nixon was his name. He subverted the senate and finally took over and he was really evil. But he pretended to be a really nice guy. Luke's father gets subverted by the Emperor. He gets a little weird at home and his wife begins to figure out that things are going wrong and she confides in Ben, who is his mentor.

On his missions through the galaxies, Anakin has been going off doing his Jedi thing and a lot of Jedi have been getting killed — and it's because they turn their back on him and he cuts them down. The President is turning into an Emperor and Luke's mother suspects that something has happened to her husband. She is pregnant. Anakin gets worse and worse, and finally Ben has to fight him

1.2 *ILM model maker Grant Imahara inspects the engines on the scale model of the Trade Federation ship, which has been fitted with lights.*
1.3 *Final frame of the Trade Federation battleship as the Republic Cruiser arrives. The sphere in the center of the ship pre-figures the Death Star. Doug Chiang: "Since we were designing spaceships earlier in the timeline, I wanted to plant visual influences that you can then see and connect the evolution of the design into the original trilogy."*

1.4 **Doug Chiang's concept art, completed on November 6, 1996 (3.5 days of work), shows detail of the Trade Federation ship's hangar bay entrance as the Republic Cruiser approaches.**

D.CHIANG

"*When I was writing* **Star Wars** *I'd sit down, lock myself up, and I wouldn't come out for months until I was finished. This takes a certain kind of stamina, because the process of writing is not easy and takes a great deal of concentration and almost, I guess, the essence of meditation. You get into a world, stay there for a while, then move around and see the things that are happening there.*"

George Lucas

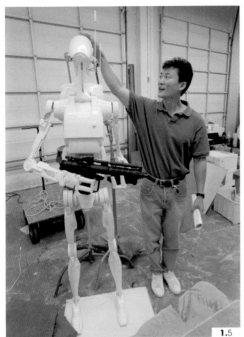

1.5 Doug Chiang reviews the full-size battle droid model. Chiang: "I wanted them to be tall because I wanted them to be menacing. They were white, like the stormtroopers, but during shooting, George said, 'Let's make them tan.'" Models like this were used during filming to give eyelines for the actors.
1.6 The first drawing for the film by Chiang, dated January 15, 1995, is of a baron droid. The droids belonged to the trade barons, or robber barons, later named Neimoidians.

1.5

1.6

and he throws him down into a volcano and Vader is all beat up.

When he falls into the pit there is hardly anything left of him by the time the Emperor's troops fish him out of the drink. Then when Ben finds out that Vader has been fished out and is in the hands of the Empire, he is worried. He goes back to Vader's wife and explains that Anakin is the bad guy, the one killing all the Jedi.

Mrs. Skywalker has had the kids, the twins, two little babies who are six months old or so. The Skywalker line is very strong with the Force, so Ben says, "I think we should protect the kids, because they may be able to help us right the wrong that your husband has created in the universe." Ben takes one and gives him to a couple out there on Tatooine and he gets his little hideout in the hills and he watches him grow. Ben can't raise Luke himself, because he's a wanted man. Leia and Luke's mother go to Alderaan and are taken in by the king there, who is a friend of Ben's. She dies shortly thereafter and Leia is brought up by her foster parents. She knows that her real mother died.

I think you can make Ben take the blame for Vader. "I should have given him more training. I should have sent him to Yoda, but I thought I could do it myself. It was my own pride in thinking that I could be as good a teacher as

1.7

1.8

Yoda. I wish that I could stop the pestilence that I've unleashed on the galaxy." His burden is that he feels responsible for everything that Vader has done.

Paul Duncan It is clear that you had precise ideas from the very beginning.

George Lucas There was no room for me to put the backstory in those films in an organic way. Also, if I had started talking about the backstory, the Whills, and the midi-chlorians, and all that kind of stuff in *Star Wars*, people would have gone, "Oh my God!" and backed off.

It wasn't until *Jedi* came out that I realized I'd lost the tragedy of Darth Vader. In *Star Wars*, it's set up as, "What is that guy? Is he a monster? Is it a robot?" They didn't know what he was. Over the three films his story dissipated. He was the chosen one of the prophecy, yet the irony was lost that it was the son bringing humanity back to the father. It wasn't clear.

I felt the story of Anakin Skywalker had enough pathos and enough of a story to enrich the prequels: how Anakin became a Jedi; how he learned to use the Force; the dark side of the Force, the light side of the Force,

1.7 *Iain McCaig's concept (December 1, 1995) could be applied to appropriate characters, whether senators or trade barons.*
1.8 *Chiang's early concept for a trade baron (February 23, 1995). Doug Chiang: "I wanted to put in a little underlying theme that the Neimoidians actually made the battle droids in their image, so I gave the Neimoidians a very long elongated head. It was like the organic version of the droids. George was worried he was going to break ILM if he made more digital characters, so he asked Nick Dudman to redesign them to be character actors in masks."*

D.CHIANG

1.9 Obi-Wan Kenobi is offered refreshments by a protocol droid while awaiting an audience with Nute Gunray. Concept art by Doug Chiang (April 16, 1996, 3 days). Doug Chiang: "Initially, Obi-Wan was the master out on this mission alone, and then he takes on Anakin as his Padawan. One day George explained that Jedi work in pairs, like the Sith, so he changed it so that Obi-Wan was a Padawan with a master."

and midi-chlorians; this is where Obi-Wan came from; this is what their relationship was; how Anakin turned into Darth Vader.

When I told Fox the next film is about how Darth Vader got to be Darth Vader they got all excited. I told them, "In the first movie, he's 10 years old." Fox, and also people at Lucasfilm, said, "You're going to destroy the franchise; you're going to destroy everything! You can't do it, this is terrible!" *Everybody*

was upset, and I thought, "This is why I own the films, and I own the company, because if I didn't, this film would never get made." If I went to a studio with this story, it would never have existed.

I know everybody wants to see Darth Vader in his black suit with his lightsaber, but the whole point of it is: How does this nice little kind kid, who has good intentions, is just like us, go wrong and became Darth Vader? And the second part of the story is: How does a democracy become a dictatorship?

I told people at Lucasfilm that they're going to have to face the reality that I'm making a movie that nobody wants to see, but I want to tell that story. I'm more interested in telling the story than I am in just doing a franchise where you tell the same story over and over again.

Paul Duncan So you made the movie for yourself.

George Lucas I make all my movies for myself. People will say, "When you release it, it belongs to the public." No, it's mine. I'm leasing it to you, $10 at a time. It still belongs to me.

November 1, 1994

George Lucas Today is my first day of writing the new *Star Wars* series. It's a beautiful sunny day in slightly drought-ridden California. Took my kids to school this morning. My oldest daughter was sick all night, until 5:30 a.m. I got no sleep whatsoever so it will be a very interesting first day of trying to stay awake more than anything else. That will be the biggest challenge. I am excited about doing this.

I've always intended to do these movies and finish them just to satisfy my own anal personality—I want to finish everything that I start.

I'm working three days a week on *Star Wars* and then I have two days a week to finish editing three *Young Indiana Jones* TV movies, shepherd scripts for *Red Tails* and the new *Indiana Jones* film, work on an educational film that I've developed to show what education is going to look like in the future, and do corporate business. I have three companies—Lucasfilm, LucasArts, and Lucas Digital (which is Industrial Light & Magic and Skywalker Sound). Lucasfilm finances these movies so there's business involved in this process that a lot of filmmakers don't have to deal with, but it allows me the creative freedom to do whatever I want without a studio overseeing the whole process, which I like a lot.

Besides that, it's an empty life. (Laughs)

I write with a pencil in a ratty, beat-up old three-ring binder. I have written everything I have ever done in the same binder. I started when I was in college. I have a bunch of them now but I still have the one I wrote *THX* in. And I wrote *Graffiti* in it, I wrote *Star Wars* in it.

The original notes and outline for the new trilogy are something like 15 pages. I have to

"Shortly after finishing the model, they destroy it inside the hangar bay. It blows up. The first couple of times they blew things up it's kind of hard, but after a while you start building them and you realize you're building it just to blow it up."

John Goodson / Model Maker

1.10 *Final frame showing the dramatic explosion and the destruction of the Republic Cruiser.*
1.11 *Steve Gawley, John Knoll, George Lucas, and Doug Chiang inspect the Republic Cruiser model.*

1.10

1.11

NUTE
They must be dead by now. Blast
what's left of them.

The hologram fades off, as a BATTLE DROID, OWO-1, cautiously
opens the door. A deadly green cloud billows from the room.
BATTLE DROIDS cock their weapons as a figure stumbles out of
the smoke. It is TC-3, carrying the tray of drinks.

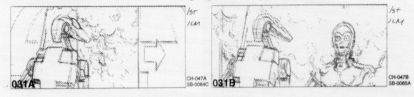

TC-3
Oh, excuse me, so sorry.

The PROTOCOL DROID passes the the armed camp just as two flashing
laser swords fly out of the deadly fog, cutting down several
BATTLE DROIDS before they can fire.

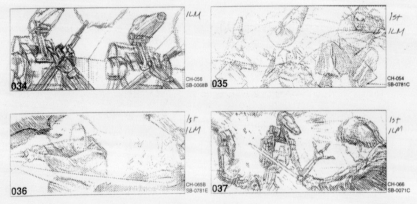

1.12 *A version of the script was made
incorporating Benton Jew's storyboards.
The two Jedi emerge from the reception
room, ready for battle, Gunray having
failed to poison them with deadly gas.*

1.13

put them into a scene form and a script form. There are a few set pieces and sequences laid out but there's a lot to do in terms of developing the characters and filling in the scenes. There is drama inherent in it because there is a lot of betrayal, but the subtleties and intricate weaving of the story haven't been done at all.

On writing days I come to my home office and I read for about three or four hours. I study mythology, folk tales, religion as well as pivotal events in history, and sociological anthropological studies about the way societies work, what they believe in, and how those things are put into practice.

Mythology is basically a psychological summation of history, taking an event in history, converting it into something that is psychologically more pleasing to an audience. I also watch a movie, look through research books, picture books, various locations, design ideas,

1.13 *Qui-Gon Jinn (Liam Neeson) and Obi-Wan Kenobi (Ewan McGregor) draw their lightsabers to defend themselves against the attacking droids in the Trade Federation battleship hallway. They have just escaped the room full of poison gas behind them. Iain McCaig: "At one time the Jedi were going to be more like a UN peacekeeping force with a regimented costume. Obi-Wan's age changed all over the place — at one point he was substantially older, like a youngish 50. For a long time we had a character who was samurai-like, with a ponytail and long sideburns, but as it evolved that character split into Obi-Wan and Qui-Gon. Now there was an older mentor, and it told us a lot more about who the Jedi were. It wasn't like a peacekeeping force — it was more like a temple, with an apprenticeship. When that happened, we revised the look. In the end, to make a strong connection between the Obi-Wan we know and the Obi-Wan in the prequels, we went back to the original costume design and said, 'Let's let everyone wear those beautiful light brown robes.'"*

D.CHIANG

1.15

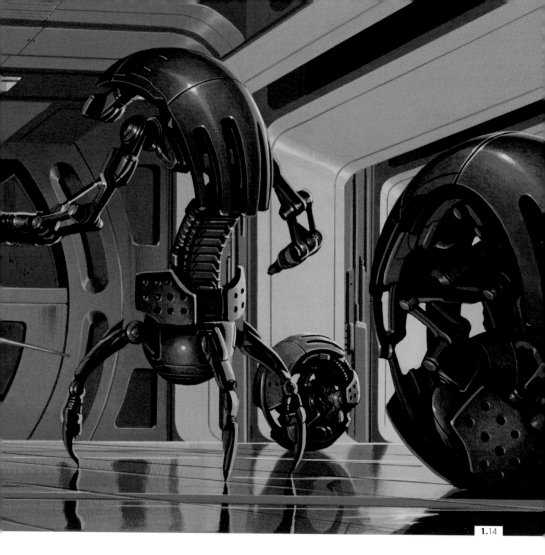

1.14 *The battle droids presented no real threat for the Jedi. Doug Chiang: "I started to explore how do we make a more menacing version. At that point George said, 'Okay, let's do a really weird mechanical droid that breaks the human form.'" Concept art by Doug Chiang (March 29, 1996, 4 days) featuring Obi-Wan Kenobi.*

1.15 *Final frame of Qui-Gon using his lightsaber to burn through the metal doors to reach Gunray while Obi-Wan attempts to fend off the attack. The filming process involved shooting the scene with the action and then filming with only the background, to get a consistent environment for the visual effects that would be added later.*

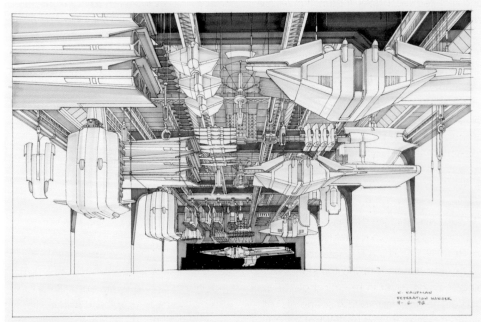

1.16

1.17

and architectural books. It's fun. It gives me a chance to think, which I couldn't do before because I was always being hit on to make decisions or to come up with instantaneous answers to everything.

Toward the end of the day I will summarize whatever I picked up during that day and put it into a notepad. I will also spend time, an hour at the most, working on an outline of scenes. Ultimately there will be approximately 50 scenes per movie, so I have to come up with 150 scenes. If I come up with a few scenes a day pretty soon I will start to get the overall flow of the movies.

It's more difficult to lay the scenes out and say specifically which scenes are going with each other, which is telling the story. I'm running the story over in my mind all the time and contemplating various scene fits. What would it be like if I did this? What if I started here? There's a lot of mechanics that have to happen, and then there's the entertainment value — Is it funny? Does it move forward? Is it exciting? — all of those kind of issues. I'm constantly running those things past a scene until something says, "Oh this is a nice scene. This feels right," and then I stick it in my little binder and I keep building.

Toward the end of this process, around Christmastime, I will start going through the outline, filling in all of the blanks and finishing it. Then in January I start the hard part, which is writing pages.

1.16 Concept for the Federation hangar by Kurt Kaufman (April 6, 1996) with ideas on how to store the ships. A great deal of thought was put into determining the ships' storage configuration and how they would be dispatched for battle.
1.17 Jay Shuster's concept, dated December 19, 1996, for the Federation Destroyer hangar shows Multi-Troop Transports (MTTs) loading onto Trade Federation landing ships.

"There is a cohesive design philosophy from Episodes I through VI that is absolutely rock solid. It grounds it in reality. It would have been easy to do X-wings and TIE fighters and Death Stars in I–III, and the fans would have loved that, but that's not pushing the art form any further."
Doug Chiang / Design Director

Writing is a very meditative experience. You have to drive a lot of stuff out of your head, you create a world, and then you start walking around in that world. It's a very psychologically interesting experience. And sometimes you want to go places and can't and you end up going to other places and it's not something you have complete control over.

There's no way to write without writing from yourself. The stuff gets made out of things that you care about, whether you have actually lived them or not. It's hard to write in the abstract, without having some emotional connection to the material. So when I write a scene I write a scene that moves me, or I care about, or it's something that is personal to me.

January 15, 1995

George Lucas It starts with me sitting here doodling in my little binder but it ends up with a couple of thousand people working together in a very intense emotional creative way to pull it off. It goes from the nannies to the producers to the publicist to my assistants to ILM to Skywalker Sound to the camera crews, sound crews, construction crews, and the actors. You can't do it without everybody pulling together in the same direction. When it's all in my binder it's just a dream. I can sit here and say, "Wouldn't it be great if…?"

D.CHIANG 1.18

but pounding that into reality takes a huge amount of effort.

Lucas formed JAK Films Inc., named after the first initial of each of his children — Jett, Amanda, and Katie — to oversee preproduction and development of the new series, and JAK Productions Ltd. to produce the movies.

George Lucas The process of working with the art department is something I started on *Star Wars* with Ralph McQuarrie. I finished the first draft of the film but when I started the second draft it took me about a year. That year I'd describe a character to Ralph like Darth Vader and say, "He's black and has a dark mask and a Samurai-ish helmet." When I'm working on the script, it is very ephemeral, and he made it real for me. If I said it's a spaceship and it's all white inside, he was able to put the detail in so I could see it. So when I go back and do a second draft I have a much clearer picture of what it is, and I can be more specific about how I describe things. It's getting closer to directing.

When you are writing a screenplay you don't know the logistics of a room. You don't know where the door is in relationship to the desk. But when you have a drawing of it you can say, "I know the door is going to be five paces from the desk." You start staging things, and think, "Does he talk as he walks from the door? No, it's too far and it won't play. I'll cut to him at the desk before I can have him talk." Those are the kinds of things you discover on a set, which means you are modifying the script to fit the reality you have to cope with. The art department helps me deal with logistical problems very early on, which means it's easier for everybody.

1.18 *Doug Chiang's concept design "Theed City" (August 19, 1997, 2.8 days).* **1.19** *Doug Chiang and Charlie Bailey inspect the models for Theed. Doug Chiang: "Once George had approved the palace concept, which captured the right architectural style, that anchored everything. Knowing that the palace was on a cliff edge, we laid out the whole city plan in foam core. I worked with ILM to create generic buildings that could be reconfigured to that footprint. On our back lot stage, we had several dozen buildings that were dressed differently on each side so we could rotate them to create different streets. It was really wonderful, because out of the puzzle piece of maybe three dozen buildings, we achieved all the backgrounds for Theed." The models were filmed outside to take advantage of natural light.*

Doug Chiang / Design Director During the autumn of 1994, George Lucas announced that he was staffing up an art department for the first of three new prequels. For many designers and artists who grew up as the *Star Wars* generation, myself included, it was the opportunity of a lifetime.

I'm a self-trained artist — I went to film school, not art school — so when I started working at ILM in 1989, I set aside almost a year, at night, to polish my art skills. I developed my own aesthetics — taking organic forms and merging it with technology. It was the mixture that George was looking for, because in *Star Wars*, 80 percent of it is real, but George makes it special by adding 20 percent that takes it into the exotic. Without knowing it, I stumbled on that process. I became the design director on the new project.

I was familiar with the original trilogy designs from Joe Johnston and Ralph McQuarrie, and I trained my whole career to design that. In January 1995, prior to starting at Sky-walker Ranch, I had a meeting with George. I thought it was just a meet and greet, but he said, "Put all those ideas aside. We're going to start fresh." It was a shock. I felt like I had been studying for the wrong test. But in hindsight that gave me clarity into the whole design philosophy for the *Star Wars* universe and how George thought about it.

He described all these things that he wanted: a new racing spectacle, which became the podracing scene; a new planet culture that had an elegant design — that was Udopau, which became Naboo. I had pages of notes but I didn't know how it all fit together.

My first day was January 15, a Sunday. I had a mental block because of the sheer amount of work to do, and the pressures of living up to Johnston and McQuarrie. I tackled that by giving myself goals: three to five designs every day, 25 by the end of the week, for George.

Paul Duncan The first day you drew the droids owned by the trade barons/robber barons, later called the Neimoidians.

1.19

1.20 *Portrait of Queen Amidala, played by Natalie Portman.*
1.21 *Iain McCaig's design for the queen's costume, dated March 14, 1997. McCaig: "I loved Natalie Portman in Léon: The Professional (1994). I think she is an amazing actress. And then I saw her audition tape: where she is substantially older than she was in that film and just a beautiful young lady. So, I thought, that by drawing her as the queen in the concept art will be my way of rooting for her, and maybe George will notice."*
1.22 *In the Naboo palace throne room, a hologram of Senator Palpatine (Ian McDiarmid) reports that he had received confirmation from the Chancellor that his ambassadors had arrived to negotiate with the Trade Federation.*

Doug Chiang The brief George gave was "Create a robotic stormtrooper." The stormtroopers were black-and-white and look like skeletons, so I thought, "How about turning human musculature into mechanical forms?" and see if that went anywhere. So I took the human anatomy and made it robotic. The stylized body shapes of African sculptures also influenced them.

Paul Duncan You did five drawings on January 15.

Doug Chiang These were all explorations and I think they're complete failures. I was trying to get all the bad ideas out to find where George wanted to go with this.

Paul Duncan But if you look at drawing number 002, the rib cage is very similar to the final rib cage. And in number 005, the elongated head is similar to the final head, and the eyes are exactly like the final design. You are finding pieces.

Doug Chiang Yes.

Paul Duncan You are working on multiple designs at the same time, but continue drawing the droids on January 25, 26, 31, and then in drawing 198, on April 24, you're close to the final form.

Doug Chiang It's very collaborative. George has exquisite taste in form language, and it's surprising how quickly he can read an idea and see if it conveys the personality and works for the story that he wants to tell. In the art reviews he'll pick out certain things that he likes — like the eyes, the head, or the rib cage — then it was my job to take those elements and make the design structurally sound.

Paul Duncan Did you have context for the story and the environments they were to be seen in?

Doug Chiang Not yet. It wasn't until a year and a half afterward that George started to share how the story all fitted together. I was designing in its purest form where we were trying to come up with elements that weren't preconceived ideas. It was empowering for me because I wasn't there just to illustrate his ideas but I was contributing my own ideas.

The art department was formed in January of 1995, based in the attic above George's

1.21

office at Skywalker Ranch, starting with Terryl Whitlatch and myself.

Terryl Whitlatch / Concept Artist I am a paleo reconstructionist and animal artist — ILM needed someone who could do animals well.

Doug Chiang We would have art reviews every Friday.

Terryl Whitlatch George would discuss the characters, the vehicles, architecture — what

1.22

D.CHIANG '95

1.24

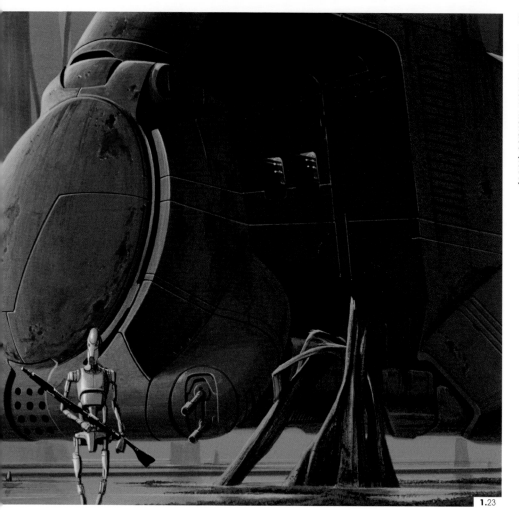

1.23

1.23 **Doug Chiang's concept for the MTTs landing on the swampy terrain of Naboo (April 17, 1995, 6 days). Chiang: "George wanted a vehicle that carried troops. He described it as a floating locomotive that could plow through anything. The first image that came to my mind was of a charging bull elephant. It worked out very well, because the whole droid army was being given an animal-like personality."**
1.24 **Final frame of the Trade Federation landing ships over Naboo, a shot supervised by John Knoll.**

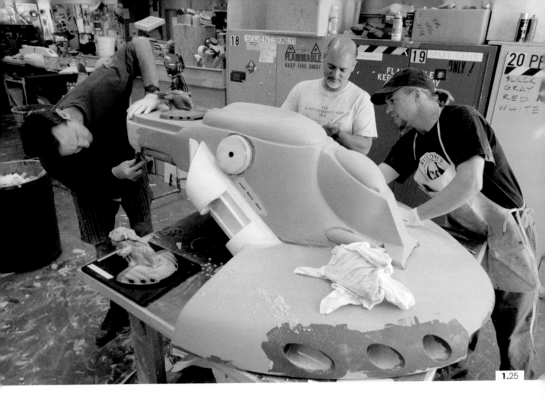

1.25

was most pressing on his mind. Then Doug would immediately hold a meeting after that meeting, to review everything that was said and send us to our respective drawing boards, imaginations quivering and assignments in hand, to design what was within our realms of expertise. Sometimes there were some crossovers, but most of the time we each had our various areas — storyboarding, environments, costume — and mine was anything having to do with an animal or creature. We'd work all week creating, mostly in traditional media — pencil and markers and acrylics — then we'd present the results to George.

George Lucas Most filmmakers do not have a preproduction process that goes on for two and a half years. We would bat ideas around, and it was a give and take of creative ideas. It was a lot of fun.

Paul Duncan You were willing to accept ideas and comments?

George Lucas As long as I could say no. I had to tell them, "Look, I'm going to reject a lot of

1.25 Sean Casey, Mark Siegel, and David Owen building the scale model of the AAT. Its smaller maquette is on the table. Maquettes were developed from the concept art. Lucas would suggest changes and the design would be finalized to become the template for the scale model. Sometimes the maquette or scale model would be scanned for CG modeling.

1.26 Chiang's sketch concepts for droid attack tanks (July 12, 1995). Chiang gave himself a target of creating five designs each day. He would begin by sketching rough drawings of shapes, then picking out some of these to expand and develop into fuller designs. To speed up his process, he later skipped this step and jumped straight to individual designs.

the things you give me. So just accept that as a given and don't worry about it. It's nothing personal. I'm trying to think of the overall movie. There are things about this I know that you won't know. I'll be making decisions that seem arbitrary but when it's done it'll make sense." We did that and they were good about it.

I can make a decision in 15 seconds. People have to perceive what's going on very quickly. In a normal movie, if the audience sees a 1945 jeep, they can jump to the conclusion that World War II is going on, and they know all kinds of things about that. We're dealing with things that people have never seen before, and they have no idea what the cultural connections of these things are. So if it's hard to understand what it is they're holding in their hand, or what it is used for, or what it is they're wearing, they're thinking about what it is that he's holding instead of what's going on in the scene. Since we have thousands of things to think about and design in a movie, you can't be obscure about anything, because once

"The secret of doing these films, like in sport, is to stay relaxed, enjoy yourself, and you come up with new ideas and try to tell a story as best you can."
George Lucas

you put them all together, it gets too obscure for the audience to follow.

Doug Chiang In one of my first meetings with George, he described the spaceships. The next week I came in with drawings that were very typical of the *Star Wars* universe. George said, "No. Let's push the envelope a little bit further. Let's try Art Nouveau as an influence. Let's try chrome." It was exciting but we weren't quite sure how that would work. As we started designing, we related our designs to the history of industrial design in the US. We equated Episode I to the early 1900s and the 1920s, where industrial design and art

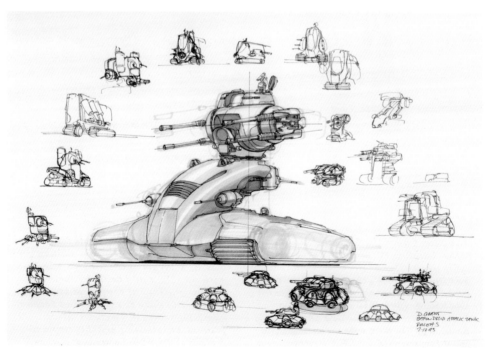

1.27 *Doug Chiang's concept for Obi-Wan
and Jar Jar fleeing from the droid army
(March 15, 1996, 3.75 days).*
1.28 *Final frame of Qui-Gon and a
number of Naboo creatures racing
from the oncoming MTTs.*

D.CHIANG 1.27

1.28

> *"Jar Jar was an alien creature, sort of insecure, but cute and lovable. Very humorous, but maybe with a touch of pathos because this is a character that had been exiled from his homeland and was trying to make do in the adverse circumstances in which he found himself."*

Terryl Whitlatch / Concept Artist

were very much intertwined. Everything was beautifully designed and had a more hand-crafted look.

As we progress through Episodes II and III, we'll slowly see the design segue into the 1970s, when assembly line aesthetics started taking over, and things began to look a little more manufactured, which is *A New Hope*'s aesthetic. It works as a design philosophy because it happened in our history.

Terryl Whitlatch George mentioned this funny, gangly, goofy character, lovable and yet cowardly. He was going by the name "Corky." At that time, George's young son was calling every vehicle a "jar jar." George thought that was cute so the character's name became "Jar Jar."

All we had was a personality, and he was a large-eyed creature that could express a great deal of emotion and feeling through his eyes. By chance I had brought a little sketch I had done at ILM for my own entertainment. George saw that and said, "These eyes are like Jar Jar's," and we went on from there.

Jar Jar is an amphibious creature; he can survive both in the water and on land. So, like an amphibian he has smooth, permeable skin. He can absorb oxygen molecules through the water to be under the water. I got a lot of my influence from hadrosaurs, duck-billed dinosaurs that were semiamphibious, at home in

the water and on dry land. One of the animals that influenced him is the emu. So, if we put an emu, a duck-billed dinosaur, Danny Kaye, and Charlie Chaplin all in one, you would end up with a Gungan.

Paul Duncan You all worked on the character throughout 1995 and 1996. Why so many designs and concepts?

Doug Chiang It was because he was going to be the first synthetic character. I remember distinctly George saying, "Don't worry about how we're going to execute this. Just design the best design. The folks at ILM will take care of that."

Terryl Whitlatch When a basic concept was officially approved, I did anatomical orthographical drawings — views of the side, front, rear, top, and often the bottom — of the skeletons, musculature, and anatomical surface for all the alien wildlife and creatures, so they

D.CHIANG   1.29

Terryl Whitlatch
9-14-95
JAR JAR BINX
VARIATIONS

1.30

1.29 Doug Chiang early artwork for an amphibious "Goonga" (March 30, 1995).

1.30 Whitlatch's concepts for "Jar Jar Binx" influenced by the attributes of frogs and dragons. Jar Jar is still very large compared with Padmé (September 14, 1995).

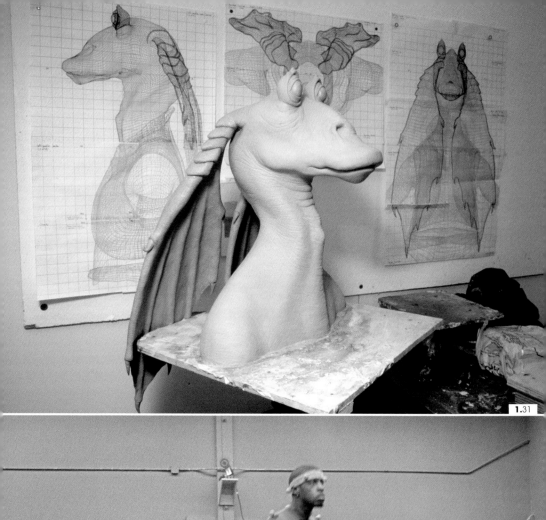

1.31

1.32

could be modeled, textured, rigged, and animated for ILM. That's at least 9 to 15 technical drawings/ paintings for each approved creature, and there were at least 50 such creatures accepted for the film.

All of these creatures needed to appear real, from their outer coloring to their inner structure. Sometimes I even had to design the dental configurations and the tongue relationships, and at times even needed to animate the creature myself in 2-D to make sure it could do certain things, or to act as a locomotion guide for ILM. A lot of what was done in preproduction was to make sure that Production/ILM (where things get really expensive really fast) had exactly what they needed.

Doug Chiang Once we designed Jar Jar in 2-D on paper and George approved it, I had Tony McVey, a creature sculptor, interpret the drawings and make 3-D maquettes. We did a series of small character personalities' looks, George picked some, and we made bigger versions. ILM scanned those and it goes into the digital realm. The character is fine-tuned with the animation director's input, because performance ties into it.

My role covered the point at which George was formulating ideas with the art department, through production, when I was designing sets with Gavin Bocquet, the production designer, then through postproduction, working closely with ILM, supervising the practical miniature builds and the digital builds. The film and the designs evolved throughout the whole process, which is why George felt it was very important that there's continuity in that.

Summer 1995

George Lucas I grew up loving cars, going fast, and racing cars. I always wanted to have a race in one of my movies. Once I was

1.33

involved in an extremely exciting race with a friend of mine at Riverside. I've elaborated on it quite a bit to create what I hope is the ultimate race sequence.

Ben Burtt / Editor In early summer 1995, George gave me a verbal description, and later a paragraph, describing the podrace.

George Lucas This is going to be like the *Ben-Hur* chariot race. They've got these pods—two engines that are like the two horses—and they're holding on in open cockpits, which are like the chariots. It's a fight to the death.

1.31 *A clay model of Jar Jar was sculpted and scanned, putting the character into the digital dimension.*
1.32 *Ahmed Best was cast as Jar Jar. Lucas recognized his abilities as both an actor and someone who had a great physical presence, who could create a character through movement. Ahmed Best: "I wore a motion capture suit covered in light sensors. As I moved, the light sensors moved, infrared cameras tracked the movement and input that data into a computer. That's how they captured the movement in the computer."*
1.33 *Jar Jar's design was finalized and this computer-generated image was produced on January 14, 1999, to check the modeling. The arrow is pointing to a horn that has detached from his ear, indicating a rework is required.*

1.34

1.34 *In Jar Jar's scripted introduction to the movie, shown in Iain McCaig's storyboards, he picks up a clam, the clam emerges from its shell to grab him, but his long tongue jumps out and he devours it. The idea was discarded in favor of Qui-Gon literally running into Jar Jar while fleeing the droid army invasion. However, Jar Jar's ravenous appetite is a recurring joke throughout the movie.*

Anakin goes down the racetrack. He bumps into this guy. This guy crashes and then Anakin has to go through the fireball and go on to the next one. The first lap he's ahead, the second lap he's behind, the third lap he's ahead, the fourth lap he's behind, and finally he wins. That's the story.

Ben Burtt I started developing that visually, which meant collecting footage from movies, newsreels, recording things on TV to VHS, and then transfer it into Avid. I built up a library of vehicle, helicopter, and airplane races. I started shooting cockpit scenes — I built a little cardboard racer at home and had a front projection system, so I put on an IMAX laser disc of flying through the Grand Canyon and had my son Benny drive against this background. I filmed a composite of that and his friend with an alien mask. If I had to put a model on a stick and fly it in front of a camera then I did that as well. I cut that together with racing car footage.

George Lucas I've done this on all the movies. In *Star Wars* I used old war footage to make storyboards in motion for the Death Star attack sequence. We did hand-drawn animation, animatics, for *The Empire Strikes Back*, and we did videomatics — using video to shoot models against a blue background — on *Return of the Jedi*. This way ILM knows exactly what they have to do, how many frames it is, and how it's going to fit into the flow of the film. It's very hard to do that on a piece of paper. You really have to see the kinetics, the cinematic qualities of the shot.

Ben Burtt I worked on that first cut, which was 22 minutes, for months. It was a race with every possible wild thing that could happen: cars colliding, cars going off the track and blowing up, someone passing somebody and sticking something in the tires and they'd crash. I put some temporary sound to it, jets and airplanes, and that's where we started. It was crude, but George loves to work that way. It gave him something to react to.

1.35

1.36

Although the footage jumped from a car to a model to an airplane, we found that it wasn't that confusing, because so much of it was cutting properly: the screen direction, the geography, the matching of speeds or the placement of the viewer's eye in the frame. For example, if your eye is directed to three quarters across the frame on shot A and in shot B your eye naturally picks up the next thing in the same place

1.35–36 *On-set and final frame of Jar Jar thanking the Jedi for saving his life. Ewan McGregor: "One of the hard things is not looking at Ahmed's eyes. They're put this dark screen over his helmet, but it's still human instinct to look in his eyes instead of looking up at Jar Jar's eyes on top."*

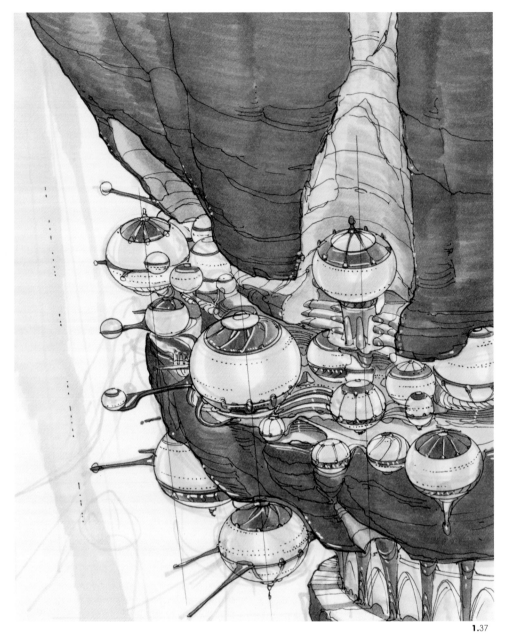

1.37

1.37 **Doug Chiang's May 25, 1995,
design for the Gungan city, then named
Otoh Botoh.**
1.38 **Final frame of the arrival into
Otoh City. Brian Flora / Matte Painter:
"I found some pictures in a book, of**

**Paris at night, where green lights were
arcing up underneath architectural
shapes. I used that as a color basis for
a light source that illuminated all these
bubbles from beneath."**

1.38

"George wanted the Gungan city to be an Art Nouveau–influenced city. I incorporated those Art Nouveau forms into the city and the Gungan aesthetics grew out of that, where the forms are considered grown or somehow crafted."

Doug Chiang

pay a tremendous amount of money for each second of film, and you damn well better know as a director going in what you need to shoot. If I can go in one day and cut 10 shots out of a sequence and it will still work, if each of those shots cost $100,000, it certainly more than paid for my salary on this film from a producer's standpoint.

then it's a successful, smooth cut. That's the magic of editing and that's where George is very adept.

George Lucas There's maybe five or 10 minutes of the movie that doesn't have digital characters, digital effects, or action sequences, so we decided to do animatics of the whole thing.

Ben Burtt That led to me tackling the film sequence by sequence: the sword fights, the underwater submarine scenes, the end battle. The idea is for it to be a living, dynamic storyboard, so that when George is on the set, he can show ILM what they need to create. "I want this angle, this speed, from this point of view." That way it's efficient.

This was an important process for George because ultimately he was going to have to

September 1995
David Dozoretz / Previsualization Effects Supervisor
I was the first computer artist hired on the film, in September 1995, and the podrace was my first responsibility. We built 3-D models of all the podracers in the terrain so that they can really zip by the camera. We filmed puppets of the pilots — Robert Barnes made them out of foam — on a makeshift green screen over in the tech building on the Ranch. Using Electricimage Animation System and Adobe After Effects, we combined all that with storyboards that Iain McCaig drew and replaced the stock footage in Ben Burtt's edit. It was also our job to figure out the continuity of this thing. If there are 13 racers and five of them die we had to keep track of where each racer was at every mile.

Animatics are this amazing visual storytelling tool because one guy on a computer can

1.39 *Best looks on as Neeson and McGregor sit on the steps of the town square set, concentrating on Lucas's direction. They are working in a predominantly blue-screen environment, where some visual elements have not yet been designed.*

1.40 *Kurt Kaufman's storyboard for shot OGB.027.010.A (OGB = Otoh Gunga Boardroom. It is scene 27 and shot 10 of the scene.) The live-action shot was completed first, then the storyboard was made incorporating the live-action material. After approval, a bubble model was built, shot, and replicated within the scene during postproduction.*

1.41 *Final frame of the scene where the Jedi request assistance from Boss Nass (Brian Blessed).*

try a million things. The computers are getting faster, but we try to keep it very low resolution, because if George asks, "Move this thing over here," we pride ourselves on trying to get it to him in 20 minutes. Our record is once we did 75 shots in a day, which is an enormous amount of work for only four guys, but we loved it.

George Lucas When Ben and I get finished he'll have sound effects and music and everything on there so it will be a finished piece of film. I'll just have to reshoot it with higher quality cameras and higher quality podracers and higher quality special effects, but the sequence itself in terms of the piece of film will be done. It will just be done at a very low quality.

March 23, 1996

George Lucas I've been working almost 18 months now and I've just finished the first draft of the first script. Part of the reason it's taken a while is I have a lot of stuff going on in my life and it intrudes when you're writing. I go into the office once a week, but I would say there is at least one other day a week that has been chewed up by emergencies and major corporate decisions that need to be dealt with.

The most difficult part is starting the script. It didn't have anything to do with writing, but with understanding the characters' personalities. Once you get that down, you don't write the movie, the movie writes itself. A character has to react to things in that character's way, so you don't really have too much of a choice if he stays in character. That takes a long time. It took me a year. (Laugh)

The story has Obi-Wan as a young Jedi in his mid-twenties. He's ambitious and takes on the mentorship of this kid who starts out about eight or nine years old. The kid is enthusiastic, good, and compassionate. Even though he wasn't raised a Jedi, he has a lot of Jedi qualities about him. Even though he's too old to start the training of a Jedi, Obi-Wan feels the Force is so strong with him that he has to train him as a Jedi. So, Anakin starts out very idealistic, very naïve, very clean of any dark side.

Why do the Jedi take the kids when they're little? I have to come up with an answer even though it doesn't show up in the script. There

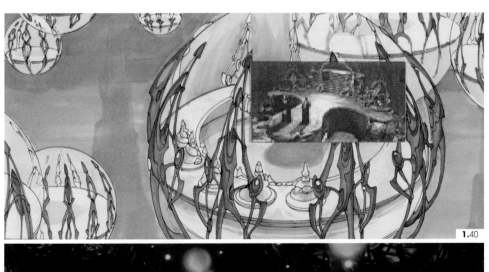

1.40

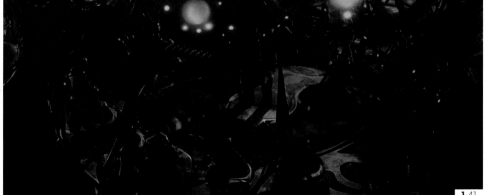

1.41

> **"There's always
> a bigger fish."**
>
> Qui-Gon Jinn

has to be logic behind why that happens. This is Anakin's Achilles' heel that ultimately comes into play when he grows up. He was too old to part from his mother. As a result, later he fell in love and he couldn't bear to part from his wife when he found out she was going to die in childbirth. Therefore, when the devil came to say, "I can bring her back," he fell for it, even though it was a lie.

Obi-Wan begins as this strong Jedi character but when you see all six movies you'll see that what Ben is doing with Luke is very close to the same mistake he made with Anakin. So there's this underlying current that he's going to make the same mistake again, that Luke's going to turn into a Sith instead of having him redeem Darth Vader. That's the big tension in this whole thing — can Obi-Wan right the wrong that he's done?

Ultimately, this trilogy is about the relationship between Anakin and Padmé. She's much more than a wife. It's a complex, slightly dysfunctional relationship and it resolves itself in a similar way to how Ben resolved the issue of Anakin, which is that when one person dies something new is born. So when Anakin's mother, who is a key player in all this, dies, something is born in Anakin that becomes Darth Vader. When Anakin is in the process of becoming Vader, Padmé finally lets go of him.

Paul Duncan And in the way that after Ben dies in *Star Wars*, it reaffirms Luke's belief and trust in the Force.

George Lucas The core of Anakin's problem is that Jedi are raised from birth so they learn to

1.42 **On their journey, Qui-Gon, Obi-Wan, and Jar Jar are attacked by an opee sea killer, which in turn is captured by a giant sando aqua monster, thus forcing the release of the submarine. Terryl Whitlatch's concept art (October 19, 1995) shows the relative scale between the submarine and the aquatic monsters.**
1.43 **Doug Chiang's painting of the opee sea killer in pursuit (January 24, 1996, 4 days) earned a "Fabulouso" stamp from George Lucas.**

D.CHIANG

1.43

let go of everything. They're trained more than anything else to understand the transitional nature of life, that things are constantly changing and you can't hold on to anything. You can love things but you can't be attached to them. You must be willing to let the flow of life and the flow of the Force move though your life, move through you. So that you can be compassionate and loving and caring, but not be possessive and grabbing and holding on to things and trying to keep things the way they are.

Letting go is a central theme of the film.

*1.44–45 **Ed Natividad storyboarded the invasion of Theed as a war story with frightening depictions of death, as well as children cowering in a window.** 1.46 **A troubled Queen Amidala observes the invasion from the palace. Closer scrutiny of the wall behind the queen reveals the wiring used to power the lights at the bottom of her dress. The wiring was digitally removed.***

April 17, 1996

Doug Chiang George wanted trade barons who were controlling the droids. I created a portrait.

Paul Duncan That was your March 7, 1995, painting.

Doug Chiang Right. He liked it, and then we put a pin in it because the idea of the trade barons evolved a little bit. So, I set that aside.

I had a wall of shame where every week I put all my rejects, to keep my sanity, because in the first weeks George was rejecting everything. The wonderful thing is that George keeps track of all that. So later on, after our art reviews he would go in there and pick out things and say, "Let's update this. I have an idea for this." Everything was always in play.

In the initial meetings where George tells us a new idea, he's generally very vague. The next week, he'll say something, and give us another piece of information. Then the third week, if we're missing it, he'll say, "Do this, and this, and this," and he'll pull out a reference he had all along. Part of the process is he wants us to explore options.

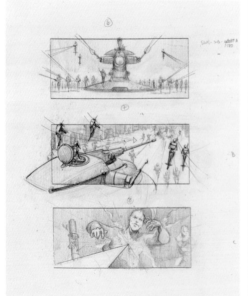

1.44

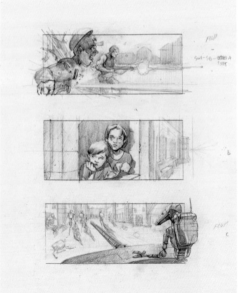

1.45

1.47

1.47 *Filming McGregor and Neeson preparing to escape from the bongo sub. The background is blue screen to enable CG environments to be added during postproduction.*
1.48 *Iain McCaig's storyboards depict the submarine about to fall over the waterfall. Qui-Gon shoots a cable that attaches itself to a railing onshore giving the Jedi and Jar Jar time to escape.*
1.49 *Kurt Kaufman's storyboard (March 13, 1998) for the bongo arriving in Theed — note that the live-action plate had already been filmed. In the script the submarine emerges into an estuary but the current pushes it toward a waterfall.*

A year later, in March 1996, he said, "Remember that portrait? Let's take that and I have a new character for you." That's when he described the cut-and-paste idea of taking the head on the portrait, putting it on a dumpy duck body, then adding bat wings and duck feet. Terryl Whitlatch, Iain McCaig, and I all heard the same thing, and put it through our filters. Iain and Terryl did beautiful drawings of exotic creatures that fit the brief.

Paul Duncan Terryl did a sweet-looking giant budgerigar, and Iain did a smoking ghost-like figure.

Doug Chiang George kept saying, "No, no, no. Do these three things." It was baffling, because we couldn't figure it out. In the end I did exactly what he said, and pieced it together.

I remember drawing it and thinking, "This is not going to work." When I drew it, it was like, "Wow, it actually worked."

Paul Duncan So this is drawing 627, dated April 17, 1996?

Doug Chiang Yeah. That was Watto. There was this whimsy about it that makes it *Star Wars* fun. That is George. He had a clarity of vision from the start. If he had the time I'm sure he would draw this himself.

Paul Duncan Watto feels like one of those malevolent characters in a Disney film like *Pinocchio*. He is a slave master, the owner of Anakin and Shmi, but he doesn't beat them. He allows Anakin to do things. There's a push-pull of emotions going on that's not clichéd.

Doug Chiang Exactly. There're layers and depth to his character. You see that when he loses the bet to Qui-Gon. Those are the things that George is thinking about when he tells us about the design. When we're drawing, George's casting. So we're trying to capture a very specific character type that he's looking for. He's looking for personality. He's looking for things that will reinforce what he's writing.

After this, I had a huge appreciation for George. As young designers you think, "I trained my whole career. I know what it is. I'm going to sell you on the idea." You know what? George is operating on a different level to us.

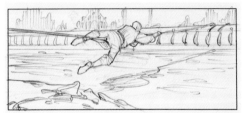

1.48

April 23, 1996

George Lucas In the writing process, I'm very focused on story. When you're doing storyboards you're more interested in the cinematic kinetics of things, of how things move together.

1.49

"*The live-action sets were built one story tall, so we had to add all of the rest of the architecture. Otherwise, Physical miniatures were made for the Theed shots due to the complex nature of the architecture and the need to provide floral augmentation. These were built to 1:30 scale and filmed outdoors to match the original live-action lighting. Filming was done at 64 FPS, to minimize the effect of wind on the miniature trees, using motion control photography, to match the original camera motion.*"

Scott Squires / Visual Effects Supervisor

1.51

1.50

George Lucas held a three-hour storyboard meeting every Tuesday with production designer Gavin Bocquet, David Dozoretz, and the art department led by Doug Chiang. On April 23, 1996, Lucas outlined the sequences he needed:

1.50 *Obi-Wan and Qui-Gon dispatch the droids and introduce themselves to the queen, telling her that the negotiations she had relied upon have failed.*
1.51 *Ewan McGregor bounces from a trampette to slay the battle droids, depicted by members of the crew wearing white suits and droid masks for reference. Ray Park, crouching next to the camera, observes proceedings.*

GWL Storyboard Meeting Notes / April 23, 1996

1. Opening
2. Bridge and conference room
3. Battle outside conference room
4. Battle outside bridge
5. Landing craft and chase
6. Underwater sequence — swimming to Otoh Gunga
7. Otoh Gunga landing platform
8. Space battle — going past blockade (into hyperspace, back out onto Tatooine)
9. Pod race
10. Jedi/Sith fight (huge) on Tatooine (like Jackie Chan film)
11. Leaving Tatooine (into hyperspace)
12. Arriving at Coruscant (ship in, city shots à la Cloud City)
13. And following... the rest back to Naboo (more details later)

Lucas then described specific shots for the underwater sequence as Obi-Wan and Jar Jar swim to Otoh Gunga, stipulating that, "all shots underwater are moving shots—camera floats with them." The descriptions of wide-screen, point of view, close-up, reverse shots are very specific as Obi-Wan and Jar Jar enter the underwater city, take the submarine, are followed by the opee sea killer, which is devoured by the sando aqua monster, go through the center of the planet, are chased by a colo claw fish, which is eaten by another sando monster, and then arrive at the Theed estuary. Iain McCaig drew these storyboards.

Each meeting followed a similar format, with Lucas commenting on past work, and adding new sequences. On August 20, Lucas described new battle ideas, which would be drawn by Ed Natividad, and commented on the Jedi/Sith fight on Tatooine.

Iain McCaig / Concept Artist I had done a sequence where the Sith Lord comes racing up on his speeder. Obi-Wan Kenobi turns round as the Sith Lord jumps off his bike, throws his cloak off, draws his lightsaber and attacks Obi-Wan before the cloak even hits the ground. I storyboarded this and tried to make it look really fast. I used all the tricks I had and when it was up on the wall, George asked, "What are you trying to do?" "To look really fast, George." "Fast. Want to see fast?" and then he took three of the boards and he rear-ranged them. He didn't remove any of them and it was 10 times faster. I thought I had that scene locked down, and I learned there's always a better way, even in areas you think you know real well.

George Lucas The work part is not hard. It's really the relentlessness of the amount of it that you have to do that's hard. It's one thing to storyboard 100 shots and it's another thing to storyboard 2,000–3,000 shots. We've been going on for several months now and it's going to go on for another year.

June 22, 1996

George Lucas I finished the rough draft and the revised rough draft and now I'm starting on the first draft. I've got a lot more to go.

In the very rough draft, Obi-Wan was essentially by himself through the first third of the film. In the first 10 pages or so there was nobody for him to play against. Then Jar Jar Binks

1.54

1.53

appears, but he's comic relief. The queen operates in a different world than the Jedi. I have to develop a relationship between her and Anakin, because that's where the real story is, but I wasn't able to develop Obi-Wan's character fast enough.

When I got through the rough draft I realized that I had a second Jedi that comes in about halfway through the script who is an interesting character and the more I thought about it the more I thought of things I could do with these two Jedi together because one alone didn't have much to react to.

Paul Duncan So you added a Jedi mentor for Obi-Wan, called Qui-Gon Jinn, which meant that Obi-Wan became a Padawan. The film begins with them dealing with a dispute between the Trade Federation and Naboo.

George Lucas The film starts with corrupt corporations doing things behind people's backs. The Jedi are trying to solve the mystery. A corporation is a shark without a conscience. All it

*1.52 **Preparing the model of Theed for shooting. It was filmed outside to make best use of natural light.***
*1.53 **The queen reluctantly decides to leave Naboo to plead for help from the Senate on Coruscant. This final frame of the royal starship leaving the Theed hangar shows the integration of the Theed model with the CG starship and background environment.***
*1.54 **George Lucas demonstrates how to attack a battle droid with a lightsaber.***

cares about is eating. It's not responsible. It's the stockholders' fault, or the CEO's fault, or the board's fault. It's always somebody else's fault, but of course the golden rule is "make money, no matter what," so that's what everybody follows. They're not doing it to be nice to people.

Our central characters—Qui-Gon, Obi-Wan, Padmé, and Anakin—are all trying to

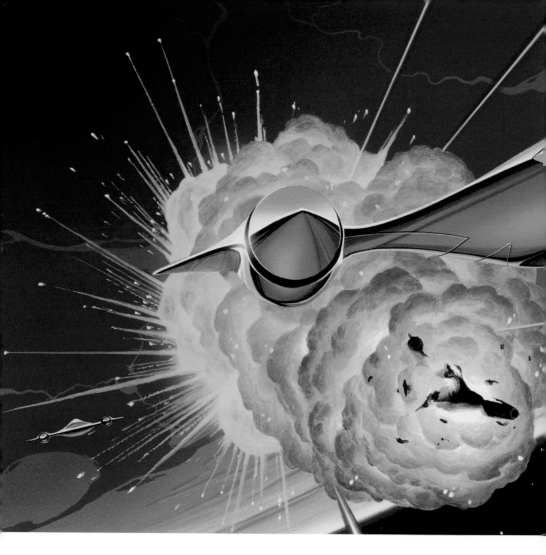

do the right thing, but they're completely overwhelmed by forces that are way bigger than they are. The Jedi Council and bureaucrats in the Senate are the inactive forces working against them; while unbeknownst to them the active one is Palpatine.

The second film is about the building of a secret army and going to war, which obviously turns the grand chancellor into an Emperor politically. The Senate gives up the Republic. It's still a Republic, but an Emperor rules it. Don't worry, as soon as things are fixed, he'll give it back. (Laughs)

The two main themes are "How do you become a bad person?" and "How do you give away a democracy to end up with a tyrant?" Because they give it away—there's no coup, there's no rebellion, there's no nothing.

Paul Duncan They vote it in.

George Lucas They vote it in, which is what happens in real life.

Paul Duncan The three movies are the endgame for the Emperor.

George Lucas The whole thing's been set up for a long, long time. He is just watching the dominoes fall.

D. CHIANG

1.55

September 1996

George Lucas I was trying to get a studio facility built here, near the Ranch, so I could shoot here, but that did not happen. But hey, they win, I lose. I'm going to England.

Rick McCallum / Producer We needed an area five or six times the size of Elstree Studios, so we rented Leavesden, a former aerodrome located on the outskirts of London, for two and a half years.

David Tattersall / Cinematographer The advantage for Rick and George was that they could lease the entire facility; they didn't have

to share anything with other productions, which is the usual situation. Because of that, many sets could be built once, and left standing indefinitely. Our production designer, Gavin Bocquet, had about 15 large spaces to work with, which gave us the room to have some 25 fully constructed sets to shoot on.

1.55 *Chiang's painting showing the queen's spaceship, and others, trying to unlock the Trade Federation's blockade (August 7, 1996, 2 days).*

1.56

Rick McCallum We've totally destroyed the barrier between production and postproduction. It means that George can direct the movie, we can keep our sets up, we have total security, we can edit for eight or 10 weeks, rewrite, then we can reshoot. We built this into the budget and the contracts with the cast and crew.

Preproduction commenced in September 1996.

Rick McCallum We have about 500 people working full time, but most of that is construction. It will slip off and then we will have a shooting crew of about 80 people. But we will be building sets throughout the whole time.

Rob Coleman / Animation Director Instead of building these huge, enormous sets as Cecil B. DeMille would have done building the Colosseum in Rome, for example, you build a little bit of the Colosseum with a lot of blue screen around it, and you put your actors in front of that. You save money and put it into digital or miniature backgrounds, then composite things together.

Rick McCallum I'd planned to build only up to six feet, just enough to get the actors shot against the backgrounds. Then we cast Liam Neeson, who's 6'4", as Qui-Gon, so we had to raise that minimum height. He ruined my budget.

September 7, 1996

George Lucas Ideas don't come into a story that easily. A lot of the time the characters have to say what you mean, and to do that the characters usually have to have differing opinions about the idea so they can discuss it.

Qui-Gon and Obi-Wan disagree about using what one would call in mythological terms "the guide." One believes in the guide. The other one doesn't. When you are walking down the street and the beggar's on the street, one character takes the beggar along with them on the trip, and the other one says, "Why are you doing this? This is going to slow us down. This is not a wise thing to do." The first one says, "Yes, but this beggar is useful to us." It's a classic mythological motif but at the same time, it's conflict.

1.56 The queen's ship has been damaged by the blockade — its shield generator has failed and power is down. A brave little blue droid goes through an airlock to the exterior of the ship to restore power to the stricken vessel.
1.57 R2-D2's first appearance is in the queen's starship. Doug Chiang created concepts for the popular little astromech droid, based on it being like an unfolding Swiss Army knife (November 20, 1996).

The characters have to grow so what happens is that eventually the character that is very much against doing this has the obligation transferred to them.

In this case, we have Qui-Gon, the mentor who takes on Anakin, and the Padawan Obi-Wan who thinks this is a bad idea, so we've got a dynamic between these two Jedi. At the end of the film, Obi-Wan takes on the obligation to train Anakin, one that he can't really fulfill because it's over his head.

His inability to train this kid properly turns Anakin into Darth Vader and drives the rest of the stories. Not only does he let his mentor down, but it plays into the collapse of the Republic. This is why he feels obligated to try to rectify the situation with Luke.

One of the reasons people connect to *Star Wars* so much is because the psychology of it is very old. Whether it's knights in armor, or Greek warriors, or Western gunslingers, you're always telling the same story where you combine the larger cosmic and spiritual issues with the temporal issues of who you are and what your limitations are. I'm amazed people aren't telling these stories anymore. People have forgotten about the reason you tell a story. They just seem to tell it without any point to it.

> *"Every time I do a Star Wars film it's like running the Indy 500 — no matter how many times you've done it, it's the same challenge. There is no guarantee that you're going to be able to pull it off at all but the driving's fun."*
>
> George Lucas

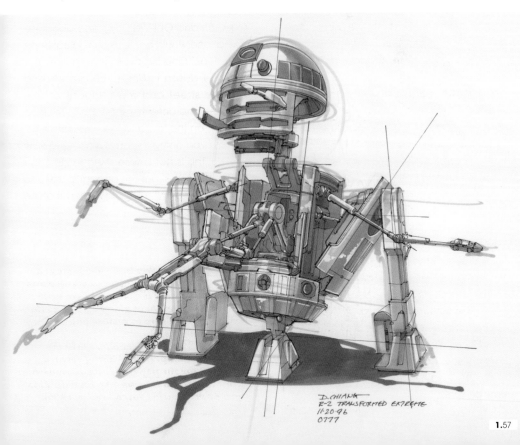

D. CHIANG
R-2 TRANSFORMED EXTREME
11-20-96
0777

OK

1.58

October 26, 1996

George Lucas Digital characters have been done before, in *Jurassic Park*, *Jumanji*, and *Casper*, but talking digital characters who are part of the scene and on screen for a long time is a huge challenge.

Jar Jar is the key character but we have about a dozen synthetic characters that will be in the movie. There's a lot of material to make, therefore we have to come up with an innovative way to cut the costs so that we can do as much of it as we plan to do. The current motion capture technology isn't suitable because you have to capture each actor on their own on a special stage then put them into the image later. We need a character that everybody can interact with, so we're trying to figure out how to do that. We want to film an actor on the set, harvest the movement data, then feed the data into software so that the character will be automatically animated, and the actor digitally overpainted. Then we put the detail on and tweak it.

We've come to the conclusion that Jar Jar's face is too complex to try to get a human face to mimic it, so we will have the actor do their part, watch the lip movement for the sync of the words, and the animator will animate that from scratch.

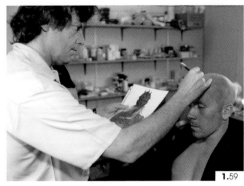

1.59

*1.58 **This Sith Lord concept (April 2, 1996) is now recognizable as Darth Maul. However, McCaig drew feathers (tied around his head with wire), and these were later replaced by horns, giving the Sith Lord an even more demonic appearance.***
*1.59 **Ray Park's transformation from martial artist to Sith Lord. The makeup process took one and a half hours.***
*1.60 **The first appearance of Darth Maul (Ray Park). Darth Sidious (Ian McDiarmid) introduces Nute Gunray (Silas Carson) to his new apprentice, indicating that he will be the one to locate the queen's missing ship.***

1.60

This week we've been testing with mime Michel Courtemanche to figure out how Jar Jar would walk, personality traits that he might have, things that would make him look different when he's the animated character. I want him to have a very distinct look and a very distinct movement pattern, so we've been experimenting with various possibilities in that arena.

A lot of the movement things though were simply me saying, "Swing your arms around, make your arms really loose, walk this way, walk that way, move your head, move your neck, and move your hips, try to put all those things together," and then say, "Let's make it more relaxed," to try to come up with something that looks right.

Going through the language with Michel was the first time I've heard it so I was able to listen to it objectively. It tends to sound a little bit like an Indian accent, so I have to keep playing around with the words until I come up with a consistent seamless foreign

1.61 A battered R2-D2 (Kenny Baker) is introduced to the queen, who offers her thanks to the little droid for saving the ship.
1.62 The queen's handmaiden, Padmé (Natalie Portman), is assigned the task of cleaning R2-D2. The queen believes in democracy, that everyone should contribute to society.
1.63 This concept for the handmaiden Padmé by Iain McCaig (May 17, 1996) was based on the Hopi Indian hair that had inspired Princess Leia's hairstyle in Star Wars.

dialogue that is not derivative of any particular current culture. And it still needs to be understandable, because I don't want to have to subtitle it.

November 16, 1996

George Lucas I'm pretty close to finishing my second draft, which is officially called the first draft, which is in reality the 25th draft. I'm up to

1.62

IAIN MCAIG
(PADMA (HAIR)
5 · 17 · 96.
0 0 0 9 8.

page 100. I've run into the stumbling block of too much script and I'm trying to figure a way of expediting story so that we can get from point A to point B faster. In essence, I've run out of room.

I don't have extraneous scenes. In theory I could cut out an action sequence with Obi-Wan and Jar Jar with a sea monster, but it's a pretty good scene and I need something to intercut with the approaching Federation army.

The podrace serves the purpose of establishing Anakin's character, his prowess as a pilot, and his extrasensory abilities with the Force. So there's a lot going on in the podrace besides just an action sequence. It's about 20 minutes now and I'm trying to get it down to about 10 or 12 minutes.

The biggest structural problem is the third act. In *Star Wars*, they flee the Death Star, go to the Rebel base, have two scenes, and then there's the end battle. In this one they go from Tatooine to Coruscant, Coruscant back to

Naboo, make lots of plans, and set up for the battle. Then they have the battle and the film ends. I've got about 15 or 20 scenes where *Star Wars* is only two, and if each of those is two minutes, that's 30 minutes right there. I have to get that down to about five or six

1.64 *Filming in Tunisia. Qui-Gon and R2-D2 need to visit the city of Mos Espa to obtain parts to repair the hyperdrive, which was damaged during the escape from Naboo. Captain Panaka (Hugh Quarshie) and Padmé follow, insisting that the queen has ordered Padmé to join them despite Qui-Gon's reservations. In the background is the gangway of the queen's starship supported by scaffolding; the rest of the ship will be added in postproduction.*
1.65 *The model of the queen's starship in the desert landscape of Tatooine was filmed on the roof of ILM in San Rafael, California.*
1.66 *Doug Chiang's concept art for the queen's starship, which has landed on the desert planet of Tatooine, with Jar Jar in the foreground (May 23, 1996, 2.4 days).*

minutes. I'm simplifying and trying to make the story cleaner and faster so I can get to the end.

This is the first really official script that everybody will have which means that it will be harder to change things after this point. This one becomes real.

I have ideal characters in my head, but when I finally get to the actors, they're going to be real people with their own personalities and they're not going to necessarily be exactly what I had in mind. They're going to be something else, but I have to accept the fact that that's now the character. It begins to drive the movie in directions that I didn't anticipate.

Robin Gurland / Casting Director It's always about who's right for the role. If it was

1.65

1.66

1.67

1.67 *George Lucas (right) and production designer Gavin Bocquet (second right) inspect the scale model of Mos Espa to determine what will be built in Tunisia. Bocquet: "George was just adamant that the light and the sand and the whole environment of Tunisia were Tatooine, and he would not go anywhere else."*
1.68 *Lucas (center) setting up a shot on the Mos Espa set in Tozeur, Tunisia, a few days after a storm had wrecked the set. Crew members worked frantically to effect repairs in time for the shoot.*

someone the public knew, fine. If it wasn't, that was just as well. We never showed them the script, which surprised most of them. They would just come in and chat with George, Rick, and myself about anything and everything — politics, religion, theater. In fact, we talked about everything except *Star Wars*. George was looking to find out who the person was and how he or she matched the vision he had of a particular character.

George Lucas We cast our very first person. We're trying to make a deal now so hopefully that will happen and fall into place. But we've cast Natalie Portman to be Padmé, which is going to be great. She's perfect for the part. It's hard in those types of situations to find a young girl who has a lot of presence and a lot of strength who can play what is in essence an adult role. She has to play the queen, who is very aloof and distant and wears a lot of makeup and has rather extreme costumes. And then she has to play Padmé, who is much more personable, much more human.

We have a couple of possibilities for each of the other major roles. The most difficult one obviously is the boy Anakin.

January 15, 1997

On January 15, a list of storyboards was made of all the sequences, which totaled 2,018 shots, with some sequences still under development. Lucas held a storyboard/set design

1.68

1.69

meeting at Skywalker Ranch with the production team and the team from ILM.

John Knoll / Visual Effects Supervisor We saw all the storyboards pasted up on sheets of foam core, and George took us through the boards one by one.

George Lucas I broke it down in terms of what parts of the image are going to be real and what parts are not real. Most movies you build a set and shoot it. We can't do that. Here we have to know who are the real characters, and who are the synthetic characters? What is the real set and what is the synthetic set? What are the real props and what are the synthetic props? A lot has to do with how much the actors come in contact with it, how much it costs to build in either environment. If a car is built for real then you might as well use it again and again. You don't want to have to build it twice, a real one and a synthetic one.

John Knoll My reaction to just about every board was "That's going to be really hard." And before you have time to think he's on to the next one. "There's 2,000 characters in that shot!" So it was a pretty overwhelming experience.

Rick McCallum It became clear this is going to be unlike any other special effects movie ever done. To put it into perspective, a big film has maybe 250 effects shots, and a monster film like *Titanic* has 450 to 500. George was thinking about somewhere between 1,700 and 2,000 shots. The thing that I was most afraid of was not "Can ILM do it?" but "Could any effects house do it?!"

1.70

June 6, 1997

George Lucas I needed somebody who could serve as the center of the picture, the way Alec Guinness did in *Star Wars*; somebody who was very soulful and wise and powerful physically.

Liam Neeson I met George and Rick in London and we talked about kids. George is a family man, and I have two little boys, and that's what we talked about. Rick called me up and said "The character was originally a 60-year-old, would you be prepared to play 55?" I said, "Sure, I'm an actor." But I thought, I'm not going to do old-man acting, because that would be stupid—this guy has to have a lot of lightsaber fights.

George Lucas I decided on Liam because I didn't want somebody that looked like a movie star—I wanted somebody that looked like a very strong Jedi.

Rick McCallum For a younger Obi-Wan, we took a bunch of Alec Guinness films from when he was younger and looked at current actors. We thought Ewan McGregor was great playing roles in *Trainspotting* and *Emma* the same year. Once we met him we knew.

George Lucas The first thing he said when he came in for the interview was "You've got to give me this because my uncle, Denis Lawson, played Wedge."

I was impressed by Ewan's charisma on screen. He's the right age, he looks a little

1.69 *Lucas asked Chiang to put the head of the rejected trade baron on a duck body and feet, and add little bat wings, to create Watto (April 17, 1996).*
1.70 *Final shot of Jar Jar, Padmé, and Qui-Gon meeting Watto (Andy Secombe) and in search of parts to repair the hyperdrive.*
1.71 *Best, Portman, and Neeson in Watto's junk shop. Andy Secombe, playing Watto, is wearing a hat that provides an eyeline for the actors so that they can visualize where the junk dealer will be floating.*

1.72 *Padmé and Artoo meet Anakin (Jake Lloyd) for the first time. "Are you an angel?" Anakin asks Padmé.*
1.73 *Iain McCaig's concept for Anakin Skywalker (October 27, 1995).*
1.74 *Jake Lloyd was eight years old when the film was shot in 1997. Lucas: "We tested literally thousands of kids. We went all over the world for two years doing tests, shooting tapes. Jake Lloyd was a natural. He reminded me of a young Luke Skywalker; and that was good because he had to embody the same presence that Luke had in the first film. Jake was somebody you liked a lot, who was a lot of fun and very alive. He was charming and witty as a person, and that carries through into his role."*

like Alec, and he's got a mischievous quality about him.

Robin Gurland George wrote Anakin knowing that it would be an incredible task to find the right child actor. He had every imaginable element built into this kid, from mechanical ability to earnestness. Usually children's roles aren't that complex.

I interviewed about 3,000 Anakins.

George Lucas We went all over the world looking for kids. We started out when they were five, six, and seven years old. We have been interviewing these kids on a six months to a yearly basis over the period of three years watching them grow, watching them progress, doing tests, doing tapes. In the end it boiled down to about a half dozen kids.

Jake Lloyd was one of several kids that we brought in. I tested them myself and worked with them. Ultimately, I felt that Jake had the personality I was looking for combined with a very real talent that he exhibited when I worked with him during the testing period. Jake has all the funny, enthusiastic qualities and the acting talent it will take to pull this off. **Jake Lloyd** Robin called my agent and asked, "How would Jake and his parents like to spend the summer in London?" When I found out, I screamed, "Oooaaah!" It was very cool. I started bawling, I was so happy. Now everyone will know who is behind the mask of Darth Vader!

Jake Lloyd signed his contract on June 6, 1997. On June 18, the principal cast read through the Fourth Draft script, dated June 13, 1997, and titled The Beginning. *The script was revised June 23, 1997.*

June 26, 1997

Gavin Bocquet / Production Designer Normally you're somewhere for a week or two, and you get a chance to catch a deep breath. But this was relentless from the first day. Every two days we were moving to a completely new environment with new characters and new action and a new style.

Production commenced on June 26, 1997, at Leavesden studios. The cast and crew were called for 8:00 a.m., the first shot of scene 77 was taken at 8:32 a.m., with the clapperboard indicating that the director was "Yoda."

Scene 77-EXT. CORUSCANT-BALCONY OVERLOOKING CITY-NIGHT

DARTH SIDIOUS and DARTH MAUL look out over the vast city.

Darth Sidious (Ian McDiarmid) tells his apprentice Darth Maul (Ray Park) to go to Tatooine,

1.73

1.74

Terryl Whitlatch
9-29-95
Nemesis Pod Racer

w/o clothes

should I add an arm
tattoo?

smaller
K scale

1.75

kill the Jedi, then return the queen to Naboo and force her to sign the peace treaty with the Trade Federation. McDiarmid had played the Emperor in 1982, aged 37, for Return of the Jedi *(1983).*

Ian McDiarmid It was an incredibly unique opportunity. I am basically myself in this film—though I got about 10 years' help from a hairpiece. Palpatine looks like me. That's fascinating. In my career as an actor I've often played older than myself, but you don't often go backwards in time—when you're really 15 years older—to play a character younger than yourself, and far younger than the same character you've already played.

David Tattersall The first shot of the day was always a master. After that, it was a matter of moving in to get two-shots, over-the-shoulders, and close-ups. We then switched to the reverse angle and repeated the process. It's a classical way of getting coverage, and so many other directors tie themselves in knots, from an editing standpoint, by not doing exactly that.

Two cameras were generally used to cover every setup—one wide and the other tighter, but at the same angle. The first camera would cover for the storyboard, while the second would get something else—it was fairly conventional. The first unit would start with George

1.75 *Terryl Whitlatch concept art for Sebulba, Anakin's nemesis podracer (September 29, 1995). Whitlatch: "George knew that he wanted a smallish (in order to fit into a racing pod) spidery character that walked on his hands and steered with his feet, was arrogant, sneaky, bad-tempered, as well as being a cheater and all-around bad guy. So I gave Sebulba the head of a sour, ill-tempered camel with hornlike structures and a spidery way of moving. It took only one day to get George's approval, and that's the way it went for most of the other podracer characters, who, after all, are rather minor characters. George saw, he liked, and we all breathed a sigh of relief!"*
1.76 *Anakin stands up to Sebulba (Lewis Macleod) to protect Jar Jar; Jar Jar accidentally caused a chuba to be thrown at Sebulba. Anakin and Sebulba are rival podracers. Whitlatch: "I think of Sebulba as 'his badness.' He doesn't care how he wins as long as he does."*

and then the second unit with cameraman Giles Nuttgens would follow up behind to pick up their material. Giles shot several episodes of *Young Indy*, so he was somebody familiar with our procedures.

The great thing about doing a wide master first is that nobody on the set is in any doubt

1.76

1.78

> *"We were looking for something that could be a slave quarters and we came across these ksour, which were old grain stores for tiny towns and villages in North Africa. They're two or three stories, and almost catacomb-like, but above ground."*
>
> Gavin Bocquet / Production Designer

about what's going on in the scene, which is important when there are so many effects. If a director begins with the close-ups, or something in the middle of the scene, confusion can very easily occur.

There were eight setups for the scene, and 20 takes, each of them with a blue screen background where the nighttime cityscape of Coruscant would be added later by ILM.

David Tattersall We had a surveying team working with us during the shoot, collecting spatial and topographical information, but the Arri Camera Data Capture System recorded everything regarding the camera itself: focus, aperture, zoom controls, the geared head, the dolly, et cetera, and fed it into a laptop. Together with the information collected by the survey team, ILM had a very good idea of what we were doing on each shot; they could replay any camera move in the virtual environment, which avoided the usual laborious match-moving process. The DCS required the camera assistant to do about 30 seconds of extra work on each take, but overall it had very little impact on our work.

The crew moved on to scene 127, where Anakin Skywalker (Jake Lloyd) and Jar Jar Binks (Ahmed Best) are in the anteroom of Palpatine's quarters listening but not understanding what is happening inside. The short scene was completed in seven setups and 46 takes. However, since Jar Jar is in the scene there are multiple reference takes with and without Jar Jar in the shot, and also shots for light reference.

John Knoll We can take a clean plate—a scene with all the actors but without Jar Jar—and add a CG Jar Jar into the shot.

That's one option. But when we started shooting in the set, the way Ahmed Best cast shadows on the walls and set, and the way that he interacted with the lighting, meant that the shots were going to be a lot better if we could use as much of his performance as possible, so that's the approach we're taking.

Also, we had two lighting exercises that we went through for every setup that involved a CG character. When you're putting a CG character into a shot you want to capture what kind of lighting was present on the set at the point where the character is standing. So we had a sphere. One side of it was a matte gray—the same 17 percent gray as our standard gray card—and the other side was chrome. For every setup we would shoot facing gray side toward camera and then chrome side toward the camera.

The chrome side was useful because you get to see where all the lights are in the room—the key and fill lights—and the ratio of all the lights.

1.77 *This slum scene by Whitlatch features the daily life around Shmi and Anakin's slave quarters (February 8, 1996).*
1.78 *Gavin Bocquet and Rick McCallum went location scouting in the summer of 1994, before there was a script, knowing that some of the story would take place on Tatooine. They found Ksar Ouled Soltane, a fortified granary, in the Tataouine district of Tunisia, and Terryl Whitlatch used photos of this location as reference.*
1.79 *Anakin offers his new friends refuge from the storm in his home. Anakin is portrayed as a kind boy who is always helping people and fixing things.*

1.79

1.80

Finally on the first day, shooting began on scene 128, where Palpatine tries to persuade Queen Amidala to call for a vote of no confidence in Chancellor Valorum. They filmed eight setups and 29 takes, with the scene to be completed the following day. Generally, there were more takes for the first setup as cast and crew learned their positions and refined the scene.

The first day finished at 8:00 p.m. after 12 hours of filming. Shooting days at Leavesden were often longer than 12 hours and rarely shorter.

July 1, 1997

Terence Stamp flew in from Australia to play Chancellor Valorum in two scenes. The first is scene 132, in the chancellor's pod at the Galactic Senate, where Valorum is attacked by a vote of no confidence from Queen Amidala, filmed on July 1.

The gray side, you can see what the key and fill ratio were, and what color the different lights were. When we were working with the image, a quick way to get the lighting is to put a CG gray sphere next to the sphere on the image, and move your CG lights around until the two spheres look like each other. Then you can put your CG character in the image, knowing the lighting is pretty close, and then start refining it.

Also for all the Jar Jar, Watto, and Sebulba scenes we had painted models that we'd film turning around in the light so we had color reference. For Jar Jar we had a full-size head and shoulders painted silicone model. For Watto we had a half-size model of the full body. And for Sebulba we had a half-size head and shoulders. This way, when we rotated the Watto model we could see how bright the blue body was, how bright the yellow belly was, how much accent and shadow the wings have, and so on.

Terence Stamp When they told me I would be playing the President of the Universe that caught my attention, but when I walked onto the set, no Natalie. "We've given Natalie the day off," they said. "That bit of paper on the post? That's Natalie. Deliver your lines to the paper."

Portman had completed her lines for the scene the previous day. Stamp asked Lucas for direction about his character.

Terence Stamp Lucas seemed rather astounded to be asked that. He paused, thought about it, then said, "He's a good man, but beleaguered, a bit like President Clinton." That was it! No more direction.

On July 2 the remaining principal actors started on the production in scene 126, on the Senate landing platform, where the queen, her entourage, the Jedi, and Anakin are met by Senator Palpatine and Chancellor Valorum.

Name

JAK/GWL Notes, 01/20/98:
(68B/1 "B")
Mos Espa Street - Revised shot: Push-in on group, they
exit R. Creature or droid in fg to cover Anakin's dialogue
flub. Add tail to shot to extend Artoo. People running from

JAK/GWL Notes, 01/20/98:
(XVV75B-3)
Mos Espa Sandstorm - Guy runs into doorway, 2nd. guy on
L. in bg. 2nd. guy is patched in.

JAK/GWL Notes, 01/20/98:
(XVV75A-1)
2 more characters run from sandstorm. Guy crossing L-R
is same guy in doorway of previous shot patched in
(MSS 071 011)

JAK/GWL Notes, 01/20/98:

JAK/GWL Notes, 01/20/98:
(71/3)
WS Qui-Gon, Padme, Anakin in doorway. Add more bg
people.

JAK/GWL Notes, 01/20/98:
(72H/2)
WS Anakin, Jar Jar, Qui-Gon into hovel. Use ref cut - Jar
Jar head replacement.

JAK/GWL Notes, 01/20/98:

JAK/GWL Notes, 01/20/98:
(72/20pu "B")
MWS Group meets Shmi. Add Jar Jar.

1.81

1.80 *The production encountered problems shooting R2-D2 in Anakin's hovel. It was an enclosed space with narrow doors and uneven flooring and the droid failed to operate correctly during a number of takes. The solution was to commission ILM and the Effects Department to construct some replacement R2-D2 units. Despite all the difficulties, the little droid endeared itself to at least one member of the cast.*

1.81 *Shot log from January 30, 1998, showing Lucas's review of the sandstorm scene, detailing the alterations he felt were needed to enhance the sequence, including adding a creature or droid in the foreground to cover Anakin's dialogue flub. Also note that for some shots, Ahmed Best's body performance is used and only Jar Jar's head is replaced, whereas in other shots Jar Jar has to be added.*

1.82

> **"George wanted Anakin's homemade version of a protocol droid. Being homemade and unfinished, George described it as 'a man of wires.' I went through many, many drawings trying to determine how naked, so to speak, C-3PO should be."**
>
> Doug Chiang

Liam Neeson Our very first scene involved coming down the platform to meet Valorum. Ewan and I were just thrilled. We kept laughing and shouting, "Yeeeahh! We're in *Star Wars!*"

This scene, like many scenes for the movie, involved acting against blue screen and alongside characters that did not yet exist.

George Lucas *Star Wars* is really make-believe, like an old-time, old-fashioned movie, which is one of the reasons why I wanted to do it. I'd never done a movie like that before—where it's all blue screen. We'd sit down the actors and say, "This is like a stage play. It's going to have no sets, just you on the stage, doing *Hamlet* or *Waiting for Godot*. You can do this." We showed them pictures of what the set looks like, or play the animatics, so they'd have an idea.

Liam Neeson We would watch the scene on these little screens with computer figures. So it was like, "Oh, yeah, I go here and there." It was great to see the scene before you shot it.

Natalie Portman The acting was so technical in many ways. It's about hitting marks and keeping eye lines.

Liam Neeson It was a new technique to be learned, I have to admit. I wanted to make the scene real and give a sense to an audience that this is an everyday occurrence, that I talk to these creatures all the time, no matter what they look like or where they are from. So I wanted to keep my acting very simple, straightforward, and truthful.

July 15, 1997

From July 10 to 15 the scenes set in Anakin's hovel were filmed on D Stage. On the last day, C-3PO appears for the first time. As designed by Doug Chiang, C-3PO was still being constructed by Anakin.

John Knoll When we saw the designs it was quite clear that it was impossible to use a guy inside a suit. We thought it either had to be computer-generated or it needed to be a puppet of some kind.

Both George and I had seen Bunraku, a Japanese puppeteering technique where a performer is all in black against a black background, the puppet is attached to the front of the performer, and it's lit so that you can't see the performer very well. I thought we could do the same thing for C-3PO.

Mike Lynch in the model shop built a crude mock-up and attached it to his front. We shot a test on video and showed it to George. It was a little funky, and it's going to be really hard to paint out the performer, but George

87 — The Phantom Menace (1999)

1.82 *Anthony Daniels (second left) read his lines offscreen during filming.*
1.83 *Very close to final version of C-3PO by Doug Chiang (October 30, 1995).*
1.84 *Doug Chiang's 1995 concept art shows C-3PO in the process of being constructed by Anakin. The concept art experimented with establishing different levels of completion for the protocol droid.*

1.83

1.84

Prod. Office: Leavesden Studios
Hill Farm Avenue, Leavesden, Herts
Tel: Fax:
2nd AD Bernie Bellew:

JAK PRODUCTIONS LTD
STAR WARS - EPISODE 1
THE BEGINNING

Date: Thursday 26 July 1997
Call Sheet No: 1

UNIT CALL ON SET: 8.00am
B/fast in canteen from 7.00am

Director: George Lucas
Producer: Rick McCallum

NO SMOKING, FOOD OR DRINK ON THIS SET

LOCATION	SET - DESCRIPTION	SCENE	D/N	PGs	CAST
MS2 STAGE	Ext Coruscant-Balcony overlooking City				
Leavesden Studio	Sidious tells Maul to dispense with Queen & Jedi	77	N	4/8	12. 13
	Int Palpatine's Quarters - Anteroom				
	Jar Jar comments on the oddness	127	D	3/8	2. 3. 6. 9. 10. 11. 47
	Int Palpatine's Quarters - Living Area				
	Amidala confers with Palpatine	128	D	1 1/8	2. 3. 6. 9. 10. 11. 47

	ARTISTE	CHARACTER	DR	P.UP	M.UP/W	L.UP	ON SET
2	Jake Lloyd	Anakin	4	08.20	09.00		10.00
3	Natalie Portman	Queen Amidala	6	07.20	08.00		10.00
6	Hugh Quarshie	Captain Panaka	1	07.50	08.30		10.00
9	Christina Di Silva	Rabe	T 1	07.20	08.00		10.00
0	Liz Wilson	Eirtae	T 2	08.00	08.20		10.00
11	Ian McDiarmid	Palpatine	2	-	-		10.00
12	Ian McDiarmid	Darth Sidious	2	06.10	06.45		08.00
13	Ray Park	Darth Maul	3	-	06.30		08.00
47	Ahmed Best	Jar Jar	3	08.00	08.45		10.00
STAND INS							
	Steve Ricard	Utility					08.00
	Joan Field	Queen					09.00
	Ray Griffiths	Anakin					09.00
	Paul Kite	Utility					08.00
CHAPERONES							
	Lisa Lloyd	For Jake Lloyd					09.00
CROWD (Total: 1)							
	John Fensom	Protocol droid	T 3		09.00		10.00

REQUIREMENTS

PROPS:	As per Ty Teiger and Peter Walpole
VISUAL EFFECTS:	Jar Jar to be tested on film for ILM when time allows
SPECIAL EFFECTS:	Wind fx on balcony
CREATURE EFFECTS:	Dressing area on set for Protocol droid
MAKE-UP/HAIR:	Optician Gemma Scott-Knox-Gore on set with lenses for Maul at 7.30
FITTINGS:	Kamay (Valorum's Asst.) at studio for fitting 15.00
ARTIST TRAVEL:	Arrivals: Terence Stamp (Valorum) arr. LHR 5.50am
CATERING:	Breakfast available in canteen from 7.00am. AM & PM breaks on set for 100 people
UNIT NOTE:	Please park milk floats sensibly to ensure entrances/exits to the stages are kept clear, and keep doorways and stairwells clear of equipment - Thank you.

ADVANCE SCHEDULE

Date/Loc	Set	Scene	D/N	Pgs	Cast
Fri 27 June (MS2 stage)	Int Palpatine's Quarters	135	N	2	3.6.9.10.11.47
	Int Hologram/Naboo Palace Throne Rm	18pt	D	1/8	11
Sat 28 June	REST DAY				
Sun 29 June	REST DAY				
Mon 30 June (B stage)	Int Alderan Box - Galactic Senate	132pt	D	2/8	3.6.9.10.11.27.62.63
	Int Queen's Box - Galactic Senate	132pt	D	2	3.6.9.10.11.27.62.63

Chris Newman - Assistant Director

1.85

1.85 Call sheet for first day of shooting. Note that the date is incorrect — filming actually began on June 26, 1997. The first scene to be filmed was scene 77, where Darth Maul (Ray Park) assures Darth Sidious (Ian McDiarmid) that he will find the Jedi and the queen on Tatooine. George Lucas: "The way I work is: first thing I'll do is shoot a wide shot. I'll just set the camera up in the corner. I'm not going to relentlessly lay out the storyboard and say exactly what's going to happen. If I forget to say 'action,' and 'cut,' someone will step in and say 'action' and 'cut.' I manage 'action' and 'cut' and 'faster' and 'more intense.' And then mostly I sit there looking miserable and quiet."

1.86

1.86 *Rick McCallum snaps the clapper-board for the very first take of the film. Note the director's name is "Yoda."*

1.87 *The final frame of Sith Lords Darth Sidious and Darth Maul discussing their dastardly plan.*

1.87

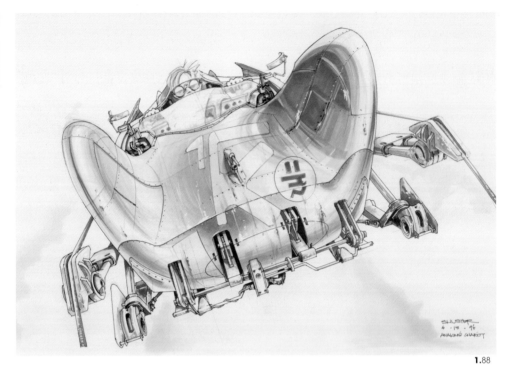

1.88

1.88 *Jay Shuster's design for a podracer (June 19, 1996). Shuster: "What was really special about the Maserati Birdcage was its really pronounced fenders. George wanted Anakin to sit really low into it."*

1.89 *Anakin is confident about winning the podrace. His friends, Amee (Katie Lucas), Melee (Megan Udall), Wald (Warwick Davis), Seek (Oliver Walpole), and Kitster (Dhruv Chanchani), less so.* 1.90 *Anakin manages to complete the construction of his pod. "It's working! It's working!"*

1.89

1.90

really wanted to have C-3PO present in the set for the lighting and for the interaction, so I thought, all right, let's do it.

During the scene, Anthony Daniels was just off camera reading his lines and Mike Lynch was performing the puppet.

Because C-3PO is so skeletal and you can see right through him in so many places, I was concerned that it would be impossible to completely remove the rods and the puppeteer, so we had Mike wear different colored suits in each scene. Anakin's bedroom is dark, so we have Mike in black to contrast with C-3PO. Likewise, out in the desert, we will have him in a light tan suit so that it is like the sandy color in the background behind him.

July 21, 1997

David Tattersall We had three distinct phases on the production. The first was to work our way through our initial 25 sets at the studio

(including the Galactic Senate Chamber, Senate landing platform, Anakin's home on Tatooine, Watto's junk shop, and Watto's box at the Anchorhead Arena). In the second phase, the company moved on to Italy and then Tunisia for location work (depicting the queen's palace on Naboo, and desert exteriors on Tatooine). Meanwhile, all of the wrapped sets at Leavesden would be replaced with new ones — we'd then return to shoot phase three, using the next 25 sets (including the Jedi Council Chamber, the starfighter hangar in Theed, and the palace's generator complex).

The advantage to this plan was that we had time to pre-rig and pre-light before we began shooting phases one and three, which allowed us to just go from one set to the next.

On July 21, the main unit moved to the Royal Palace of Caserta in Italy to shoot the scenes set in the throne room of the Naboo palace.

1.93

George Lucas We're developing the technology to create sets but there are some things you wouldn't want to create in the computer. The palace is an incredible piece of architecture and to try to recreate it digitally would be a vast amount of work, so it's much easier to take advantage of some of the creations that already exist.

Gavin Bocquet We were looking for a very specific thing: giant picture windows behind the queen's throne. We found a vestibule with a huge picture window at one end, so we dressed and changed a few things, added a few columns, and made that into the queen's throne room.

From July 22, the main and second units worked for fours days to complete all the necessary scenes.

1.91

1.92

July 29, 1997

Rick McCallum It took us about three and a half months to build the 18 podrace engines that we sent to Tunisia. It's like moving a small platoon across a desert.

The podrace engines, which were made from surplus military airplane parts, arrived in Tozeur, Tunisia, on July 17, while the main unit arrived from Naples on July 26. The first scenes to be shot in Chott el Gharsa were the Mos Espa market scenes on July 28–29.

Natalie Portman It got really hot. We'd start shooting as soon as the sun rose, so pickup was before 4 a.m., and we were shooting before 6 a.m. At 1 p.m. it was 130 degrees, so we fried an egg on R2-D2.

David Tattersall The temperatures were quite scary, photographically speaking, especially on the days when they got over 130 degrees. My main concern was whether the

1.91 *Final frame of Anakin going to bed as Qui-Gon prepares to send the sample to Obi-Wan for analysis.*
1.92 *Qui-Gon takes a sample of Anakin's blood. The entire scene was shot on August 12 and 13, 1998, with film and digital cameras. Lucas: "Midi-chlorians are a loose depiction of mitochondria, which are necessary components for cells to divide. They probably had some-thing—which will come out someday—to do with the beginnings of life and how one cell decided to become two cells with a little help from this other little creature who came in, without whom life couldn't exist. And it's really a way of saying we have hundreds of little creatures who live on us, and without them, we all would die. There wouldn't be any life. They are necessary for us; we are necessary for them. Using them in the metaphor, saying society is the same way, says we all must get along with each other."*
1.93 *Kurt Kaufman's concept art (August 26, 1998) for the background setting to be composited into the shot where Qui-Gon sits on the balcony with Anakin.*

1.94 Doug Chiang's artwork for Darth Maul's spaceship, the Sith Infiltrator (January 16, 1999, 3.5 days). Chiang: "My initial take on Darth Maul's spaceship was that it was going to have parts of the Imperial shuttle and TIE fighters we saw in the first three films, both in proportion and texture. So I took little bits and pieces from those two original designs and put them together."

film would actually melt in the camera. We'd tested the cameras during prep in Arri Media's climate-controlled box, letting them run for a day, but only at 120 degrees.

On the set, we had a routine in which the film was kept in an air-conditioned storage truck and then very gradually brought up to temperature by transferring the cans into different vehicles kept at different temperatures. We hoped that would prevent condensation, warping, or whatever. Then, after exposure, the footage was quickly brought back to a reasonable temperature.

D.CHIANG

1.94

Liam Neeson You had to watch yourself and drink a lot of Gatorade. But George never changed his costume at all. From England to Tunisia he wore the same jeans and checked shirt and baseball cap. So I thought, I'm not going to complain if he's dressed in jeans.

George Lucas The heat was draining. I tried to be conscious of how everyone was holding up, especially Jake. He would never tell me if he was having a problem, so I'd check with his mother; and there were a few times when he really needed a rest. But as difficult as it was, Tunisia looks like Tatooine, so it must be *Star Wars*!

Nick Dudman / Creature Effects Supervisor George is spending a huge amount of money and no one, I'm sure, is more aware than he is what is riding on it. He is eminently pragmatic. If you say to him, well, the guys will only be able to wear that for four minutes in the Sahara, unless we spend a fortune on running frozen glycol around their bodies with some cool suits, he says, "Okay, get the cool suits."

Ahmed Best On July 29, I was eating dinner with Ewan and George and we saw lightning streak across the sky. I turned to Ewan, and since we were in the desert I said, "Wouldn't

1.95

it be crazy if it rained?" Well, it was a torrential downpour. George was freaking out.

Addendum to Progress Report No. 24 / July 30, 1997

At approximately 20:00 on the night of July 29 a severe desert storm hit the Tozeur area. This storm consisting of thunder, lightning, rain, and sand with winds of between 70 and 100 miles per hour which affected Tozeur town; some 40 kilometers from the Chott el Gharsa locations. After a production meeting on the evening of the 29th it was decided to send a small advance party out to the location at 02:30 on the 30th to check access to the site across the desert roads and assess any damage done to sets and location facilities. At 03:00 the advance party found that access to the location was possible despite some waterlogging on the access roads.

Mos Espa Street Set: Two buildings completely destroyed. Almost all other buildings sand and water blasted removing paint and plaster finish. All props either destroyed, knocked over, or damaged. Luke's speeder moved some 50 meters. Street set impossible to shoot on until major repairs undertaken.

Watto's Back Yard: One two-ton scrap metal piece thrown 50 meters. Impossible to shoot on.

Arena Viewing Platform: Complete set picked up and thrown some 100 meters. Damage done to control panels and other parts of the set. Shooting not possible.

> *"The stands were filled with colored Q-tips to provide a reasonable crowd texture for very blurred or distant shots, but most of the shots inside the stadium were populated with live-action extras shot in groups on digital video."*
>
> John Knoll / Visual Effects Supervisor

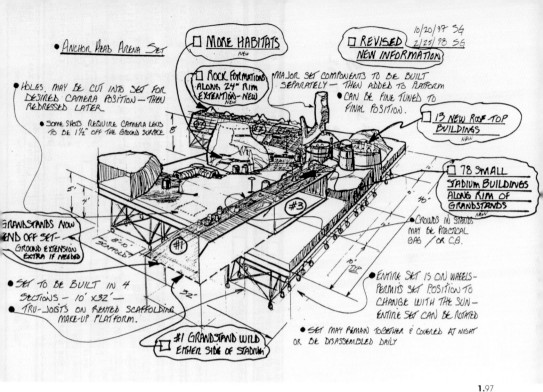

1.97

1.96

1.95 *It is easier to create a physical model than to build and render a detailed CG version, so the Anchorhead Arena (later renamed the Mos Espa Grand Arena) model was built. The entire 40 x 32–foot model was constructed on wheels that allowed it to be shot with various shadow angles.*
1.96 *There were 90 arena shots, of which 70 were static. However, some, like this final frame, required a flyover with a motion control camera.*
1.97 *The requirements of the model changed over time. This detailed set drawing of the Anchorhead Arena was originated by Steve Gawley on October 20, 1997, and then revised on February 25, 1998.*

SHUSTER
9 . 6 . 96
POD RACER #13

1.98

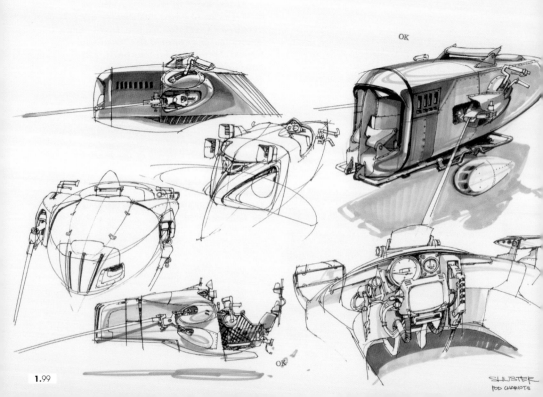

OK

OK

SHUSTER
POD CHARIOTS

1.99

Arena Grid and Pod Engines and Cockpits: Severe damage to these pod cockpits and engines. Anakin's engines smashed and broken in two. All other engines suffering some degree of damage from almost complete destruction to various parts ripped off or smashed in wind. Notably one two-ton engine picked up and hurled some 75 meters. Internal damage to scaffold "chassis" of engines, wheels, and scaffold supports bent or smashed. All pod cockpits suffering a degree of damage ranging from all but total destruction to water and sand damage. Shooting impossible without major work refitting and repairs. It should be noted that these pods and engines were constructed and fitted in the UK by both props and construction departments over a five-month period. Extremely complex structures.

Facilities and Unit Base: Three large marquee tents used by Creatures, Costume, Makeup/Hair, and Crowd Changing flattened and ripped apart.

Costume: All costumes stored in large marquees soaked and covered in sand. Crowd calls impossible without major work to dry and clean costumes. Long-term damage to costumes still to be ascertained. Principal's costumes stored on the Wardrobe Bus undamaged and enable shooting on July 30.

Action undertaken:

1. Tunisia shoot rescheduled to allow immediate shooting on Naboo Spacecraft Ramp

1.98 *Jay Shuster's concept for a podracer (September 6, 1996) became Mars Guo's podracer. George Lucas: "I love Ben-Hur — the chariot race is one of the best action sequences ever shot — so I thought, 'Maybe we could make a space version of Ben-Hur and have podracers instead of chariots.'"*
1.99 *Various ideas for pod chariots by Shuster (March 1996).*
1.100 *John Bell's October 1995 concept is dark and menacing.*

Terryl Whitlatch
7-19-96
Pod Racer

1.101

"The podracers and the creatures were developed independently. We lined up all the creatures and we lined up all the pods, and George picked what creature went into which pod. It was uncanny how the creatures matched the pods. He's a wonderful editor and is able to see what goes together well. All the creatures matched the pods; the personality and everything."

Terryl Whitlatch

and subsequent days scheduled to allow repair work to be undertaken where possible. Damage to props and sets may not be completely repaired with time allowing and may necessitate further UK shooting or CG work.

2. Additional labor, craftsmen, and materials brought in from UK, Tunis, and Medenine to allow immediate repairs to all damaged sets.

3. UK props and construction labor about to return to UK kept in Tunisia to allow repairs.

4. New facilities such as tents and catering equipment, fridges etc. hired in from Tunisia.

5. Governor of Tozeur province contacted and visits site. Military assistance and tents given by Tunisian authorities.

George Lucas I had been through the same experience on the first *Star Wars*—it was as if the storm had hidden away for 20 years, just waiting to come back.

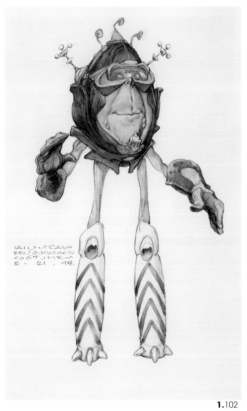

1.102

1.103

Rick McCallum Luckily we had this one set, the Naboo Spacecraft Ramp, that we could still continue to shoot on, pushing the podrace to the very end of the schedule.

On July 30, the production shot scene 60 (Qui-Gon et al. leaving the spacecraft on the way to Mos Espa), 66 (Obi-Wan on the comlink to Qui-Gon), 103 (probe droid's POV of Obi-Wan loading the ship while Qui-Gon goes back to Mos Espa). The following day was devoted to shooting the first fight scene between Qui-Gon and Darth Maul at the same location.

Liam Neeson Stunt coordinator Nick Gillard worked out a series of parries and attacks. Ray Park and I really rehearsed that scene so we could have literally done it in our sleep. If we got our lightsabers caught up in our cloaks, George would always just reshoot. We

covered it with up to three cameras, though, and we did each setup in two or three takes.

They completed 33 setups for the scene. Meanwhile, Pernilla August and Andy Secombe (playing Watto) arrived in Tozeur earlier than scheduled so that their scenes could be filmed while repair work was being undertaken.

Rick McCallum We would literally finish painting a set, and immediately bring in the actors

1.101 *This Whitlatch podracer design (July 19, 1996) becomes Boles Roor.*
1.102 *Iain McCaig's costume design for Ben Quadinaros (May 21, 1997).*
1.103 *This Whitlatch podracer concept (September 10, 1996) earned a "Fabulouso" stamp from George Lucas and became podracer Ebe Endocott.*

1.104

1.104 **Shmi (Pernilla August) tells Anakin to be safe. This was shot in Tunisia with life-size engines and cockpits.**
1.105 **The pods are in their starting positions as the flaggers move onto the track. Anakin is announced as a late entry to the race. The scene was originally much longer but the introductions to the racers were cut due to running time constraints.**
1.106 **On July 30, 1997, George Lucas and Rick McCallum assess the extensive damage to Anakin's pod engines following the storm in Tunisia the previous night.**

1.105

1.106

1.107

to start filming. In a couple of scenes, Natalie walked in and realized that her shoes were stuck to the paint.

The Arena Starting Grid scene was shot on August 5–6.

Rick McCallum I volunteered to shoot a wide shot from a crane. One of the things that I could see that was so wonderful was not only all of our pods rebuilt but beyond that sand dune was our whole base camp, which had been completely rebuilt and to see it all working, seeing the second unit about a half a mile away actually shooting, seeing the first unit

1.108

prepping for our biggest scene in the movie, it was a joy.

Progress Report No. 31 / August 7, 1997

Main unit completed call sheet as scheduled. The unit will now move to Medenine and Tataouine, southern Tunisia, for the remainder of Tunisian shoot.

The slave quarters scenes were shot at Ksar Ouled Soltane, a fortified granary, in the Tataouine district, for two days beginning August 9. They completed scenes 71 (Anakin bringing Qui-Gon and the others back to his home during a sandstorm), 88 (a probe droid patrolling the area), and 104 (Qui-Gon breaking up a fight between Anakin and Greedo, who has accused him of cheating in the podrace).

In the scene Wald (Warwick Davis) notes, "Keep this up, Greedo, and you're going to come to a bad end."

George Lucas The scene with Greedo is not about controlling your anger as much as it is placing your anger in the right place. I think it's an essay on the judicial use of your power.

The scene would eventually be cut from the theatrical version of the film, although it was included on the home video release.

1.107 *Final shot of the royal box, complete with Jabba (credited as himself) and his entourage: Diva Funquita (Amanda Lucas), Bib Fortuna (Matthew Wood), and Diva Shaliqua (Bianca Warren).*
1.108 *Iain McCaig's storyboard shows Jabba starting the race — by spitting the head of a small amphibian at a gong.*
1.109 *Lucas inspects the maquette of Jabba in the royal box.*

Rick McCallum I was very disappointed about losing the scene. I felt it showed a little bit of the dark side of Anakin.

George Lucas It does show that Anakin has a temper, that he does get in fights. In the long run of the movie I didn't think it was essential to establishing his character one way or the other.

Scene 108 was also completed, where Anakin says goodbye to his mother. He promises to return and free her. The Tunisian shoot was completed the next day, and the production traveled back to the UK on August 12.

Rick McCallum Despite the storm, we never lost a beat and we walked out of Tunisia the exact day we were supposed to.

August 29, 1997

Filming resumed at Leavesden on August 13 with the completion of 13 scenes set in the cockpit of the queen's spacecraft.

On August 29, Samuel L. Jackson joined the cast as Jedi Master Mace Windu, and Frank Oz resumed his role as Yoda for Qui-Gon's funeral scene.

Frank Oz People always say to me, "Oh, you do the voice of Yoda," but the voice is 10 percent of the performance. I do it months later in a looping booth in half a day. I asked George. Why don't you do him as a CG effect this time? He said it looks more organic this way.

1.109

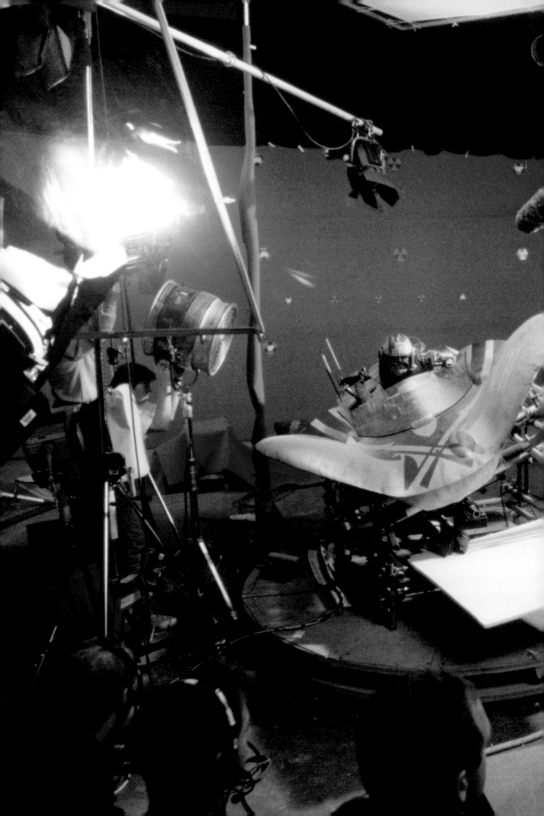

D. CHIANG

"Animatics started out as a conceptual thing. 'Let's put a racer in action; let's see it in a shot.' Then it became, 'We've got the storyboards for the podrace; let's make an animatic and cut the entire thing together.' We had at one point a 22-minute version of the race — that was too much, so George pared it down."

David Dozoretz / Previsualization Effects Supervisor

1.110 **Filming Jake Lloyd in the cockpit, which sits on a gimbal that the crew moves to simulate its motion.**
1.111 **This podrace painting (January 9, 1996, 5.25 days) earned Doug Chiang a "Fabulouso" from Lucas.**
1.112 **Doug Chiang's concept artwork shows one of the more dangerous vantage points for spectators of the podrace (March 6, 1996).**

1.114

Like many of the returning protagonists, Yoda was significantly younger than his character in the previous films but needed to be recognizable.

Paul Engelen / Chief Makeup Artist I wanted Yoda to be silicone because when you'd seen him before he was a very, very old refugee in hiding. There was an old, weary quality to him. This Yoda has to look the same, but there has to be a vitality to him. My feeling was that apart from putting a little more strength into his features, if we did him in silicone we could get a much more healthy, translucent feel to him. I think that worked, but the problem with a silicone puppet is weight. It weighs a ton. If you've got that on the end of somebody's arm, they've got a problem. In fact, Frank Oz was really good about it because he agreed that it gives movement and a feeling of skin texture that is much nicer than foam.

1.113 *Lucas directs Michonne Bourriague, who plays Aurra Sing.*
1.114 *Final frame of Aurra Sing watching the race from a balcony overlooking Beggar's Canyon.*

The Jedi Council scenes were shot over the following two days, September 1–2. Qui-Gon wants to take on Anakin as his Padawan, but even though the boy passes the tests, the Council refuses because he is too old.

George Lucas Qui-Gon is an outlier, an independent soul. Even though he's a Jedi, he doesn't just go along. He's not neutral. One could say that he's, in essence, a troublemaker, because he wants to do it his way—in that case, he's me. (Laughs)

Paul Duncan What is the purpose of the Jedi? Are they a police force?

George Lucas No. They're not like cops who catch murderers. They're warrior-monks who keep peace in the universe without resorting to violence. The Trade Federation is in dispute with Naboo, so the Jedi are ambassadors who talk to both sides and convince them to resolve their differences and not go to war.

If they do have to use violence, they will, but they are diplomats at the highest level. They've got the power to send the whole force of the Republic, which is 100,000 systems, so if you don't behave they can bring you up in front of the Senate. They'll cut you off at the knees, politically.

They're like peace officers.

As the situation develops in the Clone Wars they are recruited into the army, and they become generals. They're not generals. They don't kill people. They don't fight. They're supposed to be ambassadors. There are a lot of Jedi that think that the Jedi sold out, that they should never have been in the army, but...

Paul Duncan Do you think that?

George Lucas It's a tough call. It's one of those conundrums, of which there's a bunch of in my movies. You have to think it through. Are they going to stick by their moral rules and all be killed, which makes it irrelevant, or do they help save the Republic? They have good intentions, but they have been manipulated, which was their downfall.

Both Jackson and Oz were scripted to say Star Wars' most famous line, "May the Force be with you."

Samuel L. Jackson I had a big grin on my face every single time I had to say it. I actually started laughing uproariously...I had to wipe the smile off my face because George Lucas was getting really annoyed.

September 9, 1997

Doug Chiang One day we were storyboarding, and George said, "Darth Maul pulls out a double-edged lightsaber." I said, "Really? Cool!"

George Lucas I was looking for a kind of sword fighting that was reminiscent of what had been done in the previous films but also something that was more energized. Up to this point, we had never actually seen a real Jedi in action. We'd seen an old man, a young boy, and a character that was half droid, half man, but we'd never seen a Jedi in his prime.

1.115–116 *A physical model was built of Jag Crag Gorge and filmed with a motion control camera. The camera rig allowed tracking and panning of the shot to get different angles within the environment. Effects director of photography Pat Sweeney and gaffer Mike Olague can be seen filming.*

1.117 *The racing course was designed to emphasize both speed and danger. Jag Crag Gorge, as shown in this final frame, was so narrow it could only be navigated with the engines at a 90-degree angle to the standard configuration.*

D.CHIANG

**1.118 Doug Chiang's concept art shows
a spectacular pod crash.**

Nick Gillard / Stunt Coordinator There's no room for error in any of the fights. You won't see it because they're so fast, but if you slowed them down and freeze-framed them, they can only parry there or they can only attack there. The moves are so natural or so correct, it's the only place they can be.

George Lucas It would not be a very exciting sequence if it was all done with doubles because the emotion of the fight is on people's faces.

Liam Neeson The first time we started rehearsing the fights, of course, we started making the sound effects of the lightsabers. We looked at each other and thought, "Okay, we have to stop that."

Ray Park Nick told me what he wanted in the moves, but he also let me be very free in my

movements and the flashier the better, which was part of Maul's arrogance. He can end with a flashy pose because he's the man.

Originally the lightsaber had a short handle, like a normal handled lightsaber, but when we made it a little bit longer I could wrap and spin it around my body when we were doing the fights. So the lightsabers wouldn't touch my body, only the handle.

Liam Neeson I was amazed by Ewan's ability to remember all the moves. I had trouble remembering two or three moves at a time, but he could do 12–13 moves, having just learnt them.

Nick Gillard Liam has a beautiful style. Powerful. Ewan picked it up in a flash and now is, I think, faster than any of us.

On September 9, Neeson, McGregor, and Park started filming scenes 157 and 160 — the fight between the Jedi and Darth Maul in the Theed central hangar — with some of the

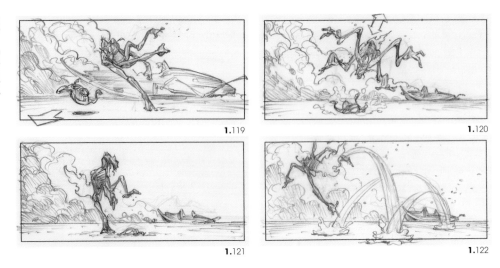

1.119

1.120

1.121

1.122

1.119–122 *Iain McCaig's storyboards for an unused idea depicting Anakin's archrival Sebulba running around after his crash with his pants on fire!*
1.123 *Against all the odds, Anakin wins both the race and his freedom.*

"*Now be brave, and don't look back...don't look back.*"
Shmi Skywalker

1.123

13 setups shot at 22 frames per second (fps) so that the action is quicker when projected at 24 fps. They rehearsed and filmed the fight (scenes 161, 166, 167, 171, 177) with the main unit and the second unit for 10 further days up until the end of principal photography on September 26. A fight unit and the second unit continued to shoot for one week. Ewan McGregor worked with the fight unit on September 29, and then Ray Park and the stunt performers continued for the rest of the week.

Nick Gillard I never thought moves on wires looked believable. Instead, we used nitrogen air rams. With air rams the performers looked as if they were flying, and the landings were hard and realistic.

October 3 was the last day of photography for the fight unit. However, fight scenes 161, 166, 167, and 171 all required future completion.

1.124 *Anakin bids his mother farewell.* **George Lucas:** *"The core story in this first film is his fear of parting from his mother, of letting go. It's emotional and it works and hopefully you don't see it as a flaw, but as a normal reaction."* **1.125** *Lucas:* *"There is an emotional scene between Anakin and his mom, when he confronts the fact that he has to let go of the woman and things he cares about. His fear of losing his mother is the little chink in his armor, which the Emperor latches onto and understands, and ultimately turns Anakin to the dark side."*

Digital Clay

Doug Chiang Episode I is a breakthrough for the whole filmmaking process. For the first time, George could treat movies like digital clay. He could tweak every moment of the movie at any time. This was driven by George. He assembled the team to create the tools to do that. It was frightening to a lot of people, because they're not used to being thrown a lot

1.124

1.127

1.126

1.126–127 *Anakin is on his way to the queen's ship to leave Tatooine. However, Darth Maul is speeding toward it, ready for a confrontation.*
1.128 *Ray Park astride his pre-CG speeder in Tunisia.*

1.128

1.129

of curves late in the production. That's part of the challenge: How do we make this fluid?

David Dozoretz We started editing before filming began and did the last animatic two months before the film came out, so we really jumbled up everything. It's really a very liberating experience, especially for George.

George Lucas I can write and shoot and edit simultaneously, and constantly upgrade what I'm doing. Like with an oil painting, I can step back, look at it, and then add a color.

David Tattersall The editing process is one of George's passions, so we provided him with plenty of raw material. I don't think it's any secret that we shot 1.25 million feet of film!

David Tanaka / Visual Effects Editor During the shoot in London all of the live-action film was processed and immediately telecined.

1.130

1.129–130 *Production stills showing fight rehearsals for the Qui-Gon / Darth Maul fight filmed on July 31, 1997, at Chott el Gharsa, Tozeur. Liam Neeson, Rob Inch (doubling for Qui-Gon Jinn when necessary), and Ray Park fought so vigorously that the aluminum lightsaber blades bent.* **1.**131 *A pneumatic ramp is used to enhance Ray Park's dramatic leap in a remarkable display of acrobatics as Rob Inch (doubling as Qui-Gon) swings his lightsaber.*

1.131

Paul Martin Smith / Editor I had everything on tape, so we digitized the circled takes and loaded them into Avid. George started coming in on Saturdays for us to go over the scenes. There's a lot of pressure to get many setups done in a day, so if, for example, you are missing anything, or if a couple of lines got flopped, I'd point out the problem. George'd reshoot it, or get the second unit to cover it. Working this way we had 80 percent of the film cut in rough assembly before we left London, minus the effects shots of course.

"We cast Ray Park as Darth Maul — he is an expert in kendo and martial arts. When one of the actors is an expert, it ups the ante for all the other actors to do their thing as well as they can. It makes a big difference on the screen."
George Lucas

After principal photography concluded, the team returned to Skywalker Ranch to commence the postproduction process.

Paul Martin Smith It became apparent with the volume of material and the amount of visual effects that we needed to have George switch between two cutting rooms. He'd cut with me for a week or so, and then he'd move over and do some sequences with Ben Burtt, which would give me the chance to work through effects and pass them off to ILM. That worked out superbly well.

George Lucas Having the freedom of being able to move people around in the frame,

1.132

change the framing, change the characters in the frame, change the actions of the characters in the frame, is kind of exciting. It gives me much more control over building a better performance and a better scene than I was able to do by just doing it on the set. Some directors are perfectionists on the set. I work with a lot of captured footage and then mold it into what I want it to be.

Tim Alexander / Computer Graphics Supervisor They had two characters that were in a scene together, and maybe not quite like the performance of one of them, so we'd have to split the take. We'd have the person on the left from one take and the person on the right from another take and cut them together to make it look like it was all the same take. One of them took place in Watto's shop, when Anakin meets Padmé for the first time, and they're having that little conversation.

At the dinner table scene, Shmi is in the foreground and looking at Anakin. We actually sliced her head off and then reverse-printed it, because she was turned the wrong way. David Dozoretz worked on a couple of shots where Anakin was talking, but they didn't want him talking, so his mouth was replaced with one that wasn't moving.

Paul Martin Smith There's one shot — scene 82, in the backyard of the slave quarters — where we wanted one of Anakin's friends to turn his head toward R2-D2 and C-3PO. In the take we used, he didn't, so we just moved earlier down into the take, got him where his head was turning, did a four-frame morph to hide the jump cut, blew it up, painted in the right-hand side of the set — just on the kid's head.

George said, "I didn't like the way I blocked this originally. Let me reblock it." We digitally reblocked the scene to move or get rid of a

1.132 *Darth Maul and Qui-Gon continue their furious battle.*
1.133 *Qui-Gon escapes and the queen's ship makes a course for Coruscant.*
1.134 *Qui-Gon: "Anakin Skywalker, meet Obi-Wan Kenobi."*

1.133

1.134

1.135 *Ralph McQuarrie had created a*
number of designs for Coruscant during
preproduction of Return of the Jedi
(1983) and these formed the initial inspi-
ration for the cityscapes in the prequels,
including this Doug Chiang concept
(July 2, 1997).
1.136 *On their way to Coruscant, Padmé*
comforts Anakin who is cold and missing
his mother. In return, Anakin gives her a
pendant he carved out of a japor snippet
that will bring her good fortune. This
scene echoes the scene in A New Hope,
after the death of Obi-Wan Kenobi, where
Leia comforts Luke by placing a blanket
around him.

1.135

1.136

character. We even shot extras to stand in for Padmé, to fix the continuity. We put new shots, like when R2-D2 and C-3PO walk away. We never had that wide shot, so that's made up of about four different shots.

There were a couple of times in the original script where Qui-Gon was giving Jar Jar a hard time. We wanted to get rid of those lines, so we added an extra walking in front of the camera to hide Liam's lips, and there went the line. Another time, Padmé said a line at the end of the movie, and George wanted her to say something different, so we changed her lips. We had her ADR the line, shot somebody's lips and pasted in the lips to match what she looped. You've seen animals talking, now we can make actors talk.

New Strategies

George Lucas We had designs and maquettes of Jar Jar, Watto, Sebulba, et cetera, which ILM used to start building their computer models. As soon as we finished filming, we began cutting sequences so that Rob Coleman

"This film is still in the style of an old Republic serial, but it's now a big city movie. The first three Star Wars were from Kansas and these three are from New York."
George Lucas

could begin animating the characters and ILM could add sets and the other VFX.

John Knoll Two thousand visual effects shots in one movie is many times more than what is even considered a huge show. These shots were not all of one type. They varied from simple splits and removals to extremely complex fully computer-generated environments filled with thousands of droids and Gungans engaged in hand-to-hand combat.

Many shots depicted in the storyboards couldn't be executed at all with the tools we had available to us at the time. New software had to be developed to handle a variety of challenges: clothed characters, very complex scenes with thousands of characters, synthetic terrains, complex models with hundreds of thousands of surfaces, synthetic pyro, rigid body and soft body dynamics that had to be integrated into character animations and motion captures, plus numerous other unsolved problems.

Rob Coleman We had been called upon in the past to create photorealistic creatures, but never had we been required to come up with so many different characters, many of which had critically important roles in a movie. There was a palpable feeling when we began the visual effects production on this film that we were not going to be able to get it all done in the time allotted. There were just too many visual effects sequences and computer-generated characters. We had to come up with new strategies for workflow, animatics,

1.137

1.138

1.139

1.137 *Keira Knightley and Natalie Portman playing Sabé and Padmé. Knightley was cast because of her physical resemblance to Portman so that she could play one of the handmaidens/decoys to the queen.*

1.138–139 *On set and final frame of the Queen's entourage being greeted by Naboo's Senator Palpatine and kindly Chancellor Valorum (Terence Stamp, right). This was the first day on set for Liam Neeson and Ewan McGregor.*

production schedules, rendering, software, hardware, and final output. We had to rethink how we went about approaching visual effects production. Episode I was like three large effects shows rolled into one.

Dennis Muren / Visual Effects Supervisor John Knoll, Scott Squires, and I divided the show between us. I looked at the storyboards and saw two sequences that looked like the most fun stuff to do: the underwater sequence and the big Gungan/droid battle at the end. So I became responsible for 390 shots including those two sequences.

John Knoll I supervised 1,073 shots. These included all of the space scenes, Trade Federation ship interiors, scenes on Tatooine (Mos Espa, Watto's shop, podrace, et cetera), and about half of the scenes taking place on Coruscant (the landing platform, Palpatine's quarters).

Scott Squires / Visual Effects Supervisor My work involved supervising close to 600 shots over a one-year period. These shots involved the scenes in Theed (Jedi battle, hangar battles, queen's palace interior and exteriors, courtyards, end parade, et cetera), the Galactic Senate sequence, and the Jedi Palace sequences.

1.140 McCaig's costume suggestion of black Jedi robes for Yoda.
1.141 Various concepts for a younger Yoda by Iain McCaig (December 12, 1996). McCaig: "In the end George decided to keep Yoda pretty much intact, but at one point he had a long beard that he knotted below his chin in a very Mongolian fashion. In another, I imagined he might be much younger, and that became Yaddle."

1.140

IAIN McCAIG
12 . 12 . 96
YODIE

1.141

D.CHIANG
JEDI COUNCIL ROOM
1.27.97
0820

The majority of shots involved not only integrating computer graphics characters into scenes but extensive use of virtual sets and backgrounds. These virtual backgrounds were made up of physical miniatures, CG sets, and digital matte paintings depending on the needs of the shot. The original rough cut of the film illustrated just how much was filmed against blue screen.

Many sequences used partial sets so it was critical to build models that matched the blueprints as well as color and textures of the original set. Most interior locations involved reflective floors that would require creation of reflections in addition to shadows for actors and CG characters.

Dennis Muren The computer gear for the high-end 3-D graphics were SGIs, we animate with Softimage, we model mainly with Alias software, and we render with RenderMan software. We have huge amounts of our own software that we use. We also use Flame and Inferno software for some compositing.

1.142 *Doug Chiang's concept for the Jedi Council room (January 27, 1997).*
1.143 *Qui-Gon and Obi-Wan brief the Jedi Council on the existence of a Sith Lord, and they also introduce Anakin as a potential Padawan.*
1.144 *Establishing shot of the Jedi Temple on Coruscant.*

1.143

1.144

We were trying to get a few shots a day out, about 30 or 40 shots a week, and we had to keep that pace up throughout the production, or we'd get behind.

Rick McCallum We used electronic projection for viewing dailies during production and to screen the various cuts throughout the postproduction process. We used an electronic system for the sound team to mix with. For dailies, we used the Digital Projection POWER 4dv. For screening cuts in progress, we used Electrohome's VistaPro 2000. The sound mix in our Mix A facility used an Electrohome Roadie.

Fred Meyers / Digital Operations There was connectivity between the editors at the Ranch

> *"There are some very goofy hair-styles here. George has had a bad rap for giving those cinnamon buns to Princess Leia, so I think he's up for the firing squad for this one…"*
>
> Iain McCaig / Concept Artist

1.147

1.145

SENATE

1.146

and ILM. They could set up their own live review sessions to show and talk about how the cut was changed that day. Everyone would look at one image that would have not only the dailies material in it but also the images of the people who were participating. Along with high-quality audio, they'd have video pointers so they could point to things on the screen.

Tim Alexander We would go to "George Dailies," on Tuesdays and Thursdays. George would come down to ILM and they would show him video, as well as film. Rob Coleman would show a sequence of shots and throw out his ideas, and then George would say, "It should be a little slower here...faster there. Maybe we should try to recut this...let's add a shot here." It was very open. When you have someone like Rob saying, "Maybe this is the way it should be cut," it's smart for Lucas to listen. That was great for us "computer" guys,

1.145 The queen in Palpatine's quarters as she decides her strategy.
1.146 Iain McCaig's concept for Queen Amidala's costume (December 15, 1995), stamped "Fabulouso" by Lucas. McCaig: "This huge hairstyle was historically accurate, but she had to walk sideways through doorways."
1.147 Lucas and Portman on set. This was the second scene to be shot on the first day of filming. Lucas: "Natalie is fantastic. It all came together. I only had to do two takes. She really had it down. Ian's always great, but I had no idea what was going to happen with her."

because usually we don't come into contact with the directors or the live-action shoots. It really taught us a lot about the editing and directing processes. It was really good for the crew as well; people felt better about it because they felt closer to it.

Cari

Rob Coleman We have about 66 creatures, and five of them have speaking parts. Jar Jar Binks alone is in 400 shots. I'm doing 800 shots with a staff of 45.

Four computer-generated characters had key speaking roles in the film: Watto, Sebulba, Boss Nass, and Jar Jar. These four characters had to hold their own against the live-action actors. Not only did they have to seamlessly blend into their environment, but they had to give a believable performance, and deliver important story dialogue while being

1.148 *The grand exterior of the Galactic Senate building.*
1.149 *Final frame of the Senate Chamber.*

1.148

1.149

also lead animators assigned to major sequences such as the Gungan ground battle, the podrace, and the underwater sequence.

To ensure that we were creating performances that would be engaging and entertaining, we took great care in studying the voice actors for each of our key computer characters. The actors' facial expressions and body movements were analyzed and then the animators set about key frame animating each computer character.

Paul Martin Smith George shot one take with the actor on set doing the voice of our animated characters. Jar Jar was in a costume. Watto wasn't. Then George would do another take with the actors off-camera. We would literally use that as a "patch." I would take out the section of the actor and his voice and put him where we wanted him in the empty plate. If George wanted, for example, Jar Jar's head staring at Qui-Gon I'd find a head turn, freeze

1.150

compared to their live fellow actors on a frame-by-frame basis. These visual effects had to live and breathe.

For the animation, we broke down the work needed for the various characters, and then into units for each. Each of the main computer characters had a lead animator; there were

1.151

1.152

it so it kept its direction, so Rob Coleman would know exactly where the eyelines should be.

Rob Coleman Jar Jar's performance really started with Ahmed Best...Ahmed's performance was a reference.

Ahmed Best I did double everything. I was there on the set, and then I went to San Francisco and did more shooting for motion capture and animation.

Jar Jar's facial features were animated using Caricature, also called "Cari," software ILM had developed for Dragonheart (1996).

Steve Rawlins / Character Animator Cari is one of the most important tools for getting the character to act and deliver a performance. It's where you start to see the character come alive — it happens right in front of your face. You start by blocking Jar Jar in the frame then flesh out his movement, the right speed, the

1.150 *Palpatine urges Queen Amidala to plead her case to the Senate, and this leads to a vote of no confidence in Chancellor Valorum's leadership.*
1.151 *B Stage at Leavesden Studio housed both the Chancellor's central podium (left) and two congressional pods (right). By filming different senators in the pods at differing angles, they can be digitally moved and stitched together to form part of the Galactic Senate Chamber.*
1.152 *Senator Bail Antilles (Adrian Dunbar) of Alderaan seconds the motion for a vote of no confidence in Chancellor Valorum.*

right weight, then Cari really makes his face come alive. Instead of a thing you're sliding around in the frame, you have an actor.

Rob Coleman We have the ability to control all of the soft tissue in the face — the muscles, eye blinks, breathing.

Six months later, after going through a continuous process of refinement, the character became more defined.

Paul Martin Smith In a sense, what ILM was giving us was the second set of rushes.

November 25, 1997

Paul Martin Smith The entire podrace was cut before George even shot anything, and we were cutting it until the week before the final mix.

1.153 *Rick McCallum: "Frank Oz will be playing Yoda again. The majority of the time he will be controlled by Frank, but in those circumstances where Yoda needs to walk, then he will be CG. CG is just a tool that helps you solve problems that you can't do in other ways."*
1.154 *Anakin correctly identifies the objects on Mace Windu's (Samuel L. Jackson) viewing screen.*

The cut was alive for a good three years — two years during the shoot and final edit, and a year before that in previsualization.

David Dozoretz After principal photography, we added the live-action footage into the animatics, and then we added the computer set extensions, and the computer ships we got from ILM.

John Knoll The first challenge of the podrace was figuring out how to create the landscapes. Location aerial plates were not a realistic option both because of the very specific terrain features George wanted to see as well as the dangerous paths he wanted to take through them.

Miniatures were possible for a few of the more enclosed terrains like the canyons and the arena, but most of the terrains were so wide open, and the speeds depicted so fast that the models would have to be huge and would be very difficult to shoot. That left it to some form of computer graphics, but what? This had to work not for just a couple of shots, but for over 300 shots in a 10-minute sequence. The solution was to greatly extend a 3-D matte painting technique that we first used on *Mission: Impossible*.

Distant objects were rendered by projecting matte paintings or photography of real objects

> *"I died and went to heaven.*
> *I looked up and there I was*
> *in Star Wars with Yoda."*
>
> Samuel L. Jackson

onto simple geometry. Closer objects (like the stone arches) were created first as miniatures. The miniatures were digitized as medium-resolution CG models. The miniatures were then photographed with a still camera out in the parking lot, and the photographs were projected onto the CG model. The result was a series of very realistic objects that could be placed into a scene, and the CG camera flown through them without any concern about depth of field, camera clearance, or limits of travel.

Finally, the ground plane was created on a frame-by-frame basis by a piece of software that created geometry only where the camera was looking, high resolution where it was close to the camera and low resolution further away. This gave us terrain with enough visual complexity using optimized geometry that could be rendered in a reasonable amount of time with a reasonable amount of memory.

Following *Star Wars* tradition, the pods had a very complex exposed machinery look. Highly detailed miniatures were used for the more static shots (like the interior of the podrace hangar), but CG models were used for all of the flying scenes. Building CG models of the extremely complex and detailed shapes of the pods resulted in the heaviest CG models we've ever had to deal with. Many shots contained more CVs (control vertices) than pixels!

Texturing dozens of models each with several hundred separate texture maps and surface material also presented problems.

1.156

New software was needed to keep them organized and make fine-tuning of shader parameters tractable. I was constantly comparing our (computerized) renders to photographic reality. If we were just slightly off, it was pretty obvious.

A number of the pods crash during the sequence. George's desire was for the crashes to not simply be big fireballs, but instead to look like Formula One car crashes, where the cars tumble end over end, shredding apart and scattering pieces everywhere. Our first thought was to build breakaway pyro models of the pods and blow them up in a miniature terrain set. But as soon as we began to work out how fast the camera would need to travel, what rigging would be necessary, how much miniature set would be needed, and what frame rate would be required, it became clear that that approach would be far too difficult and costly.

1.155 *As they prepare to disembark on Naboo, Anakin is happy to see Padmé again. The scene was deleted.*
1.156 *At the end of a somber scene where Obi-Wan expresses doubt about Anakin being trained as a Jedi, Qui-Gon tells Anakin about midi-chlorians, and the queen is escorted on board, Jar Jar jubilantly exclaims, "Wesa goen home!"*

We decided to simulate the crashes in CG using rigid and soft body dynamics, coupled with custom software to deform and break the model appropriately. The result was a system that had both the realism and randomness of a physical simulation, along with the repeatability and control of computer graphics. It was very simple, for example, to make a particular part shatter into 20 percent fewer pieces, or to make some piece tumble twice as fast.

1.157

1.158

Matthew Wood / Supervising Sound Editor There was no music during a lot of the sequence, so it was fully a visual and sound effect–driven scene. This was probably the most difficult scene to design, and Ben worked on it for a long time right up until the final mix.

Ben Burtt I tried to give each vehicle sound a personality. I considered the pilot of the craft and whether I wanted the audience to like or fear a certain ship or character. A pod sound can be powerful, angry, comical, smooth, cool, hip, old-fashioned, goofy, or dangerous.

Matthew Wood Ben has a pretty huge library of effects that he has amassed over the years. Ninety percent of the stuff we used was pulled

from his library and digitally formatted for editorial and design.

George said, "I really want a Ferrari, a Porsche, this boat, this aircraft," so I went out to Willow Springs raceway and recorded

1.157 *Doug Chiang's concept art for the meeting at the Gungans' sacred place (August 8, 1997, 4.5 days).*
1.158 *Final frame of the Gungans' sacred place as the queen and her entourage approach.*
1.159 *Lining up the camera to film the Gungans' sacred place. Only the trees' roots and trunks were required for the shot.*

exactly what he wanted. I put microphones in cement tubes in the middle of the road. It made this weird, ethereal sound combined with the cars racing.

Ben then took those files and using a Synclavier, a Kyma workstation from Symbolic Sound, and a Pro Tools system, layered them all together to make composite effects for the editors.

Anakin's podracer used sound from a Porsche, while Sebulba's came from an F-51 Mustang flyby mixed with a cigarette boat on San Francisco Bay that Lucas asked to perform maneuvers.

On November 25, 1997, Lucas reviewed the footage of the podrace sequence and listed all the shots over eight pages, making notes and corrections where necessary. Lucas deleted 47 shots but added 40, mainly reaction shots to include Jar Jar, C-3PO, and Kitster, as well as more close-ups of Anakin in his podracer.

"George's big thing is always design something from reality, and put a little bit of artificialness or exaggeration to put it into another world. We took real trees that were 100 feet tall, and made them 300 or 400 feet tall, and added weird root structures. That's all you need."

Doug Chiang

March 2, 1998

The first cut of the film was completed on February 24, 1998. Its running time was 02:06:34:15, consisting of 2,175 shots, of which 1,919 required VFX.

Pickups were needed to complete the re-edited scenes and the fight between Darth Maul and the Jedi so these were shot at Leavesden from March 2 to 7.

Paul Martin Smith On pickup shoots, they'd have the list of everything they needed and

1.160 *The sculpture of Jar Jar's head is mounted on a C-stand as a lighting reference and Ewan McGregor is holding a mirrored ball which ILM will refer to in postproduction to achieve consistency between the lighting of the scene as filmed and the CG elements that will be created.*

1.161 *Brian Blessed: "I'm playing Boss Nass, the King of the Gungans. It was a marvelous moment when George Lucas said, 'They want your help. They're all kneeling in front of you, Brian. And all these Naboo, about 50 million Naboo, they're all kneeling in front of you, Brian, and they're asking for your help.' I'm a kind of reluctant hero in it and I've got a massive army. And he said, 'What are you going to say when they ask for your help?' And I went [Blessed makes a hilarious aquatic holler], and he said, 'Bring that, I knew that I was employing a mad bastard. Bring that, that's exactly what I wanted, Brian.'"*

1.162 *Padmé reveals herself to be the queen and kneels before Boss Nass to beg for the Gungans' help.*

they'd have a tape of what the element was on the set so they would reshoot and reframe as per the tape. They'd send the shots back to me and I'd cut in the one I liked best.

There were 119 setups over the six days covering moments from the whole movie, from scene 2 (shots of the back of Qui-Gon and Obi-Wan in the Republic Cruiser) to scene 178 (Yoda and Mace Windu at Qui-Gon's funeral, reshot with Yoda's hood down). Other key moments shot include Darth Maul's introduction as he steps into the hologram (scene 53), Maul's jump from the speeder on Tatooine (scene 110), the battle on the power generator walkway (scene 166), Obi-Wan's reaction to the death of Qui-Gon (scene 171), and a new scene where Obi-Wan declares to Yoda that he will fulfill his obligation and take on Anakin as his Padawan (scene C177).

A camera fault was discovered on the VistaVision camera, which meant that shots

1.160

1.161

taken on March 3 and 4 had to be retaken. After further problems on March 5, it was agreed with John Knoll that the Vista-Vision shots — the larger format was for VFX shots — could be shot on 35 mm camera.

The third cut of the film was locked on March 13, 1998, with a running time of 02:17:42:06 — 11 minutes longer.

March 30, 1998

Steve Gawley / Model Supervisor I started in April 1997, and my responsibility is to provide miniatures of sets and models. The effects supervisors decide what will be a practical model or digital, and then they give us a call. They tell us their needs — it's to be seen from so many angles and in so many shots — and I'll draw up a schematic based on the design

1.162

1.164

1.163

1.163 *Doug Chiang's artwork depicting the Gungan army emerging from the swamp includes the lumbering fambaa, based on a dinosaur concept, and the kaadu, inspired by an ostrich (September 16, 1996, 6 days).*

1.164 *Final frame of the Gungan army marching to battle, featuring a fully CG cast of thousands.*

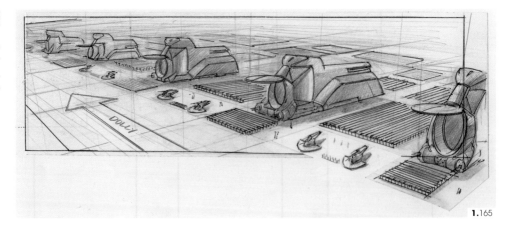

1.165

1.165 *Ed Natividad storyboard showing the camera tracking past the MTTs as the droid army prepares for battle.*

and estimate the cost and the amount of time. And then they say, "How about sooner?!"

We are busier now than we've ever been in the model shop because it is often quicker to design and create in the three-dimensional world than in the digital world. We provide reference models that are scanned by the digital folks, and background sets that will have the digital characters added. As a matter of fact I've had times when I can't find enough people.

The Podrace hangar was the first model to be set up and shot, from February 3 on the Windward stage, while the Trade Federation hangar bay was shot on the Vista Cruiser stage from February 9, both supervised by John Knoll.

On March 30, 1998, filming began of the Trade Federation ship for the opening scene as the Republic Cruiser approaches it. This ship and the Droid Control Ship were filmed up to August 17 on the Vista Cruiser stage under the supervision of John Knoll.

John Knoll The space scenes were executed as a mixture of miniatures and computer graphics. The queen's ship and the Naboo fighters were done using computer graphics in part because of the chrome surfaces that needed to reflect their environments. Because the space battle involved choreographing large swarms of Trade Federation and Naboo fighters, computer graphics was the most expedient option. Since the Trade Federation battleship was a motion-controlled miniature, we developed an automatic translator to convert camera moves from the motion control system to computer graphics and vice versa. Custom animated reflection environments were created for all scenes of the chrome ships. For example, when Anakin's starfighter flies through the Federation battleship's hangar, we rendered the hangar as six 90-degree field of view cameras: top, bottom, left, right, front, and back. These were stitched together to create a 360-degree view of the environment around Anakin's ship.

Plasma

George Lucas The Gungan battle was like the Charge of the Light Brigade. It illustrated a theme that repeats in my films — a non-technological society taking on a highly

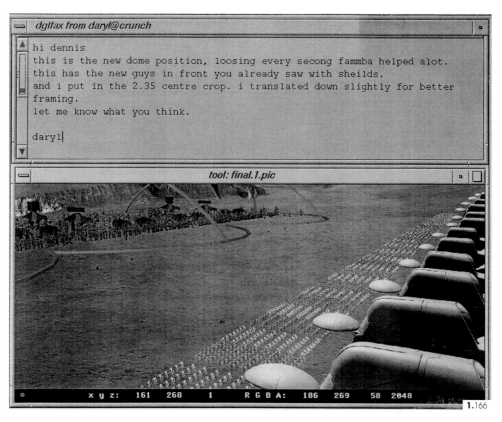

dglfax from daryl@crunch

```
hi dennis
this is the new dome position, loosing every secong fammba helped alot.
this has the new guys in front you already saw with sheilds.
and i put in the 2.35 centre crop. i translated down slightly for better
framing.
let me know what you think.

daryl|
```

tool: final.1.pic

x y z: 161   268   1   R G B A: 186   269   58   2048

1.166

1.167

1.166 *This digital fax from digital effects artist Daryl Munton to Dennis Muren shows how the team changed the number of and positioning of fambaa and other elements to find the most dramatic and logical compositions.*

1.167 *As the droids prepare to attack, the Gungans erect an energy shield for defense.*

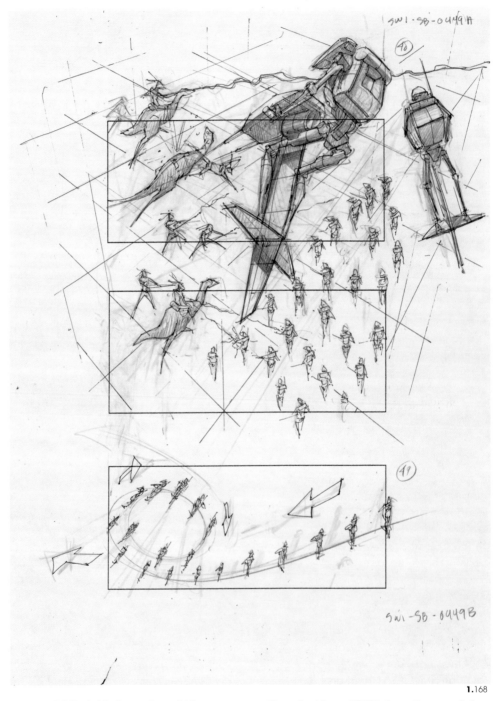

1.168

1.168 Ed Natividad storyboard ideas showing the dynamics of the battle between the droids and Gungan.

Here droids on STAPs launch an aerial attack to support the ground troops.

1.169

1.170

technological society. Like the Vietnam War, the people without the technology were the victors because they had the heart and soul. So it's another version of the Ewok battle.

Dennis Muren This sequence was primarily made up of thousands of animated CG characters, miniature battle tanks, enhanced still-photo backgrounds, and dozens of 1/3-scale pyro elements.

The challenge for me was to do the shot design. First, we looked at war footage to see what reality was like.

Paul Duncan Doug Chiang drew up helicopter shots of the armies massing, and there were action and gag ideas supplied by Ed Natividad and Iain McCaig.

1.169–170 *Storyboard circa October 1998 and final frame of the droid and Gungan confrontation. The droids have conventional blasters whereas the Gungan use booma projectiles.*

Dennis Muren I distilled it down to make it easier to understand, and also so that we could do it with the tools we had and in the time we had.

For the background, we found a place out in Patterson, Southern California. The mountains are green in the background because it had just been the rainy season. We shot 250 pictures and we would cut and paste

1.171

the hills and valley floors together to give the size needed for the battle. Most of the clouds came from stills shot near Carlsbad, New Mexico. By treating the still-photo backgrounds as composite elements, we were able to change and add shots as needed. The same hills could be reused with new clouds and look different.

Rob Coleman I can't tell you what it's like to get handed a sequence like this. The entire sequence exists only as a visual effect. A typical line from the script could read, "The Gungans march to meet the Battle Droids." That simple statement translated into months of work to create the amazing shot of 7,000 computer-generated Gungans and their various computer-generated animals parading off to war. Nothing moving in the shot is real.

1.172

Dennis Muren I repeated shots, like you do in live action, where you go back to the same angle, so that the audience can follow the action. For example, I have a shot of a bunch of the droids walking toward camera, then a few shots later I'd have exactly the same angle and a droid is hit and falls down. If I had a different angle, it would take longer for the audience to figure out where they were and that's time lost.

The Gungans had huge shields that cover and protect them is made from the same technology as their underwater city bubbles. George started talking about it one day, and said that the Gungans mined the plasma that powered the city and generated the light. It could be molded into a hard, round object with the energy sealed inside, and a hard crust that would crack and spew out the energy plasma that would short out the energy circuits of the droids. It's interesting to me that he'd thought out how they were mined — and George does that with so many things. Everything has that sort of history to it. They're not just neat ideas — they're logical ideas.

*1.171 **George Lucas tried to include air whales in** The Empire Strikes Back **(in an early script Luke is helped at Cloud City by a noble race of aliens riding air whales) and** Return of the Jedi **(air whales transport the heroes to the rebel base in an unused scene). Here Terryl Whitlatch has the air whales as part of the Gungan air force (September 20, 1995).***
*1.172 **Doug Chiang depicts a sky battle between droids on their single trooper aerial platforms and Gungan-mounted air whales (April 10, 1996, 2.3 days).***
*1.173 **On March 25, 1996, Doug Chiang completed an extensive series of storyboard proposals for the Gungan battle, showing the forces of both sides mobilizing into position, including this "helicopter" shot of a Gungan air force over their ground troops.***

August 10, 1998

The Anchorhead Arena model was filmed from July 7 to August 11, 1998, supervised by Dennis Muren and John Knoll, with additional filming on October 2 and 5.

John Knoll Anchorhead Arena was built as a 40-foot-long miniature. It was photographed outdoors for a real sunlight look. The stands were filled with colored Q-tips to provide a reasonable crowd texture for very blurred or distant shots.

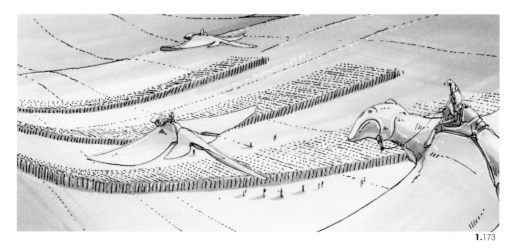

1.173

1.174

1.175

Michael Lynch / Chief Model Maker It had an airplane hangar on a track to cover it up at night. It was placed on a rotating base so we could position the set properly in natural sunlight.

John Knoll Most of the shots inside the stadium were populated with live-action extras shot in groups on digital video.

These were filmed on August 4–6 with pro-sumer digital cameras. There were five days of reshoots and new scenes at Leavesden on August 10–14, 1998.

George Lucas We were trying to develop digital cinema at the same time as we were preparing and shooting the movie. We were testing cameras, projectors, all that stuff.

For new scene 128A, shot on August 10, Anakin goes to see Padmé on Coruscant but instead meets the queen in her dressing room. As a test, some of this scene was shot on a Sony HDC-750 digital camera, which ran at 30 fps, and recorded onto an HDD-1000 videotape recorder. Likewise, on August 12, some of new scene 83A, set on the slave quarters porch at night, where Qui-Gin takes Anakin's blood and tests for midi-chlorians, was shot on the HDC-750.

Rick McCallum We were worried about pulling this off because in the intervening months Jake had grown about four inches.

1.174 *Full-size model of the AAT in the Theed plaza, with Lloyd, McGregor, Portman, and Neeson, at left, waiting to enter the hangar. The set for the plaza was built one story tall on the Leavesden lot, with additional buildings added digitally in postproduction.*
1.175 *Gian speeders and Flash speeders were used by the Naboo soldiers to attack the droids and provide a distraction so that the queen and the Jedi could access the Theed hangar.*

George Lucas I had originally written and shot Qui-Gon getting the blood sample for the midi-chlorian count in the arena hangar, but I rewrote it and put it on the balcony at night so that Anakin could talk about the stars. I wanted to get a sense of Anakin's future, and his dreams, and where he expected to go, so I needed this introspective moment.

I like the theme of symbiotic relationships that goes throughout the whole movie, of people helping people, and the idea that there may be a completely different life-form living inside your body, completely independent of you, but has some influence over you.

Fred Meyers After the Leavesden shoot, the one-inch analog masters and deck shipped to us at ILM, where we digitized the 1920 x 1035 60i material into four Quickframe SD servers, reconstructed RGB DPX frames, and de-interlaced and retimed the shots to 24 fps for editorial and VFX.

Paul Martin Smith There are two shots in that sequence that are digital, a close-up and a wide shot. If you look at it carefully, the footage is problematic—the contrast is slightly different—but only because of the conversion from 30 fps to 24 fps. But Sony is in the process of making a couple of 24 fps cameras for us for the next film.

September 25, 1998
Jeanne Cole / Publicity / E-mail to all Lucasfilm
Just a few minutes ago the following announcement was posted on www.starwars.com:

September 25, 1998: We're happy to report that George Lucas has decided to name the new movie *Star Wars*: Episode I *The Phantom Menace*. As announced earlier, the new movie will appear in theaters in the United States and Canada on May 21, 1999.

1.176 Filming the Jedi and queen entering the Theed hangar on August 19, 1997. During one take a squib sparked in Natalie Portman's face, so she was taken to a specialist to check that her eyes were okay.

1.177 Final frame of the Naboo star-fighters flying off to destroy the Droid Control Ship orbiting the planet. Anakin and Artoo are in one of the fighters.

November 12, 1998

Scene 166, part of the battle between the Jedi and Darth Maul along the Power Generator Walkway, was not straightforward. The Change Notes show that after the live action was shot, the background was added on March 19, but on September 24 Lucas expressed concern with the design of the light tubes, and on November 12 requested they be "refilmed" by ILM.

Scott Squires This was a horrendous sequence to deal with. The design wasn't totally locked down before live action was shot. This meant removing flashing colored lights from shots so they would work with the new design concept. Some shots were done with doubles and required face replacements of the real actors. The live action was filmed on a short section of walkway against blue screen. The rest of the environment was done with CG. Extensive use of rotoscoping was used for the lightsabers with special software to duplicate the look from the original films. Some scenes required replacement of body parts of the actors and doubles when they became obscured in airbags or other items.

The last change on the scene was on March 5, 1999, when the tube glow had to be fixed on shot JDB.166.027, where Obi-Wan grabs his lightsaber.

February 10, 1999

On February 10, John Williams started recording the film's score with the London Symphony Orchestra at the Abbey Road Studios.

John Williams / Composer The first time I saw *The Phantom Menace* was October 1, 1998. I began to write the score in the middle of October, so it gave me three months plus to write two hours of music for orchestra. Very difficult, just in logistic terms.

I would say, conservatively, that 90 percent of it is new. The remaining 10 percent are "quotes" from earlier themes. The first minute and a half has the "Star Wars Theme." In the middle there are very brief quotes of "Darth

Vader's Theme," "Yoda's Theme,""Princess Leia's Theme," when there are hints of what they will become as the prequel advances. But the 90 percent that is new comes something like this: I was able to take some of the old themes and "de-compose" them—take them apart and write them in a sense backward.

"Anakin's Theme" is the kind of theme you would have for a young boy, very innocent, lyrical, and idealistic. But it's made up of intervals from "The Imperial March." I made Anakin's theme out of those intervals by inverting them or rearranging them rhythmically or accompanying them harmonically in a different way. It sounds familiar, very sweet, but if you listen to it carefully, there's a hint of evil.

"Duel of the Fates" is for the great sword fight at the end of the film. The decision to make that choral was just the result of my thinking that is should have a ritualistic or quasi-religious feeling to it, and an introduction of a chorus might be just the thing.

Williams selected the following lines from the Welsh poem "Cad Goddeu" (The Battle of the Trees), and had them translated into different languages, including Sanskrit.

Cad Goddeu / English Translation / Lines 33–35

Under the tongue root / a fight most dread, and another raging / behind in the head

John Williams "Korah," "Rahtahmah"—I've chosen these Sanskrit words because of the quality of the vowels. The medium of chorus and orchestra would give us a sense that we were in a big temple.

I've been uniquely fortunate to accompany George on this great journey that he's on, which seems now to be a life's work journey.

"Fighting someone single, all your attention is at that one person, but when you're fighting two, it's a lot harder because they come from different angles, not just straight lines. To me, it's more fun because I know that if I don't do this move I'm going to get hurt, so I have to react quickly. I get an adrenaline rush out of it."

Ray Park

1.179

1.178 **Darth Maul reveals his double-ended lightsaber and prepares for battle with the Jedi.**
1.179 **Lightsaber choreography rehearsal with Liam Neeson, Ewan McGregor, and Ray Park.**
1.180 **The fight begins. George Lucas:** "We finally get to see Jedi do what Jedi were designed to do. Before, in the first films, the sword fighting was extremely limited and was really between a fairly old Jedi who was ready to go and one who had been reconstructed and who was half human, half machine and not really very flexible. The only other Jedi who comes along is Luke, who's semi-trained by Yoda, but he never really gets the full-on training. So you've never actually seen a Jedi do what real Jedi do, until now."

1.180

1.181

1.182

"Ray [Park] is 5' 10". There's not a lot of dialogue in that part and Rick [McCallum] thought it might be better for a stunt guy to play it. I got Ray in. He is trained in five or six martial arts and he is a really good gymnast. It was just a matter of teaching him the double-ended lightsaber, but he is now so good at it that he has left us way behind."

Nick Gillard / Stunt Coordinator

March 20, 1999

Rick McCallum George called me up and said, "There's a wonderful opportunity here for Palpatine to acknowledge Anakin."

On March 20, 1999, Jake Lloyd, Ewan Mc-Gregor, and Ian McDiarmid were recalled to Leavesden to shoot an additional scene, 176A.

Rick McCallum Palpatine comes down the ramp, thanks Obi-Wan, and then his lips get very wet and juicy when he takes a look at Anakin and says, "We will watch your career with great interest." It's a wonderful throw-away line. That shot cost about $18,000 to do. We shot that against blue screen and we used a digital matte painting, and then we zapped it in. That's how easy that stuff is now.

May 4, 1999

The last Change Notes, dated April 16, 1999, indicate the final minor changes to be made. For the scene in the queen's dressing room, John Knoll is to make a change to the queen's face so that it matches the previous shot.

Meanwhile Scott Squires is to extend the beginning of the Jedi Council scene by 10 frames and to sync the ships in the background to match.

Squires also had to add VFX to the shot in the final duel where Obi-Wan looks down as Darth Maul falls, turns off his lightsaber and runs to Qui-Gon — the shot had been omitted, and was now back in the movie.

The JAK animatics department had concluded their work, and David Dozoretz e-mailed staff to thank them for their work.

David Dozoretz / May 4, 1999 JAK Films Statistics
— Pre-Visualization Stage —
Total shots pre-visualized (approximately) — 8,600
Maximum shots/day — 75
Average # of takes/shot — 3
Minutes of footage produced — 573 (9.5 hours)
Bottles of Coke consumed — 4,000
Nights working spent at the Ranch — 40
Number of frantic phone calls received from the editor, Martin — 7,300
Number of years spent working on the film — 4
Man-years spent working on Episode I — 13

— Final VFX Production Stage —
Total # of shots completed — 104
Total amount of data backed up — 3.16 terabytes
Total minutes of final footage — 11.4
How many hours have computers been powered on — 315,360
Number of pixels processed — 238,953,356,800
One stolen car (a practical joke. Though, it wasn't very funny to David.)
Number of back-up CDs burned — 700

1.181 *Each character has a different fighting style. Qui-Gon uses his height and controlled strength.*
1.182 *The fight was filmed almost entirely against blue screen and the setting of the power generator room added in post-production. Air rams were used to add spectacle and dynamism to the fight.*

May 19, 1999

Rick McCallum When you're making a film and spend millions of dollars trying to get the best answer print and also create the best soundtrack, nothing is more depressing than going down to the local multiplex on the day the film opens and watch your release print in a theater where the projector is running at 50 percent of its luminance, the sound system sucks, there's no surround, there's no bass at all.

There are about 32,000 theaters in the United States, and less than one percent can accurately reproduce any film that any film-maker makes. It's pretty mind-boggling. We're

practically into the year 2000 and we can't even create an atmosphere for an audience where they can see the film the filmmakers made. It's impossible for someone to judge *The Phantom Menace* in 95 percent of the theaters it screens in. Viewers don't have access to some of the emotional tools we have to be able to express ourselves.

USA Today / April 23, 1999 Current digital sound systems in theaters use six channels: left front, center, right front, subwoofer, left surround, and right surround (usually on the side walls). As many as 2,000 theaters will have sound systems with added force when *The Phantom Menace* lands May 19. Many are

1.183

upgrading to Dolby Digital Surround EX, which improves on current Dolby Digital surround by adding sound from behind moviegoers.

The Phantom Menace *was released on May 19, 1999. It made over $64 million on its opening weekend and over $430 million that year in the US alone. It made over $1 billion worldwide.*

George Lucas Episode I became the highest grossing *Star Wars* movie of all time, but they were all successful. The people who loved I, II, and III the most were 10- and 12-year-olds. They loved Jar Jar. There was a completely different reaction from the critics, who loved *Star Wars* when they were 10 years old and wanted to feel the same way about the new films. Twenty years later they never understood that it was a movie for 12-year-olds.

The movies pretty much turned out the way I wanted them to. There are scenes that are in my personality, that other people might think, "Why did he do that"? Most of the stupid

1.183 *Terryl Whitlatch artwork showing the Gungan cavalry mounted on their kaadu and other creatures charging into battle, supported by a division of air whales (April 8, 1996).*

D.CHIANG

"**Jar Jar tries to be brave but is insecure and clumsy. He's a blend of Charlie Chaplin and Danny Kaye.**"

Terryl Whitlatch

1.184 *Doug Chiang's dynamic painting (April 25, 1996, 2.1 days) shows the AAT firing on the Gungan and forcing a retreat.*
1.185 *Jar Jar is blown off his kaadu and ends up hanging on a tank turret.*

1.184

1.185

1.186

1.187

1.186 *Maul has a defense for every attack by Qui-Gon.*
1.187 *Darth Maul impales Qui-Gon.*
1.188 *Obi-Wan screams in despair, trapped by the energy field, as his master is killed.*

1.188

1.189

things are done because I liked them. For example, I thought Jar Jar getting his tongue grabbed by Qui-Gon was funny. The 30-year-olds thought it was stupid, but the 10-year-olds thought it was great.

Jar Jar became controversial. The media decided that Jar Jar Binks was black, and a racial stereotype, which meant they couldn't like him. The critic for *The Wall Street Journal* wrote that he was a "Rastafarian Stepin Fetchit." Somebody in the *Los Angles Times* said it was racist. Another complained that he had a Caribbean accent. Well, it's not a Caribbean accent; it's a South Sea Island accent, where people speak in pidgin English. In a lot of cases you can't immediately understand what they're talking about because, like Cockney rhyming slang, they substitute words. But the viewers have to follow the movie, otherwise we've got to subtitle the whole thing, so I wrote a modified version of that in the script.

Paul Duncan Before you cast?

George Lucas Yeah. A lot of people tried out for the part, and I hired the best actor for the job, who just happened to be black. The inspiration for Jar Jar was Goofy. He looks like Goofy, and is goofy. Maybe Goofy was not as famous and well loved as Mickey Mouse, but he still had followers and nobody condemned him.

June 18, 1999

Dave Schnuelle / Engineering Consultant, THX On June 18, the first full-length feature film was projected in conventional cinemas through digital projectors for a paying

1.189–190 *Obi-Wan must now take on Darth Maul and they battle fiercely. Nick Gillard: "You could show Ray something five minutes before filming, and he would still be better than you on the take."*

> *"George was always telling me Obi-Wan was very straight and Qui-Gon is always breaking the rules, but I get annoyed with my master for being wayward. However, when I'm fighting it seems that I do lots of twists and spins and twirls and showing off a bit."*
>
> Ewan McGregor

a cinema-quality digital projector. The *Star Wars*: Episode I digital cinema release was planned as a technology demonstration of the newest digital cinema projector prototypes. Four theaters were chosen, two in Los Angeles and two in New Jersey near New York City. A theater in each city was equipped with a Texas Instruments prototype DLP cinema projector, and the other theater in each city was equipped with a Hughes-JVC light-valve projector.

Getting *Star Wars*: Episode I *The Phantom Menace* into four theaters for a full month of showings required unusual postproduction techniques and innovative thinking on theater presentation. In the end, nearly 500 showings were provided to over 100,000 paying customers and were met with a very enthusiastic response, a historic event in digital cinema.

audience. The Lucasfilm THX group had been looking into the possibilities of using digital projection in the theater for some time. After a year of research, in March of this year, THX announced a set of specifications to define

1.190

1.191

1.192

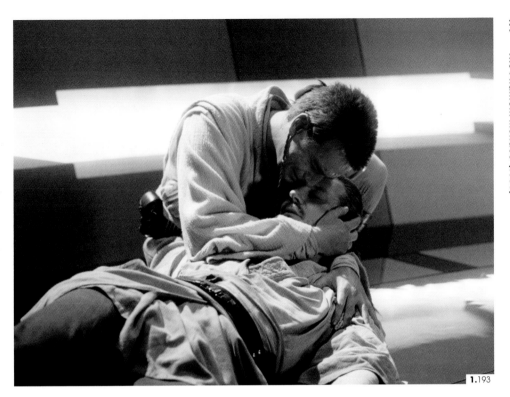

1.193

1.191 On set, Ray Park falls onto a mattress to film Obi-Wan's face.
1.192 At the last moment Obi-Wan jumps out of the pit, uses the Force to guide Qui-Gon's lightsaber to his hand, and slices the Sith in two. Darth Maul falls into the melting pit to his presumed death.
1.193 Obi-Wan cradles his dying master and promises he will train Anakin to become a Jedi Knight.

Traveling in Circles

George Lucas One of the basic concepts of human nature is personal responsibility. You either take responsibility for what you are doing, or you do not. But to deny that you have anything to do with the world, that you don't influence it in any way is ridiculous. We all influence the world. We all teach. Some of us have larger voices than others, but everybody

teaches every day of their lives. And everything you teach you are responsible for. I have a very loud voice and therefore I take it very seriously that whether you are influencing one person or a million people, the burden of responsibility still exists upon the individual.

Paul Duncan Obi-Wan Kenobi tells Boss Nass, the Gungan leader: "You and the Naboo form a symbiont circle. What happens to one of you will affect the other. You must understand this." Also, Qui-Gon later tells Anakin that we are symbionts with midi-chlorians, and that symbionts are "life-forms living together for mutual advantage." This idea of symbiotic relationships is key to the understanding of the film and of the *Star Wars* universe.

George Lucas Whenever you're telling mythological stories, you're traveling in circles. Like in a mandala there are small circles and bigger and bigger circles until finally you encompass the universe. It's the same thing telling

1.194

stories, in that every person, or relationship or group of symbiotic relationships, is always traveling in a circle. It goes back to either where it started or it intersects with other circles. At the end they survive because they're all connected.

In Episodes I, II, and III all the symbiotic relationships are torn apart. In Episode I, the senators are more interested in themselves than they are in helping each other. They have fallen out of the symbiotic circle. They couldn't agree on anything because their interests became so divergent, so they couldn't get anything done as a Republic, and the chancellor uses this division, which he helped create, to become Emperor.

In Episodes IV, V, and VI the Rebels form their own symbiotic relationship from the Old Republic to fight the Empire. They're trying to restore balance.

If you get into the ecology of it then everything is connected. Everything. If something happens to one part, then it happens to all parts, and that, ultimately, is one of the main movements in *Star Wars*.

Paul Duncan You introduced midi-chlorians in Episode I as indicators of the Force.

George Lucas This is the cosmology. The Force is the energy, the fuel, and without it everything would fall apart.

The Force is a metaphor for God, and God is essentially unknowable. But behind it is another metaphor, which fits so well into the movie that I couldn't resist it.

Midi-chlorians are the equivalent of mitochondria in living organisms and photosynthesis in plants — I simply combined

1.194 *Captain Panaka holds Nute Gunray captive while Queen Amidala renegotiates the trade treaty.*
1.195 *Sabé distracts Nute Gunray and his droids, giving Padmé time to access the pistols hidden in her throne.*

D.CHIANG

them for easier consumption by the viewer. Mitochondria create the chemical energy that turns one cell into two cells.

I like to think that there is a unified reality to life and that it exists everywhere in the universe and that it controls things, but you can also control *it*.

That's why I split it into the Personal Force and the Cosmic Force. The Personal Force is the energy field created by our cells interacting and doing things while we are alive. When we die, we lose our persona and our energy is assimilated into the Cosmic Force.

If we have enough midi-chlorians in our body, we can have a certain amount of control over our Personal Force and learn how to use it, like the Buddhist practice of being able to walk on hot coals. Some people can't because they just don't have as many midi-chlorians — that's just genetics. So the more midi-chlorians we have, the more accessibil-

ity we have to the Force. So we have to be trained how to use it.

For example, we can be good at math and on the piano, but to become a physicist or concert pianist, you have to be trained. You have to be trained to use the Force, to use the genes that give you a talent that is different from everybody else.

So you have to be found and fostered. If you have more than a certain number of midi-chlorians, you can become a Jedi. The Jedi will train you to connect to your Personal Force, and then to connect to the Cosmic Force. You don't have much power to control the Cosmic Force, but you can make use of it. The Jedi by nature of their genetics have more midi-chlorians than most people, but there is no direct connection between our human world and the microscopic world.

The Jedi are good, but they're not fantastic. They were never designed to be a superhero

> **"On the starfighter alone we went through easily three dozen drawings."**
>
> Doug Chiang

1.196 **This Doug Chiang concept painting of the space battle shows an early design of the droid fighter (September 4, 1996, 3.5 days).**
1.197 **Setting up a shot of Anakin flying the Naboo starfighter.**

1.196

1.197

"The big Trade Federation Control Ship at the end of the picture is a motion control model. Most of the shots that it appears in have been executed in an animatic form, so George has worked through the composition and timing in a way that he's pretty happy with. We've been getting those files from the Ranch so we can do an exact match on the motion control system."

John Knoll

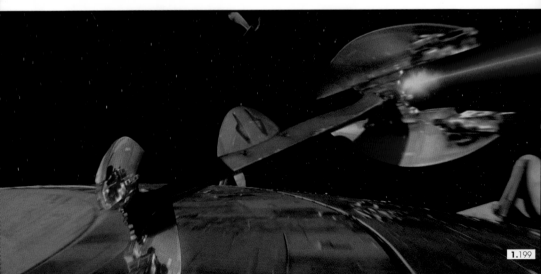

1.198 *Jake Lloyd sits inside a gimbal, which simulates the movement of the starfighter.*
1.199 *A vulture droid is firing above the Trade Federation Control Ship.*
1.200 *Anakin destroys the control ship, thus deactivating all the droids on Naboo and ending the war.*

or anything like that. They were designed to be a Buddhist monk, who happened to be a very good warrior. And they became the peacekeepers of the human world.

As explained in *The Clone Wars* episode "Voices," Qui-Gon Jinn spent time with five Force Priestesses on their planet the Wellspring of Life. They explained to him how he could keep his persona when he died and joined the Cosmic Force.

Qui-Gon learned how to hear the Cosmic Force, and when he died in Episode I he joined the Cosmic Force with his persona intact and was able to talk to Yoda in Episode III. When he was there, he learned more about how to become a Force ghost to keep your identity. Qui-Gon passed that information along to Yoda, Yoda taught Ben, and Ben was teaching Luke how to do that.

So that's how that symbiotic circle of people learned how to go from heaven to Earth, so to speak. It's based on Greek mythol-ogy—how to become a God, but in a much more practical sense and without the ego, without the identity.

The Whills

George Lucas I was going to put more about the midi-chlorians and the Whills after Episode I, but everybody freaked out and said, "We don't like this. It's terrible," so I didn't. Also, I had an investment in the whole thing financially so I was forced to relent because I knew it was self-indulgent. But I was very keen to have it be in the movies, and if I had gone on to the last three, it would've all been explained there.

The Whills are a microscopic, single-celled life-form like amoeba, fungi, and bacteria. There's something like 100,000 times more Whills than there are midi-chlorians, and there's about 10,000 times more midi-chlorians than there are human cells.

The only microscopic entities that can go *into* the human cells are the midi-chlorians. They are born in the cells. The midi-chlorians provide the energy for human cells to split and create life. The Whills are single-celled animals that feed on the Force. The more of the Force there is, the better off they are. So they have a very intense symbiotic relationship with the

1.200

1.201

midi-chlorians and the midi-chlorians effectively work for the Whills.

It is estimated that we have 100 trillion microbes in our body, and we are made up of about 90 percent bacteria and 10 percent human cells. So, who is in service to whom?

I know this is the kind of thing that the fans just go berserk over because they say, "We want it to be mysterious and magical," and, "You're just doing science." Well, this isn't science. This is just as mythological as anything else in *Star Wars*. It *sounds* more scientific, but it's a fiction.

It's saying there is a big symbiotic relationship to create life, and to create the Force, but if you look at all life-forms in the universe, most of them are one-celled organisms. I think of one-celled organisms as an advanced form of life because they've been able to travel through the universe. They have their own space-ships — those meteorites that we get every once in a while. They've been living on those things for thousands of years; they've been frozen, unfrozen, and can survive almost anything.

The one-celled organisms have to have a balance. You have to have good ones and bad ones otherwise it would extinguish life. And if they go out of balance, the dark side takes over.

The Force is split into two: the positive/light side, and the negative/dark side.

The dark side is very greedy and possessive. Greedy people want everything, and when they get everything they're insecure, constantly afraid that somebody's going to take it away from them. Fear is the doorway to the dark side. If you're fearful, you're going to do bad things, and you end up in World War II with 85 million people being killed. If you keep that up, there won't be anybody left.

If you're not afraid and you're willing to jump into the river to save a baby, regardless of the consequences, that's compassion. That's the good side of the Force.

A Global Entity

George Lucas In the beginning, the rules would be given by tribal leaders and other human entities — "You can't do that. You're disrupting everybody. So I'm sending you out into the woods." — but then it became supernatural. "If you go against the Ten Commandments, which came from God, bad, bad things are going to happen to you." It's a mechanism to control society, to keep it civil. Ultimately, fear doesn't work. Look at the history of humankind. Humans have killed billions of people and it hasn't solved anything. We're still doing it. And compassion has been overwhelmed by fear and anger and hate.

In the past people living in Jerusalem did not have any real contact with people in Rome; the chances of them meeting was zero, so they could have their own individual set of values. But now we're going through this transition into a global entity. That means everybody on the globe has to pretty much have the same values, and it's going to be a rough road to achieve this. We now know that what we do here in America is going to

*1.201 **Neither Yoda nor the Council agree to Obi-Wan taking Anakin as his Padawan. Obi-Wan insists that he will honor the wishes of Qui-Gon and Yoda relents. This scene was shot on March 5, 1998.***
*1.202 **Qui-Gon's funeral pyre and the mourners honoring his memory. Among the mourners are Anakin, Padmé, and Chancellor Palpatine.***

affect what goes on in Ireland and around the world.

We'll get there because we won't survive if we don't. But as we evolve into this, we're getting a lot of greedy people and isolationists and nativists and xenophobes who say, "I don't want to be with those people." That stuff has to fall away.

Paul Duncan It's a fear of the other or blame of the other without taking responsibility for your own faults.

George Lucas To me it's a denial of symbiotic relationships, of understanding that you need each other as part of the ecosystem. People think they are special, but they're not. Who said humans are special? Anybody who's lived with an animal knows that animals talk, have emotions, and feel sorrow. They are not as evolved as humans are, but they're no different than we are. Thinking that we're the im-

1.202

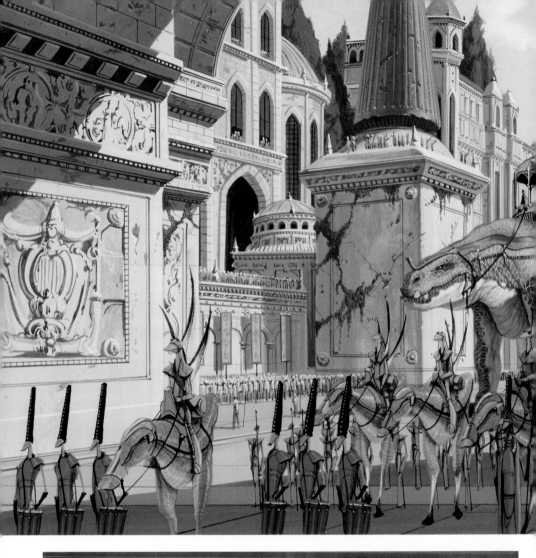

1.204

1.203 *Doug Chiang's concept painting
for the victory celebration in Theed
(October 10, 1996, 8.3 days).*
1.204–205 *The triumphant Gungans
march through Theed in a victory parade.
All the cultures of Naboo are reconciled
and Boss Nass signals this by holding up
the Globe of Peace.*

portant ones and the only things that matter is solipsistic nonsense. When you start pulling people and things and processes and everything out of the ecosystem, the whole system is weakened until it fails. Then we'll all die.

Everybody says, "Oh, global warming. We're going to destroy the planet." Well, we don't have the power to destroy the planet. We can't even come close. What we're talking about is destroying humankind. The worst that's going to happen is Earth is going to look like the Sahara Desert. There's not going to be any living things on it except for microbes under the sand or under the ice.

There are two ways that humans are going to survive: migrate, or adapt. Or both. Why are we going to Mars? Migrating in the solar system is a lot harder than migrating on the planet, but we have to learn how to do it. We have to adapt to Mars. Maybe we can terraform and make the trees grow, or maybe not. But in the end, you have to gain the knowledge because knowledge is the only thing we have to survive.

Paul Duncan The Gungans and Naboo have to make this decision about how to survive and save their planet.

George Lucas The Gungans are more sophisticated; therefore they don't want to have anything to do with Naboo, who they don't like. They rule the underworld, while the Naboo rule the upper world. The Gungans are an organic

1.205

society so all of their technology is organic, while the Naboo are mechanical. They coexist but do not cooperate, so they ignore each other.

Paul Duncan The only way to save the planet is by them joining together and cooperating, of completing the symbiont circle, as Obi-Wan suggests.

George Lucas The *Star Wars* universe is based on these integrated concepts, which are repeated over and over again within the story. Some people think these cosmic rules don't exist, but like gravity or time, they affect our daily lives.

"This film is an enemy of the status quo. This film is pro-change and about the acceptance of change."
George Lucas

1.206

"One of the principal themes is
symbiotic relationships, which
means how different life-forms/
entities/people live together for
mutual advantage."

George Lucas

1.206 *A dynamic Darth Maul publicity
photo.*
1.207 *McGregor, Lloyd, and Neeson pose
for a publicity shot.*

Attack of the Clones

Episode II: Attack of the Clones (2002)

Synopsis

Ten years after *The Phantom Menace*, the galaxy is on the brink of civil war. Under the leadership of a renegade Jedi named Count Dooku, thousands of planets threaten to secede from the Galactic Republic. When an assassination attempt is made on Senator Padmé Amidala, the former Queen of Naboo, Jedi apprentice Anakin Skywalker is assigned to protect her. In the course of his mission, Anakin discovers his love for Padmé as well as his own darker side. Soon, Anakin, Padmé, and Obi-Wan Kenobi are drawn into the heart of the Separatist movement and the beginning of the Clone Wars.

RELEASE DATE May 16, 2002 (US)
RUNNING TIME 142 minutes

Cast
OBI-WAN KENOBI EWAN MCGREGOR
SENATOR AMIDALA / PADMÉ NATALIE PORTMAN
ANAKIN SKYWALKER HAYDEN CHRISTENSEN
COUNT DOOKU CHRISTOPHER LEE
MACE WINDU SAMUEL L. JACKSON
YODA (VOICE) FRANK OZ
SUPREME CHANCELLOR PALPATINE
    IAN MCDIARMID
SHMI SKYWALKER PERNILLA AUGUST
JAR JAR BINKS / ACHK MED-BEQ AHMED BEST
SIO BIBBLE OLIVER FORD DAVIES
JANGO FETT TEMUERA MORRISON
C-3PO / DANNL FAYTONNI ANTHONY DANIELS

R2-D2 KENNY BAKER
KI-ADI-MUNDI / VICEROY NUTE GUNRAY
   SILAS CARSON
SENATOR BAIL ORGANA JIMMY SMITS
CLIEGG LARS JACK THOMPSON
ZAM WESELL LEEANNA WALSMAN

Crew
DIRECTOR GEORGE LUCAS
PRODUCER RICK MCCALLUM
SCREENPLAY GEORGE LUCAS, JONATHAN HALES
STORY GEORGE LUCAS
EXECUTIVE PRODUCER GEORGE LUCAS
PRODUCTION DESIGNER GAVIN BOCQUET
DIRECTOR OF PHOTOGRAPHY DAVID TATTERSALL
EDITOR AND SOUND DESIGNER BEN BURTT
COSTUME DESIGNER TRISHA BIGGAR

CONCEPT DESIGN SUPERVISORS
   DOUG CHIANG, ERIK TIEMENS, RYAN CHURCH
VISUAL EFFECTS SUPERVISORS JOHN KNOLL,
   PABLO HELMAN, BEN SNOW, DENNIS MUREN
ANIMATION DIRECTOR ROB COLEMAN
HIGH DEFINITION SUPERVISOR FRED MEYERS
MUSIC JOHN WILLIAMS

**2.1 *Poster for Episode II: Attack of the
Clones designed by Drew Struzan,
released in theaters and online on
March 12, 2002.***

Life Is a Pendulum

By Paul Duncan and Colin Odell & Michelle Le Blanc

George Lucas I'm a strong proponent, for better or worse, of making a film that works. By that I mean the audience can follow the story, be entertained by the story, be moved by the story, or educated by the story. I'm not that interested, ultimately, in having it technically perfect. I've discovered that has nothing to do with telling a story.

So when people analyze digital as opposed to the photochemical process, they're talking about things that nobody, except for a highly trained cameraman, lab technician, or special effects person could ever see. They're focusing on things that aren't issues that the public would ever know about or care about. To not use a process simply because of some very esoteric techni-cal issue is not something that I can relate to very well.

There is a lot of controversy about the fact that we're shooting Episode II digitally. People ask why am I doing this? The real question is, "Why not?" It's vastly superior in every way. It's cheaper. You'd have to be nuts not to shoot this way. As far as I'm concerned, we should have been shooting digital cinema 20 years ago.

Rick McCallum / Producer The very first time that George ever discussed with me his concept of a digital future for cinema and television was in 1989. I'm amazed now how precise that vision was about what he wanted to achieve. The idea was to make a digital pipeline, not just to have a camera to shoot digital, but to do visual effects, to do post-produc-

2.3

tion—the editing, the sound, the music—and then most importantly to make sure that an audience actually got to see the film projected digitally. That was the dream.

George Lucas Digital cinema didn't just happen, and it didn't happen because a lot of independent little people invented stuff. It happened because we convinced a lot of people from big companies to put up big money to advance the technology to make it happen.

Rick McCallum What was extraordinary about the whole experience is that we had about 62 companies come together based on George's dream, investing serious money without a single contract, without a single lawyer.

George Lucas Over $100 million. Sony put in about $30 million to build the camera. Panavision put in about $20 million to build the lenses. And you just go down the line.

Rick McCallum It took years to make this happen. All on people giving their word.

George Lucas And, of course, the Hollywood studios fought us the whole way.

2.2 *Ryan Church's concept art shows the senator's ship landing on the Coruscant platform (June 7, 2001).*
2.3 *Final frame of Senator Amidala's Naboo cruiser approaching Coruscant.*

George Is Not Kidding

Rick McCallum We produced the *Young Indiana Jones Chronicles* TV series nonlinearly by thinking of the 28 episodes as one giant film. If I was shooting in Paris and George was editing in San Francisco and we needed a pickup shot, George would send me mock-up footage and, although we'd each be working on a different episode, we could get it shot because of the way we structured our deals with our cast and crew.

In 1991, digital technology evolved to a level where we were able to do 100 VFX shots for every episode. We were shooting mostly on 16 mm, and sometimes on Super 8, but never on 35 mm. We knew that the whole mythology about film formats is all BS. You can be deeply untalented and be shooting on 70 mm, and it's still going to look bad. You can be deeply talented and shoot on Super 8 mm, and it's going to look fantastic. It's not a format issue; it's a talent issue.

We had to spend an enormous amount of time transferring the film onto videotape, and then onto laser discs, to edit on the nonlinear EditDroid system. Once it was edited, the tapes would be color corrected using DaVinci, the effects composited on Quantel's Harry, and the completed tapes sent to broadcast.

We then used the same techniques on a 35 mm feature film, *Radioland Murders* (1994), which was edited on an Avid, a nonlinear editor. No one had a problem with the digital effects on that film — they're imperceptible. Even though the film wasn't successful, that part of the process was incredibly successful for us. So, we started to make films in a very different way, and once you start doing that you say to yourself, "If I could only capture this stuff electronically!"

We got into partnerships with people that we thought could help us move into digital acquisition and production.

Larry Thorpe / Vice President, Acquisition Systems for Sony Electronics In late 1995, Rick purchased a widescreen Digital Betacam from us — to support the shooting of behind-the-scenes material during their movie and television productions.

Rick McCallum It was so mind-breaking that there were sequences we could shoot in the field with a camera that weighed 20 pounds. All the while, we're trying to create software to give that footage more of a film look, so it could be integrated with the 16 mm and 8 mm footage that we were shooting for TV.

Mike Blanchard / Technical Supervisor We did a number of DigiBeta (Digital Betacam)

2.4 Captain Typho (Jay Laga'aia) insists that Senator Amidala (Natalie Portman) hurry to a safe place after an assassination attempt kills the senator's faithful decoy, Cordé (Verónica Segura).
2.5 Lucas supervises as finishing touches are applied to Verónica Segura's makeup and costume to highlight the extent of Cordé's injuries following the explosion.

2.4

camera tests to figure out, "Okay, what would that look like if you filmed it out (printed digital onto film) and watched it on a big screen? What are the things we need to fix?" For example, during the shooting of the Jedi Rocks scene for the *Return of the Jedi* Special Edition...

Paul Duncan That's last week of June 1996?

Mike Blanchard Right. We shot DigiBeta side by side with the film camera. DigiBeta is standard definition (720 x 486 pixels) running at 30 frames per second (fps). When we converted it to 24 fps and transferred it to film — which is the speed film projectors run — it was soft. We lost so much resolution when we interpolated it to 24 frames it just wasn't going to work on a 50-foot screen. It was clear we needed more resolution and a 24 fps system to maintain a one to one frame relationship to match the prints that go to the theaters.

Digital cameras — they were called video cameras at the time — run at 30 fps because that's the frame rate for American television. People call it 30, but it's actually 29.97. One of the problems we had is that for George to edit or view 24 fps material on a monitor it would need to be at an actual rate of 23.98 so it could better integrate with existing equipment and could be done sooner to meet our schedule.

Since there were no monitors that would refresh at 23.98 fps, Fred Meyers, the chief engineer at ILM, and I went to a technical standards committee meeting. We had been told that was how the process worked — try to get a consensus from standards committees so manufacturers and broadcasters will support new standards and technologies. I had George write letters just to say, "Guys, stop dragging your feet. Approve 23.98 as one of the frame rates that you'll support." Whenever we asked for a standard to be approved they said, "Well, the next meeting is in a few months and then the standard has to go to

2.5

Europe." "How long are we talking about here?" "Not sure, could be months or it could be years."

That was another part of the process that we had to learn, which was that we didn't have time for standards bodies. We realized we needed to talk to the people that were building these products, and convince them to help us. It didn't make us any friends, but it was the only way we were going to get it ready in time.

Larry Thorpe I arranged a special dinner meeting in October of 1996 (during a Los Angeles SMPTE (Society of Motion Picture and Television Engineers) Fall Conference) between a management team from Sony Japan and a team from Lucasfilm. Rick made a strong case for Sony to work with them on a 24-frame system. A very key point that was made by Lucasfilm was that they would work with the technology of the moment — and not demand anything beyond what Sony was

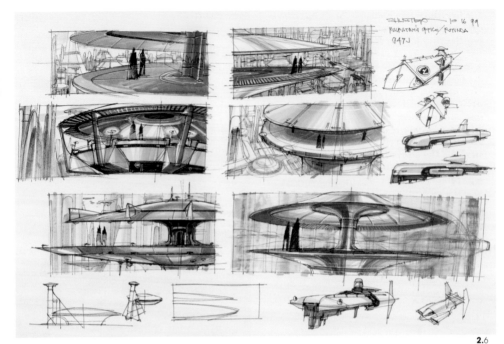

2.6

2.7

capable of developing and manufacturing at that time. George Lucas repeatedly said he would avoid technical specification debates, and would instead make all judgments and decisions based upon careful test shoots, transfers to films, and subjective assessments on the big screen. However, he said it MUST be a 24-frame system. This was a major issue for Sony; 24-frame systems had been discussed for a number of years but there were serious apprehensions about the potential market size.

Mike Blanchard Sony's broadcasting division is very profitable, but there was always the feeling that television was the little brother to the film industry. You had the film people high up in the stratosphere, with the directors of photography using 35 mm cameras and being very particular about the image, and way down

2.6 Jay Shuster's concept for Palpatine's office / rotunda (October 16, 1999). The implication is that Palpatine's office can only be reached by ship, thus retaining a large degree of isolation and privacy.
2.7 Final frame showing Palpatine (Ian McDiarmid) in his office discussing the political situation with Mace Windu, Yoda, and other Jedi.
2.8 First assistant director James McTeigue listens as Lucas composes the shot for the scene in Palpatine's office. Although Yoda would be a CG character a puppet is positioned on a box so that the actors' eyelines match.

here was broadcast doing their little television thing. They could not understand why the film guys were coming to them saying, "Hey, we want to use your equipment up here."

I believe we lost some critical time early in the project just trying to convince them that George was serious and would shoot a *Star Wars* movie with "broadcast" equipment.

Rick McCallum We had this extraordinary meeting with maybe eight or ten Sony engineers, led by Takeo Eguchi, plus Fred Meyers and me at a Japanese restaurant. The Sony head didn't speak any English so it had to be all through translators. You could see he wasn't interested. Then I gave this passionate speech about how important it was and everything else. And then he said, "Well, what do you want me to do?" And then Fred took over. Fred had come up with the idea of the 24-frame camera and had figured out exactly what was going to be needed for the whole postproduction workflow, which was the most important part, because even if we got the 24p and lens, we still needed to extract the information, convert it, and see it. So Fred drew it all on the paper table cloth. The head engineer stood up, he looked at it, he walked around the table a couple of times, and then he sat back down and did not say a single word for 25 minutes.

2.9 **Ryan Church concept art for the ribrant metropolis, Coruscant, showing the detailed exterior of Padmé's apartment (left).**

So for 25 minutes, everybody just sat there as he looked at it and then he raised his fist, slammed it down on the table, stood up, and said, "I can do it. I'll do it for you." Walked off. That was it.

Larry Thorpe George Lucas subsequently requested that we partner with Panavision as he wanted to use their lenses. In early 1997, we showed George and Rick the new HDCAM camcorder, and again we did film-out tests.

David Tattersall / Cinematographer I did a series of tests at The Culver Studios with the highest spec camera Sony had. I said to George that it's no good shooting a camera test for the new camera unless we shot with a film camera side by side without changing the lighting. We did a variety of shots with ac-

tors. We did macro close-ups, some fast-moving shots with motion blur, and with contrasty highlights — all the things that are normally a problem for video cameras. Sony and Panavision sent representatives to make sure that we didn't cheat.

Then we took both film and digital through the process of producing a negative, an IP (interpositive), an IN (internegative), and a release print, and then we had a big presentation at the Stag Theater at the Ranch for George and all the companies where we compared both versions side by side. You could see on the digital test that there were strange artifacts, step blur, and halos behind the highlights.

George was not happy.

George Lucas I told them, "Please take this camera and make it 24 frames so we can use it in the film. We can't convert the whole industry. What we can do is convert your camera." Sony said, "But then it's not as good!" I asked, "How are you going to break into the market?

SCENE 8 - INT. ELEVATOR TO PADME'S APARTMENT - AFTERNOON

PAM.014, 018

Obi-Wan - "You seem a little on edge."

Anakin - "...Not really."

Obi-Wan - "I haven't seen you this nervous since we fell into that nest of Gundarks!"

Anakin - "You fell into that nightmare...I rescued you, remember?

Obi-Wan - "Oh yeah..."

They laugh.

PAM.016

Close shot Obi-Wan

Obi-Wan - "You're sweating! Take a dep breath, relax!"

Anakin - "I havent' seen her in ten years."

Obi-Wan - "She's not the Queen anymore, Anakin. She's only a senator."

Anakin - "That's not why I'm nervous."

Obi-Wan smiles

PAM.017

Close shot Anakin

END -SCENE 8 - INT. ELEVATOR TO PADME'S APARTMENT - AFTERNOON

TOTAL SETUPS 3

2.10

2.10 *A new scene was shot on November 6, 2001, with Obi-Wan (Ewan McGregor) and Anakin (Hayden Christensen) in the elevator before they reach Padmé's apartment. Anakin is nervous about meeting Padmé again after 10 years.*

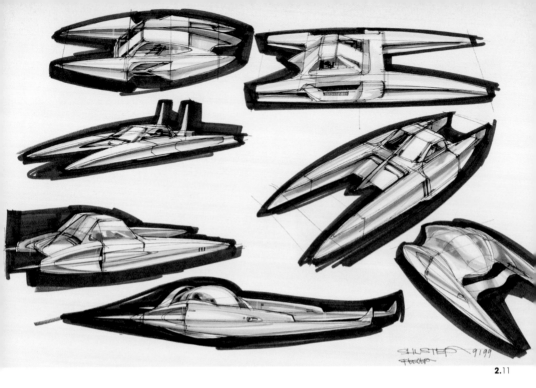

2.11 *Jay Shuster's concepts for bounty hunter Zam Wesell's speeder (September 1, 1999).*
2.12 *Doug Chiang's speeder concept (September 30, 1999).*

Look, we're going to shoot *Star Wars* on it, so it'll be a great showcase."

David Tattersall All the Sony guys went down to the front of the screen and had a huddle. They came back and said, "We know what we have to do. We have to produce a camera that shoots at 24 fps." That's where it started — the moment digital cinema began — when they agreed to make a 24 fps camera, progressive, not interlaced.

Larry Thorpe A working group made up of Sony Japan, Sony USA, Panavision, and Lucasfilm was formed and meetings were held at Skywalker Ranch every three months.

Rick McCallum We thrashed out thousands of details in relation to lookup tables, metadata,

the camera itself, and what it needed to be able to do for us as well as the lenses.

Mike Blanchard I went through all the camera reports for Episodes IV, V, and VI and worked out the focal lengths of the lenses that George uses when he shoots a *Star Wars* movie. Then we went to Panavision and said, "Can you build two zoom lenses that will cover this range?" That's what we got, instead of having primes like you normally would. There was just not enough time to get primes built for the new camera.

George Lucas I wanted to shoot *The Phantom Menace* on digital cameras but they couldn't get the cameras built fast enough.

Paul Duncan But you used a digital camera during the August 1998 pickups.

Rick McCallum The midi-chlorian test scene with Qui-Gon and Anakin was shot on Sony's HDC-750, the traditional 30 fps, studio high-definition (1920 x 1080) camera. That scene also had a digital background and a digital sky, and we were reverting back to 24 frames.

D. Chiang
9/30/99
0088

2.12

Mike Blanchard It was recorded onto the HDD-1000 videotape recorder, which was a reel-to-reel one-inch tape system. They had to have this ridiculously fast-spinning head to get HD resolution — rotating at 5,000 rpm or whatever it is — so it sounded like a jet taking off. Obviously, you can't have it on a set, so we had a long umbilical from the camera and located the VTR off stage.

Rick McCallum We had to move the set closer to the stage door because the cable wasn't long enough. We shot for a week with that.

Mike Blanchard Putting those midi-chlorian shots into Episode I was great because it showed Sony, "Wow, George is not kidding. He will put something shot by broadcast cameras into a film."

Emotional Tools

Mike Blanchard As word started getting out about us trying to shoot a film with digital cameras, whenever Rick and I would go to LA all

"There were huge demands made on all of us; we had to draw faster and better. It was trial by fire."
Jay Shuster / Concept Artist

we heard from cameramen and other people in the industry was, "a film negative is 8K resolution" (7680 × 4320 pixels).

Rick McCallum Most cameramen, when they've done a film, they have a print struck off the original negative. That print is shown by the Academy at a wonderful theater. But that's not how everybody else sees the movie. The cameramen and industry people don't go to Orange County or Kansas City or anywhere else and watch a typical film that's being projected.

Mike Blanchard The reality is you shoot the camera negative, you splice all the shots together to make the final cut, you copy it to make an interpositive, and from that make

Power 2/00
dp 209

Padme Nightgown — Cuffed Sleeved Version —

2.14

multiple internegative copies, and then from those you make thousands of copies for the release prints.

Paul Duncan So people in the theater see a third generation copy.

Mike Blanchard Correct. Sony and others have done studies on the actual resolution of a projected film print. Between the generational loss and the way film moves through the gate there is a major loss of quality and the image gets soft. The conclusion was that the resolution of the image was about 700 lines.

Paul Duncan So it was a similar resolution to high definition.

Mike Blanchard And this is without scratches, dust, dirt, hair, or taking into account the quality of the duping by the labs. More than anyone else in the business, George was acutely aware of how grim it was in theaters because he founded THX & TAP (Theater Alignment Program) in 1983. TAP would go

2.13 *Dermot Power's costume design for Padmé's nightgown (March 3, 2000). With much of the film's design created digitally, it was common for multiple designs to be created simultaneously with slight variations to give Lucas a choice. Power notes that this is the cuffed sleeved version.*
2.14 *Lucas (right) directs Ewan McGregor inside Senator Amidala's sleeping quarters.*
2.15 *Ed Natividad's design for the insidious and highly poisonous kouhun creatures that Wesell sends to attack Amidala as she slumbers (April 12, 2000).*

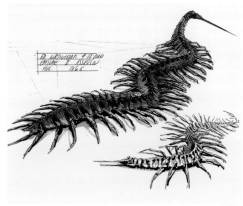

2.15

around to theaters and test the screen luminance: "Guess what, you've only got eight foot-lamberts on the screen here, it's supposed to be 16fL"; they'd do reports on image quality, image distortion, framing, masking, sound quality: "Oh, and by the way, you only have one speaker working"; and every other aspect of the exhibitor experience. You'd look at the reports and think, "You've got to be kidding me." They would assess the quality of release prints—the quality of prints coming out of the labs would vary—and grade them A, B, or C, so the A prints went to

the best theaters with the best screens and best sound, down to the C prints going to the worst theaters.

So George had hard data about how bad it really was.

Rick McCallum We spend millions of dollars trying to get the best print and create the best soundtrack, so nothing is more depressing than going down to the local multiplex on the day the film opens and watch your release print in a theater where the projector is running at 50 percent of its luminance, the sound system sucks, there's no surround sound, there's

2.18

2.16

2.17

no bass at all. Considering there are about 32,000 theaters in the United States, less than one percent can accurately reproduce any film that any filmmaker makes. It's pretty mind-boggling. We're practically into the year 2000 and we can't even create an atmosphere for an audience where they can actually see the film the filmmakers made. It's impossible for someone to judge *Star Wars: The Phantom Menace* in 95 percent of the theaters it screens in. Viewers don't have access to some of the emotional tools we have to be able to express ourselves.

George Lucas This is the major reason for digital projection. All the sound and image problems go away, and whatever you see in the screening room at the studio is the same quality you get in the movie theater. That had never happened before.

Visual Clarity

Doug Chiang / Concept Design Supervisor In May 1999, about a week and a half before the release of Episode I, George came in and said, "Okay, let's start Episode II." I thought we were all going to take a break...

George asked me and Iain McCaig to start conceptualizing. Even though he didn't tell us what the story was, he vaguely gave us an idea of who some of the characters were, what types of environments, and so we just sat down and started drawing.

We had already developed some of these worlds, like Coruscant, so the foundation was there and we knew the aesthetic guidelines. For Episode II we were honing that vision and then adding a handful of new designs that George wanted, like the rock world Geonosis and the water planet Kamino, where the clone troopers are grown.

Paul Duncan The very first thing that you drew were clone troopers on what looks like spider droids.

2.19

"What took you so long?"

Obi-Wan Kenobi

"Oh, you know, Master, I couldn't find a speeder I really liked, with an open cockpit... and with the right speed capabilities... and then, you know, I had to get a really gonzo color."

Anakin Skywalker

2.19, 21 *Ewan McGregor lands on the speeder, which was mounted on a gimbal. The gimbal, background, and crash mats were all blue so that they could be digitally removed in postproduction.* **2.**20 *Obi-Wan falls after the probe droid has been shot down.*

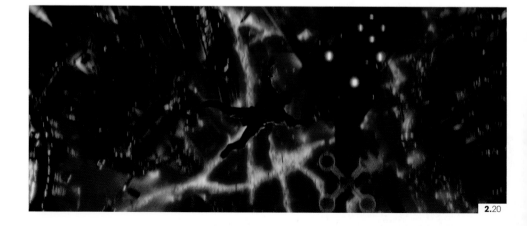

2.20

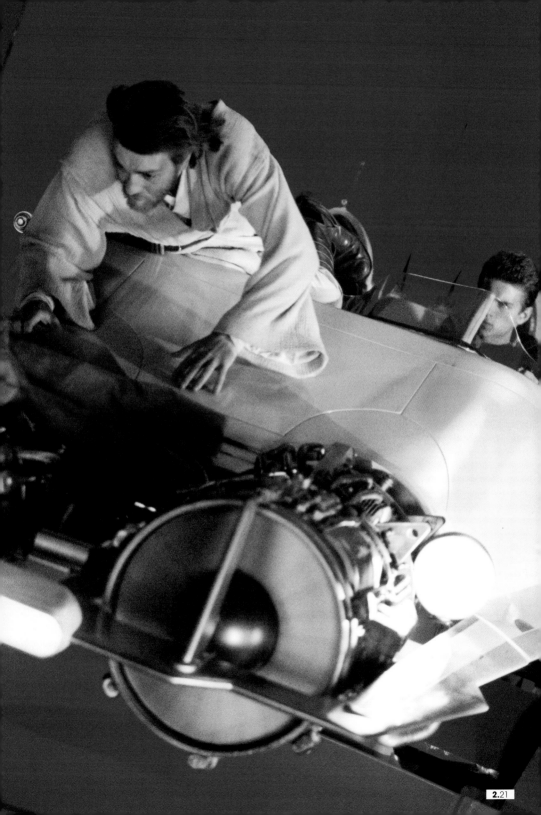

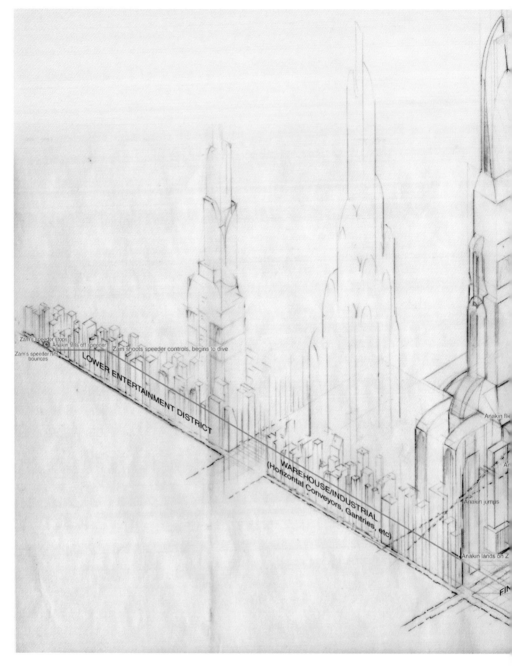

Zam's speeder stops
Anakin falls off speeder
Zam's speeder hits bounces
Zam shoots speeder controls, begins to dive

LOWER ENTERTAINMENT DISTRICT

WAREHOUSE/INDUSTRIAL
(Horizontal Conveyors, Gantries, etc)

Anakin fli

An

Anakin jumps

Anakin lands on Z

FIN

2.22–23 **Detailed route of the complete journey of the speeder chase through the districts of Coruscant, drawn by Robert E. Barnes in 2001. Precise notes indicate exactly where particular events in the** sequence happen (beginning top right) and the zones (upper, financial, warehouse) through which the speeders fly, notably where Obi-Wan falls (top right) and Anakin jumps from his speeder

2.22

2.23

(center), as well as the trajectory of the
speeders during their in-flight battle.
It culminates with Wesell's speeder crashing in the entertainment district.

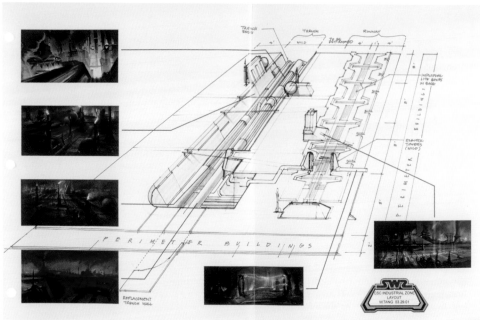

Doug Chiang When we were designing Episode I there was no Empire or Rebels so the shape language was blended. For Episode II he wanted to begin delineating a difference.

When you look at the original trilogy, the Empire and the stormtroopers are technology-based, while the Rebels and the good guys are organic and nature-based.

So that spider droid idea was to convey the idea that the clone troopers are going to deviate toward the Empire. Let's give them technological walking creatures, mechanical beasts. In contrast, the good guys would be riding animals.

Paul Duncan That idea is used explicitly in Episode III when Obi-Wan is on the boga and General Grievous is...

Doug Chiang On the wheel bike. Exactly. It's just like on Hoth in Episode V when you have

2.24 Concept art by Erik Tiemens for the refinery's power couplings through which the Jedi will have to fly, receiving a nasty electric shock as they do (February 1, 2001).

2.25 Plan view by Wilson Tang showing a more precise layout of the industrial zone, augmented with concept artwork (March 29, 2001). ILM built this as a 20 x 30–foot model at 1:72 scale and filmed it for the scene.

the AT-AT walkers and Luke and Han ride the tauntauns. The original trilogy has a visual clarity in terms of good and bad, color palettes, and shape language, and we're laying the foundation for that in the prequel trilogy.

But George took a little detour and wanted to try something a little bolder for Kamino.

He was very fond of 1960s science fiction so specifically asked us to come up with a similar look, which was this very slick, high-tech world, very clean white surfaces with plastic vacuum-formed furniture. It's a look that hadn't really been explored yet and it was fun to get into ultrasleek shapes.

The Kaminoans are stylized *Close Encounters*–type aliens — very tall characters with long necks and small heads. We had developed some of those aliens for Episode I and George wanted to explore that even further here. These elegant, graceful figures fit very well in a water environment where everything was clean, sterile, and sleek.

George wanted the Geonosians to be like termites. They had two different classes; the upper class would have wings that would fly; the lower class would be the drones who would do all of their labor.

For Episode I I designed the Neimoidians with long heads, with the idea that they had built the battle droids in their own image. The head design for the Neimoidians changed, but we revisited the original idea by turning the Geonosians into the engineers who created the battle droids, and so the Geonosians had the long heads. This fit into the idea that they were insect-like creatures. They are the Gungan equivalent in this film — an exotic society with exotic technology. But it has a slight twist. Instead of the Gungan Art Nouveau look, we're going more with a Gothic rock look for the rock world.

A Continuity Issue

George Lucas Episode I was made in Leavesden in the UK, and it was great. The only reason we didn't go back there was because Warner Bros. took it over for the first *Harry Potter* movie. They asked, "Can we use it while you're gone?" But by the time we wanted it back, all their roots had been planted in the place and they were not going to give it up.

Rick McCallum We planned to shoot in New Zealand, but they didn't have enough construction crew — we needed about 650 people.

Gavin Bocquet / Production Designer We made two trips to Sydney in July and August 1999. We needed to find out what we could achieve there with local labor and facilities, and what we'd have to bring in.

Rick McCallum Fox were contemplating making the former Sydney Showground at Moore Park into a studio and theme park.

The studio director, Kim Williams, said, "If you make the commitment for two films, we will finish the studio." So we said, "Let's go for it."

Gavin Bocquet Rick said that he couldn't take the film to Australia unless he was allowed to

2.26 *Anakin has jumped from his own speeder and lands on Wesell's in this final frame.*
2.27 *Filming Anakin hanging onto Wesell's speeder.*
2.28 *The full-scale build of Wesell's speeder, mounted on a gimbal that can move in multiple directions. The glass on the cockpit's passenger screen is broken where it is pierced by Anakin's lightsaber.*

2.27

2.28

2.29

bring his group of outside technicians. It was a continuity issue; there were various sets that were going to be repeats from the last film, and that would be hard to have a completely new group of people building those sets. There was logic in taking people who'd worked on the first film, people who knew Naboo and Tatooine and Coruscant. Rick negotiated all of that before he agreed to take this movie to Sydney.

Rick McCallum Another factor was the cost. The Australian dollar crashed so the first year it was something like 60 cents to the US dollar, and the third year was like 55 cents to the US dollar. So, for example, I think we made Episode II for around $32 million after the rebate, and then the rest were visual effects.

In England it would have cost another £15–20 million and there wasn't a rebate system at that time as there was in Australia. Of course the Australian crew was 25 percent cheaper

and we were going to shoot during their winter, when the weather was very mild, so it was perfect.

*2.29 **Ed Natividad's concept for the street-level districts of Coruscant shows crowds of citizens on multiple levels (November 4, 1999). Lucas specified the inclusion of a train, a detail that made it into the film.** 2.30 **Stephan Martiniere's concept for street-level Coruscant and the denizens within (November 7, 1999). All the concept artists had free rein to create designs wherever their imaginations took them. Lucas made his films in a nonlinear way. This process enabled concepts to form and develop, providing inspiration for the plot as well as the overall aesthetic. These designs could then be reviewed and revised, allowing the story and imagery to evolve as the production progressed.***

> *"We were going down to street level to see a Coruscant we'd never seen before. George threw down the gauntlet when he said it'd have to look better than Blade Runner."*
>
> Doug Chiang / Concept Design Supervisor

A Human Saga

George Lucas When *The Phantom Menace* came out in May 1999, I had to do some publicity in Europe. I went on vacation with my family, and looked for locations at the same time. I needed another view of the Naboo Palace, but I couldn't build one as I had done on *The Phantom Menace*, because it was only one scene. So I had to find something that would fit into the environment that we'd already created. I also needed some hideaway where I could tell the love story. When I saw the little Villa del Balbianello on Lake Como in Italy I thought, "this is perfect for the romantic scenes where Anakin and Padmé fall in love." It's the same with the Plaza de España

in Seville, Spain. So I picked both locations before I wrote the scenes. For a change I had the exact locations, but not the exact scenes.

Star Wars is a human saga about the struggle between what is good and what is evil; it also deals with more personal issues of growing up, family, and politics. I have tried to bring together a lot of the ideas that have existed over the last few thousand years and put them into a new story primarily for young people, to understand human heritage, not just of one particular country, but the human heritage that we all share.

Paul Duncan You started the screenplay in September 1999.

George Lucas The major story that is being told is actually two stories that are running parallel to each other on the grander picture. They are, how does good become evil and how does a democracy become a dictatorship, which is the social version of how does good become evil. That's the main theme of this one; not simply good vs. evil.

Episode II has a love story, so it's less of a kids' movie because they don't like to sit

2.30

through all of that yucky stuff. But it's still aimed at the same age level, so it's going to be a real challenge for me to get them through that part.

Paul Duncan We're seeing Anakin turning to the dark side through the prism of the love story. Padmé comes across as a very strong character because she's both active in the political arena and she's a fighter.

George Lucas She's grown up. The whole idea is that the characters grow; they become something. They're not the same character in all three movies. In the first movie she's young, she's a queen, she's feisty, but she's still 14. Anakin's 10. In the second movie they are 24 and 20. She's now been in politics for 10 years while Anakin's almost a Jedi.

But Anakin's also naïve, especially around her. He's falling in love, but he doesn't really know it. And it is forbidden.

Anakin had a crush on her when he was little. She dismissed him because he was just a little kid, but she liked him, like as with a puppy. Then when he came back and he was much more petulant and much more of a person, that changed the dynamic between them in terms of that love relationship.

Paul Duncan Even though she says, "No this can't happen," she still has the token that he gave to her as a boy. And then at dinner, she dresses seductively. Whether she's aware of it or not she's sending signals counter to what she is saying.

George Lucas And he's falling for it. It's inevitable that they're going to get together.

The films were always political — it's just that in Episodes IV–VI the Empire had already taken over so the politics were distant. Also, we didn't have the money to show Coruscant, only what was going on in the outer reaches

> *"We go chasing through the streets. That was lots of fun to shoot, knocking extras over and I fell down a few times. You get lots of cuts and bruises filming this."*
>
> Hayden Christensen

2.31 Ryan Church's concept for a brightly lit entertainment district as Wesell's speeder (shown in yellow here) is about to crash (February 1, 2001).
2.32 Shooting Anakin as he pursues Wesell through the streets of the entertainment district. The set was compact, so for some shots Christensen ran in a circle, which meant it was easier to keep him in focus.

2.31

2.32

2.33 *A number of members of the cast and crew appeared in the nightclub scene as extras. Here, Katie Lucas (left) and Ahmed Best (right) play a couple of patrons. Eagle-eyed viewers can also spot Anthony Daniels in another shot in the scene.*

2.34 *Final frame as Anakin and Obi-Wan enter the nightclub to see if they can flush out the bounty hunter.*
2.35 *Dermot Power's costume design put a great deal of thought into repurposing existing clothing accessories with the simple application of paint and glue (November 12, 1999).*

of the galaxy. And I was loath to have Obi-Wan and Luke sit and say, "Back in the days of the Republic . . ." "What happened to the Republic?" "Well, it was given away by the people . . ."

Paul Duncan Exposition.

George Lucas Yeah. I just won't do it.

The Vietnam War and Richard M. Nixon informed the development of *Star Wars*. At one point, Nixon thought he might try to change the constitution so he could run for a third term. That set me off thinking about how a democracy fails, and doing research on all kinds of democracies from Greece to Rome . . .

Paul Duncan Julius Caesar becoming dictator for life.

George Lucas The elites solved that by killing him, but then they turned around and gave power to Caesar's heir, Augustus, and he did get to be emperor.

In Episode II Darth Sidious / Palpatine creates a war. It's all manufactured. It's not real. "We've got to defend ourselves against the droids and the Separatists. It just so happens that the Kaminoans are building clones, so we should buy the clones." And everybody cheers. This is how freedom dies. With cheers.

Paul Duncan Sidious is a master of presentation. He's manipulating and controlling the news and the information.

George Lucas He does it all behind the scenes, in the shadows. He doesn't come out of the dark until he's sure he's got control of everything. Of course, until then, he uses everybody, like the queen in Episode I, as a front to put forward his agenda.

Paul Duncan Jar Jar proposes giving powers to Palpatine, and Bail Organa is with him surveying the clones at the end of Episode II. Everybody is being used. Everybody's a pawn.

When you were writing, was there any discussion or interaction between you and Rick about the story line, the characters, the meaning, or subtext?

stretchy orange balaclava

vac formed bubble maybe built onto motorcycle helmet and gas mask

oversized bouyancy jacket

ski pouches available in lots sizes and shapes

Image number:dp077
D.Power 99
© 1999 Lucasfilm Ltd.

space suit made from available sports wear. I think it would be best if it were sprayed dusty brown and sandy colours to make it less high tech looking and more lived in. Maybe it could be sprayed with glue and covered in pigment.

OK

2.35

George Lucas No. I never discussed it in that way with Rick, or any of the producers I've worked with. The only thing we discussed was . . .

Rick McCallum If I didn't understand something.

George Lucas But it was mostly Rick saying, "Do you really have to have a scene with 3,000 banthas stampeding across the desert?"

Rick McCallum (laughs) "Can we do it with 2,500?"

The Motion Business

George Lucas Once I had written the script, I had to explain it to people. To explain a scene to someone, something they'd never seen before, never heard of, and didn't have any idea what it is—you're starting in a really deep hole. On any given shot I may have 100 different people working on it. You have to get everybody up to speed very fast. The design of the characters, the design of the props, the location, and how you shoot the movie are all interrelated and everybody's got to understand it and get it without misinterpretation.

My credo is "a picture's worth a thousand words, so let's not talk," which is where storyboards come in. But we're not in the still business; we're in the motion business.

So that's why we have to make animatics, or "previs" as it's called.

Rick McCallum A sequence would take months for George to refine.

George Lucas And at the same time we are designing costumes and sets, generating concept art for the digital matte paintings, as well as regular storyboards — all to feed into the previs.

Daniel Gregoire / Previsualization Supervisor The first scene we worked on was the Coruscant speeder chase.

2.36 *Rehearsing Wesell's death scene. She is shot by Jango Fett from a high building on the opposite side of the street. Once the character actions and camera position are agreed, the actors will dress in full costume and makeup while lights and camera are set up.*
2.37 *Shot information sheet showing Obi-Wan trying to glean information from Wesell as she lies dying. Each shot contains a list of work to be carried out, including Wesell's head morphing back into a Clawdite as she dies. Obi-Wan finds the poison dart in CNC 400, which runs for 244 frames.*

Doug Chiang Obi-Wan and Anakin chase a bounty hunter through the city, and we go through all the different levels of Coruscant for the first time. In fact, the flying cars originally developed for the Kaminoans were repurposed to be used as the two speeders for the chase.

2.36

Shot # CNC350   Frames   65

Shot Type	2D
Compositor	
Reel 2.02 Roto	
CMM	

Animator	
Rebel	
Digimatte	
TD	
Sabre	

Description: 3S OBI-WAN, ANAKIN & ZAM

Ranch Editorial Notes:

Bid Notes:
- arm removal
- Stage elem: dart hole
- Zam starts morph into CLawditehead

Status1
Bid Complete

Sort Ordr

CNC.350

Notes: _____

Shot # CNC370   Frames   157

Shot Type	3D
Compositor	
Reel 2.02 Roto	flux
CMM	

Animator	
Rebel	
Digimatte	
TD	
Sabre	

Description: O/S ZAM

Ranch Editorial Notes:

Bid Notes:
- 3d morphing Zam into clawditehead
- arm removal, severed arm
- cg Zam
- cg clawditehead
- Stage elem: dart hole
- BG plate

Status1
In Progress

Sort Ordr

CNC.370

Notes: _____

Shot # CNC400   Frames   244

Shot Type	2D
Compositor	
Reel 2.02 Roto	
CMM	

Animator	
Rebel	
Digimatte	
TD	
Sabre	

Description: CS ZAM

Ranch Editorial Notes:

Bid Notes:
- 400W wipes into JTA
- replace face with clawditehead
- work on this shot after CNC370
- Stage elem: dart hole
- BG plate

Status1
Bid Complete

Sort Ordr

CNC.400

Notes: _____

Original ILM Matte

E.Tiemens sw2 10-2-01

ILM Matte: Modified Plate to show pockets of sunlight on city surface

/ Angle of sun

* Note - a bit more 'smog' color near horizon in the afternoon here
  If Possible keep things less blown out in values on bg. Light pools are
  the payoff here visually in the frame in an otherwise low key value scheme.

Lighting can give contrast in distance & warmth to the cooler palette

Example of matte comp

Original ILM

Original ILM

2.38

2.38 Erik Tiemens's lighting plan for the Jedi Council scene. Having received the images from ILM Tiemens sent notes back specifying the adjustments to be made — e.g., pockets of sunlight on the city surface. CG technology had advanced significantly since The Phantom Menace and ILM had the ability to enhance the texture of the light.

2.39 *Final frame showing a CG Yoda (Frank Oz), sitting in the Jedi Council chamber, contemplating recent events.*

Ben Burtt / Editor It started with a one-page summary that George typed up so I had the basic gist of who was there and what was going on.

George Lucas To start the process we would take images — an object moving across the screen, up, down, going away from us — that would show you the motion of what was happening, and intercut that with the pilots. We didn't have pilots and people yet, so Ben and his assistant editors would go out to in a little barn with a blue screen to shoot various characters flying around in the cars.

Ben Burtt We used George's Ferrari for the speeder. I think we put a few scratches on the roof.

Rick McCallum Then Ben cuts it together and shows it to George, George makes his changes, George takes it and bends it and molds it.

Daniel Gregoire Once Ben was done with his videomatics we were able to bring that into the digital realm. The previs team, using Alias Maya on Windows PCs, was able to do more complex animation. With Maya's advanced feature set, which included strong character animation, dynamic simulations, and many other complex digital tools, we built the CG versions of the speeders, and the characters, and flew them digitally though the city. We removed the need to shoot extras on camera.

Adobe's After Effects on the Macintosh was still the foundation of compositing the final previsualization shots that were often combinations of digital elements, photo images, character stand-ins, and reference footage.

George Lucas And then we take that and we blow it up, move it around, cut it out, change it around, and give it back to the animatic department and they would make a finer representation of that until we got the shots the way we wanted them.

Daniel Gregoire This worked out so well that it marked the last time a video camera would be used in the preproduction of the film.

For the next scenes we worked on, the Obi-Wan vs. Jango Fett rain battle and the asteroid chase, we went 100 percent digital. The Obi–Jango rain battle posed a particular challenge in that it was an all-out brawl and fistfight. This would take a lot of complex character animation to pull off. We simply didn't have the time to animate characters thoroughly enough to convey the fight. At this point, previsualization supervisor David

2.40

2.41

2.42

2.40 *The model shot of the exterior of Dex's
Diner and the surrounding environs.
The backing is green screen to allow the
Coruscant cityscape to be added later as
a digital matte.*
2.41 *The Coruscant cityscape was created
digitally.*

2.42 *CG models of the vehicles and steam
elements on the street outside the diner
are combined with live action of Obi-Wan
and others walking on the street. CG
trains were also added to crisscross in
front of the camera.*

2.43

2.44

2.45

2.43 *A blue cloth laid in an outdoor space, called "the slab," was used to shoot exterior figures and crowds for multiple sequences in the film. When shooting on the slab, the sun's projected position and luminance for the day was used so that the camera would be at the correct angle at the correct time to achieve the required lighting and shadows. This was essential to accurately composite the digital elements during postproduction.*

2.44 *Model maker Kevin Wallace (doubling as Obi-Wan Kenobi) walks from a blue pavement up some blue steps into Dex's Diner.*

2.45 *The final shot of Dex's Diner with all the elements composited together.*

dp472b dexter 5-col

2.46

Dozoretz decided to use ILM and its motion capture facilities to form the basis of the fight. In one day we captured what we thought would be a really good base for the sequence. Using that data in Maya we were able to pull off a first version of the sequence that was very believable and was closely followed on set during shooting. However, this marked the last time we would use motion capture on a sequence. Overall it produced good results but it was a technological challenge that at the time took more time than it was ultimately worth.

Rick McCallum The previs has huge economic impact. If you're reading a script and there's a scene that takes place on a street, the production designer, costumes, and set decorators are going to want to protect themselves by buying lots of extra pieces of set and costumes and props so that if the director asks for anything at the last moment — "Gee, it'd be great if to have another wall over here" — they have it to hand. That costs a fortune. But if you have an animatic then you only need to build the part of the street shown in the shot, not the whole length of it.

George Lucas I could play the previs for the cast and crew on the set, whether the set is blue screen, green screen, partially or fully built.

Rick McCallum You could then block and shoot the sequence quickly because it would all have been worked out.

George Lucas Likewise, I could show the previs to ILM: "This is the shot; this is the way it fits into the movie." There's no other way to do that. It's too complex. Writing millions of words, or thousands of storyboards just does not express what you really want to say.

Eventually we came to rely on that department to define how the movie would go together.

The Quality of the Cloth

Paul Duncan We begin with Padmé's ship descending into a fog on Coruscant. You're telling us that we're delving into a murky world, the world of politics, and you're expressing it visually. In comparison, Episode I seems to be dry and without weather.

George Lucas That's simply because weather is hard to shoot. We were winging it with the technology on Episode I and we couldn't do expensive stuff like weather.

2.46 *Dermot Power's concept for Dexter Jettster (August 11, 2000).*
2.47 *Ewan McGregor playing opposite Ron Falk, the voice actor for Dexter Jettster. Although Falk would be replaced by the CG Dexter in postproduction, Lucas found performances were enhanced if the actors could interact with each other face-to-face; rehearsing could lead to discoveries about the rhythm of the sequence. In further takes, McGregor played the scene on his own.*
2.48 *Final frame of Obi-Wan requesting help from Dexter as he tries to solve the mystery surrounding the poison dart. Dexter says it is a Kamino saberdart.*

"We've learned through the years that no matter how strange a character is audiences have to be able to connect to a face of some kind. So Dex had two eyes, a nose, and a wide mouth. We also gave him a bum leg so that he would walk with a limp, just to add some character to his movement."

Rob Coleman / Animation Director

2.47

2.48

Paul Duncan There's almost a film noir aspect in the first half of the movie, with Obi-Wan acting like a private eye.

George Lucas The movie is constructed as a mystery. Which is, who's behind all this? Obi-Wan traces the bounty hunter's dart back to Kamino, then discovers the clones, that Sifo-Dyas ordered the clones... What's going on here?

Paul Duncan We get fog, clouds, and twilight on Coruscant, water, rain, and storms on Kamino. The palette is becoming more complex.

George Lucas It's getting progressively darker because we know where we're headed: the rise of the Empire, and the main event, the showdown between Anakin and Obi-Wan. Episode I is bright and sunny with a little kid, and as we go down the road it's black and red with everybody dying. There are fewer jokes.

Paul Duncan In terms of color-coding, through the story Anakin and Padmé both have or-ganic colors, with Padmé leaning to lighter shades, and Anakin darker. But after the death of Anakin's mother on Tatooine, Padmé wears white in stark contrast to Anakin. This is all completely planned.

George Lucas Yes. Costumes are very big for me. I think I told you before about the Rebels

2.50

2.49 *Final frame showing Obi-Wan searching the archives to locate the planet Kamino as advised by Dexter. The miniature was filmed in multiple passes to make a depth of 10 bays and two floors. Richard Miller carved some of the miniature busts in the likeness of crew, like Rob Coleman, Pablo Helman, John Knoll, and George Lucas.*
2.50 *Preparing the minimal archive set, which comprised the flooring, the desk, and some of the busts of the "Lost Twenty" in front of the columns.*
2.51 *Model maker Jesse Thomas working on the detailed miniature model of the Jedi Temple Library on ILM's Windward Stage. It was 12 feet long and five bays deep.*

being earth colors, and the Empire being black and white in the first trilogy.

It wasn't as consistent for this trilogy because we were going to so many different places. In the wilderness you can restrict the palette, and reserve red for the Emperor, but Coruscant throws off all that planning—there's red in Coruscant and you're going to have to deal with it.

When we were doing the conceptual stuff we had to figure out the harder stuff, which is, "That looks great on a piece of paper, but what's behind it? Turn her around." Or, "She's going to have to jump through a

2.51

2.52

2.52–53 *Final frames showing Yoda consulting the younglings about Obi-Wan's conundrum — Master Kenobi has lost a planet. One of the younglings suggests that the planet existed, but somebody had deleted it from the Jedi archives.*

2.54 *Ewan McGregor entertains the young Padawans before the take. More than 20 children were cast with many being identical twins. Since filming with children is restricted to four hours, after that time they could continue shooting with their twins. Ahmed Best can be seen in the background — he was the life and soul of the party on set.*

2.54

2.53

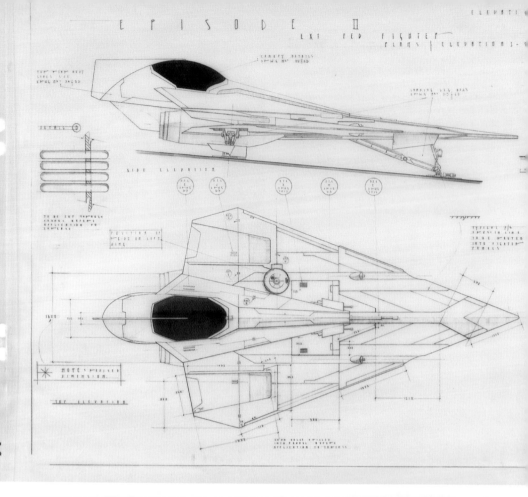

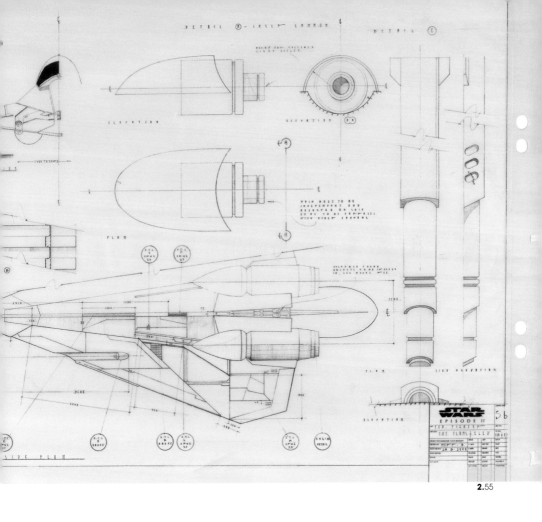

2.55

2.55 *Mark Bartholomew completed the hand-drawn blueprint for the Jedi starfighter on March 28, 2000. Doug Chiang: "George will typically pick up a pencil or pen and add his modifications to the designs or say, 'Let's take the cockpit of this drawing here and put it on here.' When I initially designed the ship into a single fighter there was not any logical place to put an R2 unit."*
2.56 *Concept for the deleted Jedi landing bay scene as Obi-Wan and Mace walk out to the landing platform.*

E. TIEMENS
7·23·01

NABOO
SPACEPORT
AREA
SWII

hoop and have a fight so she can't have a dress like this." So the design was not just the color or how it looked, but costume designer Trisha Biggar and I were worried about and focused on how this would play in real life. What were the actions that Natalie had to go through in that wardrobe and how did that fit? She had to assess the quality of the cloth, and how it moved. Is it going to be stiff or blow in the wind?

And there's a whole bunch of things that aren't in design that have to be in the ward-

2.57 Erik Tiemens's concept for the Naboo spaceport as Anakin and Padmé arrive in the freighter (July 23, 2001). The idyllic Naboo countryside contrasts with the mechanical, impersonal cityscapes of Coruscant.

robe. Costumes develop character, so each costume has to be designed to tell you what their function is and who they are.

Trisha Biggar / Costume Designer As George progressed with the script he realized more that he wanted to show a softer, friendlier side to Padmé, where she could be looking sexy and gorgeous and young, in skimpy clothes.

Natalie Portman I'm allowed to show tummy now, I guess.

George Lucas Padmé's costumes are sultrier in nature this time.

Iain McCaig / Concept Artist We wanted costumes that looked like they'd fall off if she sneezed. It was about peeking at things, about intimacy.

Dermot Power / Concept Artist The culture we live in provides us with a certain index of shapes that gets exhausted very quickly, so our designs become repetitive. So I look at

other cultures from around the world and societies through history to pool their shapes. It's a good way of getting other sensibilities into your design.

Trisha Biggar I went to the Natural History Museum and looked at the hues of coral and shiny beetles. I also looked at original photographs from Japan, Korea, Russia, Africa, Turkey, and even North American Eskimos from the 19th century. George likes to take an idea and give it a twist; this gives me free rein to gain inspiration from just about everywhere.

George Lucas The costume design is very complex, much more than on *American Graffiti*, for example. For that movie we just gave them a T-shirt or a shirt — one wardrobe through the whole movie — and that's it.

A Texture of Reality

Doug Chiang George constantly revised the script throughout preproduction but by January 2000 there was a first draft so the design department's focus shifted to the sets Gavin Bocquet would need to build for George to shoot by June.

Gavin Bocquet George told us that Episode II was going to be a much smaller, more intimate film than Episode I, with, presumably, fewer sets. It didn't turn out that way.

Doug Chiang It's the same relationship that we had on Episode I, which is essentially we work with George to get everything designed, and then once the designs are approved I hand it over to Gavin who builds set models and figures out what needs to be constructed, and what materials to build them out of. Sometimes he or I enhance the designs again because of stage space or budgets,

and present them again to George. It's a fluid exchange of information. This is becoming more of a virtual shoot than the first one, since a lot of the actual sets will be built after the principal photography as miniatures or as digital sets.

Gavin Bocquet By talking to John Knoll at ILM, and George, and Rick, and Doug, we can come to some conclusion about the best way to get a particular scene. For a one-shot or two-shot scene it's probably more cost-effective for ILM to make it than for us to physically build it. Once you start having 10, 20, 30 shots on a set, then it becomes much more expensive for ILM to construct what we could con-struct for real. In fact, the more that we build the better, since it added a texture of reality to the backgrounds, but obviously there are limits to the size that we can build.

2.58 *Final frame of the Theed palace grand courtyard.*
2.59 *Final frame as Padmé (Natalie Portman) and Anakin, accompanied by R2-D2 (Kenny Baker), walk through the palace passageway to meet with Queen Jamillia and brief her on the current situation. This was shot at Plaza de España, Seville, Spain, on September 13, 2000.*

2.58

2.59

2.60 *Discussing the scene set in Padmé's parents' house. Padmé's sister Sola tells Anakin, "You're the first boyfriend my sister's ever brought home."*
2.61 *Lucas directs Portman. This is the first scene where we see Padmé outside of her official duties and relaxing with her family. This scene gives a taste of what Anakin has always yearned for: a family life. It also highlight's Padmé's sense of duty because although she has a loving family she still dedicates herself to others. Anakin can see for the first time what was missing in his life.*

Chitchat

*Lynne Hale / Press Release /
February 11, 2000*

George is still working on the script for Episode II so at the moment Robin Gurland is only casting Anakin. Thus far, Robin has seen 700 tapes and submissions, and met with 300 candidates. She does not have a short list yet and is still exploring many possibilities. I know there have been many reports of actors saying that they have met with George Lucas and have done readings for him, or are the number one choice for Anakin. These are false rumors (but fun to read!). Regarding other characters, Robin will not begin to cast other parts until she gets a character breakdown from George.

Robin Gurland There were no auditions; everything was done by meetings. It was basically sitting down for 20 minutes to two hours and finding out who they are as an actor and what experience they have.

Hayden Christensen had two of the characteristics that I was really seeking for the character of Anakin: he has the vulnerability, and he has the edginess that's needed. We had to have that combination, and it's rare to find an actor who can go back and forth so well. There is something so interesting going on behind those eyes; you just want to know more. I think that's what my initial attraction was given that he fulfilled all of the other things that I was looking for as far as his look, his age, his temperament, and his innate quality. But, besides that, to me, he is just an amazingly seductive and intriguing actor.

Rick McCallum When you go through the process of casting, some actors illuminate themselves in a way about what the part is and what you think it should be. And that happened with Hayden.

2.62 *The sequence where Anakin is introduced to Padmé's family was filmed but deleted. Padmé's nieces meet Anakin but are far more enamored of R2-D2.*

2.62

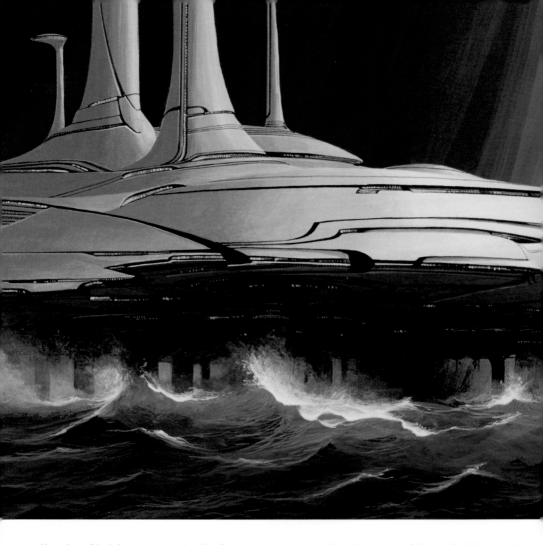

Hayden Christensen I met with George at Skywalker Ranch. And that was nothing but cool. We sat down and talked—not about *Star Wars.* We didn't even talk about the film industry. It was just normal chitchat, about my experiences with acting, my training, my thoughts on different places in the world—he was just trying to get an idea of how I was as a person more than anything else. Afterward, they gave me a couple of hats and a *Star Wars* mug. I was happy. I never felt like it would lead to anything.

George Lucas He's charming and he's young, but at the same time, he's got a real nice edge to him. He's one of these slightly brooding young Turks in the Marlon Brando / James Dean mold. He's very good with anger and these kinds of qualities, which were not only important for this film but more important for the next film. Because the boyish quality begins to drift away in the next film.

2.63 *Doug Chiang's concept shows Jango Fett's Slave I starship approaching Tipoca City's landing platform (March 30, 2000).*

D.CHIANG

2.63

Hayden Christensen Then I took a screen test. Then there was another screen test with Natalie in May. Finally, I got the call that I had the part. But I was never sure until then.

Subtlety of Performance

George Lucas The biggest technological breakthrough in Episode II is Yoda. When I started making Episode I, I knew I'd eventually have to create a digital replica that would look enough like the original puppet that viewers would believe he was the same little green guy.

"George described Kamino as a planet consumed by storms but with very hi-tech, sophisticated cities built on stilts. That image was very appealing, since I've always liked the striking image of oil derricks in the North Atlantic. When I was painting, I was trying to capture that mood where there's a break in the weather and a shaft of sunlight is highlighting the city, but the rain and winds are still powerful."
Doug Chiang

2.64

2.64 **Ed Natividad's concept of Tipoca City retains the curved design, but the supporting stilts of the city are proportionally broader and provide more stability (October 20, 1999).**
2.65 **The Kamino landing platform set with Obi-Wan's Jedi starfighter.**

The digital camera is on a telescopic camera crane jib so that it can be positioned and moved behind the starfighter. The camera crew would rehearse the moves before filming with the rain turned on from the pipes running above the set.

Rob Coleman / Animation Director It was possible to do a digital Yoda during *The Phantom Menace* but there was a lot of concern, from Lucasfilm and from ILM, about whether we could get all the digital characters that we were doing for the film done in time. Rick and George did not want to add a very sophisticated, very important character like Yoda to our plate.

I kept needling George during the production, and we came to an agreement that we would do two digital Yoda shots for *The Phantom Menace*. There's a high shot of Yoda talking to Obi-Wan, after Qui-Gon has been killed, and Yoda is walking. There's also a high shot establishing the funeral pyre. Yoda is digital in that shot as well, standing beside Mace Windu. So we got two shots in the first film.

A number of us wanted to do a computer-generated Yoda, and after *The Phantom Menace* we started talking about it again. I went to see Doug Chiang and Iain McCaig and we did a proof of concept for George. Iain did some drawings, Doug supervised the sculpt that was made of what Yoda would look like in Episode II, it was approved by George, and Geoff Campbell, our digital modeling supervisor, built the new computer-generated Yoda.

The proof of concept test was for the face, so that we could do a subtlety of performance. One of the first things that George said to us was, "I don't want this performance to stand out. We've already set the tone of what Yoda is like. I know that you guys can do all kinds of things with the face, but if it's not reminiscent of the puppet's performance then it's not going to get in the movie."

I got three of my top animators together — Linda Bell, Hal Hickel, and Kevin Martel — and we decided on six shots using *The Empire Strikes Back* as the cornerstone of Yoda's performance. We sat for a week or so and really tried to distill what was it about Frank Oz's performance and what was it about the puppet that made it as magical as it was.

We looked at what was going on with Frank's hand. What were the shudders and movements in Yoda's body? How did the ears overlap and jiggle in the latex or in the ma-

2.65

2.66

terials that were used in the original puppet? How much did the eyes move? How did the jaw move? We discussed whether we should put the jawbone where it should be, or where the jawbone would be if you had a hand inside and where the foam would be, because that really changed the performance of the character. We've gone in between the two of them so that we have both control over the jaw and the lateral side-to-side movement of the jaw that Frank did when he was operating the puppet. We also have a range of motion that he was never able to achieve simply because of the little tiny gizmos that had to be stuffed into the skull of that puppet to move the eyes and squish the skin—we, of course, are free of that.

Then we tried to transfer that to the animated character. We have the ability to make the lips do all kinds of nuances that they couldn't do with a puppet, but it didn't look like Yoda so we dialed back on those. We were able to do some different things with the eyes, and the way the skin wraps around the eyeball, but we didn't go as far as we could because it was becoming distant from the *Empire* performance.

We did three shots of him talking and three shots of him not talking, just acting with his face and face muscles. James Tooley, my

*2.*66 *Final frame of Obi-Wan surprised to learn from Lama Su that the Kaminoans have been commissioned to build a clone army for the Jedi. Obi-Wan improvises—allowing them to think him an emissary of Jedi Master Sifo-Dyas—and goes along with the Kaminoans so that he can tour the city.*

technical animation supervisor, figured out how the chaining is going to work—how the character holds together and how we animate it—and Tim McLaughlin handled all the clothing and skinning of the character.

Once we spent a couple weeks on it I felt that we were getting pretty close, so I presented it to George and he loved it. It was at that moment that he said we're going with the CG Yoda. It was very exciting for me to come back to the studio and tell everybody, because it was a huge team effort.

Once we'd achieved that subtlety of performance, we moved down to the body. Now we're trying to figure out the length of his limbs and how he walks. We studied how Frank moved him around when we animated the shot with him walking with his cane—we saw the up and down beats that Frank had put into the character when he was moving.

EP2 Matchmove Infosheet

SHOT: KOA 260   **DATE:** 7/17/01 Tues.

CAMERA SETUP: sticks dolly crane/remote steadicam car

CAMERA MOVE: lock-off pan tilt boom dolly roll

MOVE DESCRIPTION: Booms slight up & left & slight tilt down.

LENS: 9.5 mm

PERF: 4 / 8 / HD

Height	Tilt	Pan	Focus	Miniatures:
Start: 8½"	Start: 3.4° ↓	Start: straight on scene	~ 4'	
End: 12"	End: 6.5° ↓	End: ≈ 25° R	**Dutch** none	

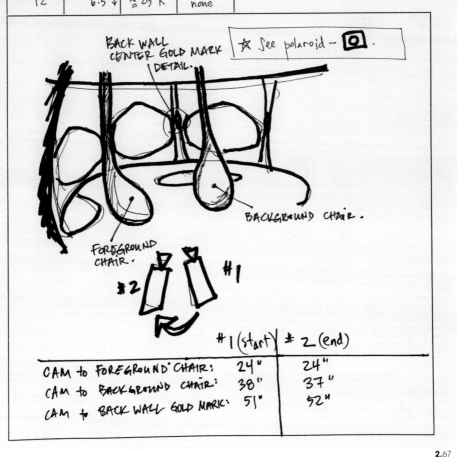

BACK WALL CENTER GOLD MARK DETAIL.

☆ See polaroid — 📷.

BACKGROUND CHAIR.

FOREGROUND CHAIR.

#2   #1

	#1 (start)	#2 (end)
CAM to FOREGROUND CHAIR:	24"	24"
CAM to BACKGROUND CHAIR:	38"	37"
CAM to BACK WALL GOLD MARK:	51"	52"

2.67

2.67 Matchmove information sheet for model shot KOA 260 (July 17, 2001). For every shot, whether live action, model, or digital, a record of the camera position in relation to the set, objects, and actors is made so that the geometry and camera movement can be reproduced precisely. This shows the camera movement from #1 to #2 when Pat Sweeney photographed the model of Lama Su's office.

2.68

2.69

2.68 *Anakin steals an audacious kiss.*
Anakin: "When I am around you,
my mind is no longer my own."
2.69 *Lucas directs Christensen and*
Portman at Villa del Balbianello,
Lake Como, on September 1, 2000.
2.70 *Dermot Power's costume design*
for a flowing gown for Padmé (May 26,
2000). The image notes that she has
"shell hair."

P3 with shell hair
dp335

2.70

We are trying to figure out what's happening with the feet.

George has told us that Yoda's going to be much more active in Episode II. I've yet to find out or see storyboards of exactly how active, but in anticipation of that we're trying to come up with new ideas of how to put his bones into his body, and the controls that we'll need to give him that subtlety of performance that he may need to be a Jedi Master in action.

I haven't seen the script so I have a lot of questions for George. "Was Yoda one of the greatest warriors ever, or is he much more cerebral, like a teacher, as we've seen him?" "We've seen him lift Luke's X-wing out of the swamp by using the power of the Force through his hand. Is his technique of battling the same, or does he actually wield a light-saber like the other Jedi?" "Does he have the ability to zip across the room or make himself invisible or levitate?" "Is he affected by his age? Do his bones hurt? Does he get tired?" All that will affect how you animate a character in a sequence.

I approach it with as wide a view as possible, and then George will help rein us in and give us an idea of how Yoda is going to move, because we haven't seen it before.

Make This Work

David Tattersall Early in 2000, I got back from New Zealand, where I'd shot *Vertical Limit*, and Phil Radin at Panavision rang to tell me that the prototype Sony HDW-F900 camera with the Panavision zoom lenses had arrived, and asked if I wanted to test it. I went along to his office and he pulled me aside to tell me, "Look, we've spent so much money on these lenses you have to make this work." We got a model, props, cars, and a bunch of stuff, and shot tests for two days with Panavision paying for everything including the lighting and crew.

"George really loves the genre of romanticism, the Pre-Raphaelite look. We leaned heavily toward that, which meant looking back to the 1920s and '30s."

Iain McCaig / Concept Artist

The camera recorded high definition at 24 progressive frames per second.

Larry Thorpe On March 10, 2000, a film-out screening was held at Skywalker Ranch.

Mike Blanchard I'll never forget that because I was about as nervous as I've ever been. We had been working on this for years and I was afraid we were going to fail and let George down. David had done a lot of tests because we needed to figure out the ILM pipeline — how John Knoll and others were going to work with the footage — the editorial pipeline, postproduction, and distribution. So we showed the film-out tests to George. The project leads from Sony and Panavision were there.

The source was from an HD camera so each frame was 1920 x 1080 pixels, but because it's *Star Wars* it had to be 2.35:1 aspect ratio, so we cropped it to 1920 x 818. Afterward, someone started to talk about some of their concerns and George said, "I don't know what you guys are talking about. What are you guys

2.71

looking at? This looks great. Make it as good as you can by the cutoff date."

Rick McCallum Anyone who thinks for a moment that we would risk $100 million of our own money if we didn't think the quality was not only better, or that we would go through all this pain if we thought the image quality was less, is just full of it.

Larry Thorpe The commitment had been made to shoot Episode II entirely in 24 progres-

2.72

2.71 *Final frame of Padmé and Anakin enjoying a romantic picnic in the glorious countryside.*
2.72 *Padmé and Anakin share a kiss in this publicity still.*

"We had to struggle with the bad design mojo of monotony and repetition. In time, the cloning facility designs adopted their strongest and most apparent theme — vast amounts of white space with strong graphic elements."

Jay Shuster / Concept Artist

2.73 *Final frame showing the young clones (Daniel Logan) in their classroom. Obi-Wan learns that Master Sifo-Dyas ordered over one million units of clones on behalf of the Republic 10 years previous.* **2.**74 *This design for the clone hatchery includes shot KOT 060 depicting Obi-Wan learning from the Kaminoans (February 15, 2001).*

2.74

2.73

sive frames per second. Six prototype systems were made.

Rick McCallum They sent the gear in boxes. There were no manuals, nothing. The Sony executive wrote a letter, saying, "We can't be held responsible for this."

Into the Maelstrom

George Lucas Writing isn't my favorite thing to do. It's just hard.

Rick McCallum When George would get into periods that were difficult for him to find the space to write, I would say, "Listen, Jonathan Hales's waiting. I just have to give him a call." I hired Jonathan as a screenwriter on the *Young Indiana Jones Chronicles* and he did a fantastic job for us for a number of years. George resisted it, like any writer does, until you get to a point where you realize there's no other choice.

George had already written his first draft, and we were putting enormous pressure on him for information virtually every day by satellite transmission from Australia. It got to the point where we were sending models of sets to him and he was basing the script around those sets because otherwise there was no way we were going to be ready. At the beginning of April, two months before we were due to shoot, George needed to get the script out and have somebody work with him on it. Jonathan came in and they never left each other for a month.

George Lucas Sometimes it was dialogue; sometimes it was fixing a scene that wasn't really working. Having someone else look at it and do a critique—I needed that support, because I was about to walk into the maelstrom.

Rick McCallum We got the script three days before we started shooting.

PREDECESSOR TO
BABA FETT —

ED NATIVIDAD
10·8·99
EPISODE II
"EARLY STORMTROOPER"

2.75

2.76

2.77

Environment

Rick McCallum The biggest problem in the film industry — and I'm talking about the American film industry — is that it's based on fear. It's based on the fear that you can be fired at any minute, that you have no control over your life. There are people who are animals, who behave outrageously badly toward each other for political reasons — that is repugnant to us.

For us ego, pride, and vanity are the three things that keep you from working collectively as a group. It's one thing to have ego about wanting to get the best job done, but once it starts to interfere with the process and the people, forget it. When we started *Young Indy* we had a group of people we didn't know. It took about three or four months to get rid of the people that manifested one or more of those characteristics. After that we kept everybody.

You have to create a positive work environment for your crew. If they think they're being taken advantage of or used in any way,

*2.75 **Between June and October 1999 multiple artists submitted designs for the clone armor, each of them trying to capture the essence of both the stormtrooper and Mandalorian armors. Ed Natividad's ideas were instead used to develop the design for bounty hunter Zam Wesell (October 8, 1999). Natividad: "For my early stormtrooper sketch I wanted to indicate it was a human not a robot, so I had the mask detached from the breastplate. George stamped it 'OK' and chose it as the bounty hunter. I tried to do some modifications, but George always wanted more of the original sketch."***

*2.76 **Jay Shuster (September 23, 1999) successfully merges the eyes of the bounty hunter helmets with the mouth of the stormtrooper helmet.***

*2.77 **Doug Chiang's concept for helmet and armor (September 20, 1999).***

you're going to lose them completely. They'll put up with it for a while because they've got to make money and make a living, but not in the long run and not at the level that we're working at.

We don't want any tension. We don't want any freak-outs. We don't want any narcissistic behavior. We want to have fun. We want people to joke but be absolutely serious and committed to what they're doing. If you do that, then you can achieve anything.

Paul Duncan To make a movie requires a real physical and emotional commitment since you are often away from home for months.

Rick McCallum That's part of the fun and the joy of it, to say, "Let's just go for it." But you have to have a family that understands; my wife was the number one commercials producer in the Czech Republic for 15 years, so she knew what the life was like. But if you don't

have somebody who understands that and you care about your family, you're screwed.

When we were doing *Young Indy*, some people couldn't cope with being away for a year. For the prequel trilogy, we were away in London and Australia for about four and a half years over a six and a half year period. You've got to have a pretty good relationship and you have to have a good environment to make sure that their families understand.

Even though you're making great money for your family, you have to have the mutual respect with your partner, they have to understand this is what you love doing more than anything, and that the quality of life they have is because of the sacrifice you're making now. If you have kids, it's tough on them—you miss their birthdays, their school plays, everything.

We encouraged our English crew to bring their families with them to Australia so they

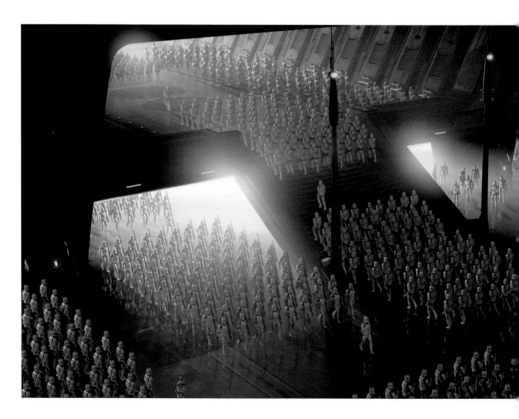

2.79

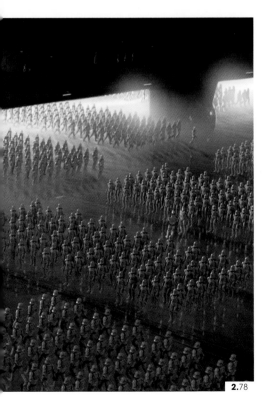

2.78

2.78 *Final frame of the clone parade ground. There are 200,000 units ready to ship.*
2.79 *Alexander Laurant's concept for the clone training area in shot KOT 160 (March 21, 2001). The red line defines which areas would be constructed as practical models and which would be developed as CG. George Lucas approved it on the following day.*
2.80 *An aiwha ("air whale") flies over the stormy oceans ridden by a Kaminoan. Winged creatures had featured as concepts in previous films but had never been realized until Episode II.*

2.80

2.81

2.81 *Doug Chiang's "Boba Fett's armor" design (March 21, 2000).*

2.82 *Final frame of Obi-Wan meeting the clone template, Jango Fett (Temuera Morrison).*

2.82

would have a relatively normal life. We'd write their schools that their children would do their homework, get tutored, or they'd go into a new school in Australia — anything to keep that balance. We wanted them to know that we care about them as much as we care about any actor on the movie.

When John Knoll came, we got him a huge house because he has, like, six kids. When Rob Coleman came, we did the same. We always encouraged their families to come and be with them and have a great time. One of the great things about the Fox Studios is that it's so central you can't live more than 10–15 minutes away from them, so we'd wrap at 6:30–7 p.m., and by 7:30 the crew'd be with their family having a barbecue out on the beach.

"Jedi won't lead droids. Their whole basis is connecting with the life force. They'd just say, 'That's not the way we operate. We don't function with nonlife-forms.' So if there is to be a Republican army, it would have to be an army of humans."

George Lucas

The Vision

Rick McCallum George and I have always been in total sync, since the day we started working with each other. We'll joke and have fun, but in terms of the script, in terms of what he wants, it was a blissful 23 years for me because I knew exactly what he wanted and needed. We see each other every day, usually over lunch, talking politics, or I would ask something about the film if it wasn't clear what it was he wanted.

A director is looking for two things. He wants the truth without being humiliated or beaten up. Also, more importantly, he wants to know that he has a partner who is going to exhaust all the possibilities to get him every single thing that he needs and wants to express the vision inside his head.

Some directors can plan out a film exactly, with precise storyboards and a very clear vision of what they are shooting. George doesn't do that. With George that vision changes. He has his idea. He starts to make it, and then it evolves. He needs that process and the ability to be able to shoot for very little money so that he has more time. Over time the movie is changing and growing in his mind. He sees a creature that has been created by the design department. "No, I'd like to see bigger ears and maybe forget the chin.

2.84

2.83 *Iain McCaig's costume design portrays Padmé as being significantly more mature (January 6, 2000). Lucas deemed the artwork to be "Fabulouso."*
2.84 *Final frame of Padmé and Anakin together in the fireplace alcove. Anakin wants to kiss Padmé once again but she resists. She says she has more important*

things to do than fall in love. Anakin proposes that they keep their love a secret, but she declares that they would be living a lie.
2.85 *Lucas directing Portman during the dining room scene. She has to imagine that Anakin uses the Force to move the fruit.*

2.85

2.86 *Jango Fett is preparing to leave with Boba in Slave I, but Obi-Wan Kenobi, lightsaber at the ready, has other ideas in Doug Chiang's concept art (April 10, 2000).*
2.87 *Iain McCaig's speculative storyboard of a Jedi fight on Tipoca City (March 3, 2000). At the time, the concept artists didn't know who would be fighting whom nor where the battles would take place.*

2.86

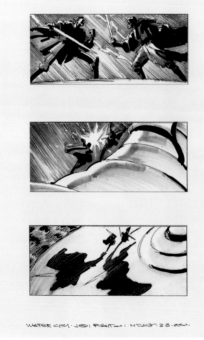

WATER CITY · JEDI FIGHT · 1. M'CAIG. 3 3. 00~

2.87

Let's make his legs shorter. No, I made a mistake with the ears. Let's do..." And then, over the process of weeks or months, it's changed and morphed into something else until he gets it. He can't express it exactly inside his mind's eye, but he understands exactly what it is he wants and that you have to go through a process to get it. But you also have to be patient and keep your crew in a place where they don't get frustrated. Luckily, they understand the process because we had the same crew that had worked for five years on *The Young Indiana Jones Chronicles*.

So by the time they were on *Star Wars*, we had a group of people that were completely and utterly in sync with each other and who understood that, whatever changes there are, we can accommodate them.

We were under very strict limitations of money and schedule. He planned to shoot 60–70 days, do maybe a week of pickups six

weeks later, and then do the same again six weeks later.

They weren't reshoots. They were additional shooting. George is learning from the performances and the editing, and then making changes to the story to make the film stronger.

Paul Duncan Each set has its own unique atmosphere and its own set of rules about what people can and cannot do. Could people make suggestions?

Rick McCallum Absolutely. It's a very collaborative set. Sometimes George listens, sometimes he doesn't. But in relationship to achieving a day's work, he always listens. When George comes in in the morning he's got three stock phrases. I don't know if he even thinks about them, but they are: "What if we did this?" or "Wouldn't it be cool if we did this?" or "You know, I was thinking, maybe it'd be great to try this out," and you have to be completely flexible. If you have a deer in the headlights look

with him, you're toast, because he's looking to work out an idea. He needs to know that if I go to him and say, "Look, we can't do this," that I spent days thinking about it, and I've exhausted all the possibilities, that I can't do it. If I just say, "I can't do it," there's no relationship.

At the end of the day, it's a director's medium, and he needs to know that the crew will do everything they can to help him achieve his vision.

Leap of Faith

Rick McCallum Seven days before we started shooting we got the cameras in Australia.

George Lucas They gave us the first six.

Mike Blanchard The serial numbers were 00001, 00002 . . . They didn't have a manual yet, so it really was like a beta test. We've spent the last five years trying to figure out how to make this work and I'm thinking,

"There's no way this is going to work." I had a stomachache for months leading up to filming because if we failed, not only would we have let George down, but everybody in the industry wanted us to fail. There were some pieces that were just held together with spit and baling wire, and so many things could have gone wrong.

It was scary as heck. Fred and I knew where all the pinch points were because he was the architect of the workflow and we worked together on the post side of things. I didn't let George know how afraid I was that this may not work. I voiced it to Rick, obviously, to make sure he knew what the risks were, but, in the end, you take a big leap of faith.

Rob Coleman The script was given to us on a Friday and we started shooting Monday morning. So we had three days of prep.

The script, dated June 24, 2000, was titled Jar Jar's Great Adventure.

Ahmed Best It was George's joke because he knew the title was going to leak to the press. That was George's middle finger to the whole "everybody hates Jar Jar" thing.

Principal photography commenced on June 26, 2000, on Stage 6 of Fox Studios Australia with scene 5—in the Senate Chamber Palpatine announces the death of Amidala before

2.88 *Stuntman Nash Edgerton doubles for Obi-Wan during the combat.*
2.89 *Final frame of Fett using his rocket-powered suit to gain the high ground and fire at Obi-Wan, who uses his lightsaber to deflect the energy and defend himself.*

Padmé arrives to confirm the assassination attempt and to state her opposition to the creation of an army to fight the Separatists. The crew was called at 7 a.m.

Mike Blanchard George and Rick made a wonderful decision early on, before the shoot, that there were no film cameras as backup, so everybody had to be committed. I thought that was a really psychological important thing to do. There's no other option.

David Tattersall George likes to work with two cameras, A and B, usually running close to each other with slightly different focal lengths. We had a camera always on the Techno-crane ready balanced. Then there were two cameras set aside for the second unit. There's one left, which was a reserve in case anything went down.

Mike Blanchard These were camcorders. You had the HDCAM tape inside the camera, and an umbilical was run to the video village. We had a guy from ILM write some software so we could see the status of all the camera

2.89

settings on a laptop. We'd spent a lot of time testing various settings to maximize contrast and detail to give us the best picture possible out of the camera. If the camera lost power for a nanosecond it would automatically go to some default state, so between every take Fred Meyers would hit a button to automatically reset the camera settings.

Paul Duncan So Fred Meyers is the first DIT (digital imaging technician)?

Mike Blanchard Absolutely. And he had to reeducate everybody on set about the new way of working. For example, the camera

2.90 Final frame showing Fett flying toward Obi-Wan and shooting out a cable with which to capture the Jedi.
2.91 Preparing Ewan McGregor to be dragged by the cable. Note that the digital camera equipment is covered in plastic because the scene uses artificial rain to simulate Kamino's climate.

crew was used to pulling the battery off a film camera, moving the camera, and plugging the battery back in, but if you did that on an electronic camera you'd have to reboot it. So they had to make sure that they left the cameras plugged into a battery all the time.

Rick McCallum We had two 40-inch plasma screens set up in Fred's little tented area that were color corrected under instruction from David Tattersall.

George Lucas In the past, with film, we had to work on faith, perhaps looking at a little black-and-white video assist. And if it didn't look right in dailies—it was out of focus, or it was overlit...

Rick McCallum You're screwed.

George Lucas ...You lost a day of shooting, which was about a half a million dollars. But now with digital, I can see exactly the way it's going to look in the theater. I would stand next to David looking at the actual shot—not at a black-and-white video, or through a little

2.90

"*George wanted Jango Fett and Obi-Wan doing these big jumps and flips as they're fighting on Kamino. But with real-life performers, you have to shoot Fett jumping, then him flying, and you cut again to show him landing. George felt that forced an artificial style of editing and cinematography that he would rather not have to deal with.*"

John Knoll / Visual Effects Supervisor

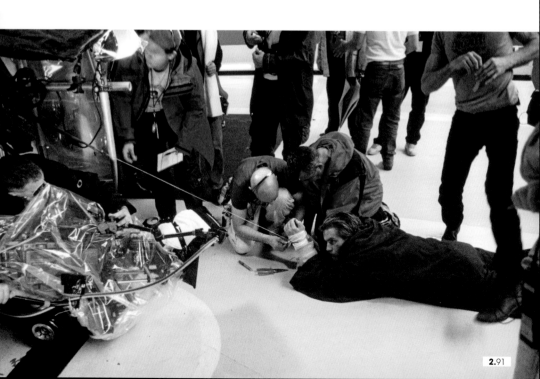

2.91

glass—and say, "You know, the problem is I want more backlight over on this side." He would go off, adjust the lighting, and five minutes later I would say, "That's great. That's what I want."

David Tattersall We're laying the foundation onto which ILM builds the finished movie. We've got to try and make it as good a quality as possible, for the blue screens to be even and flat and correctly illuminated. We have to light the foregrounds in such a way so that the atmosphere will be harmonious to what we know the background will be eventually.

Rob Coleman John Knoll was responsible for being on set for every visual effects shot in the movie. John is making sure that the shot is composed in a way that we'll be able to composite in the background, other characters, digital vehicles, and even my foreground characters. He's really experienced at the lighting and later on will be dealing with the compositing and making sure that everyone looks photorealistic.

I'm there to look after the acting and the performance of the animated characters—how a character will walk and breathe and talk. John is making sure that the char-

*2.92 **Final frame of Padmé's starship arriving on Tatooine. This is shot TWO 010, a combination of model shot (which has a lot of detail), digital ship and set extension, and live-action figures on the streets.***
*2.93 **Model makers Dave Murphy, John Goodson, and Lauren Abrams working on the model of the Tatooine spaceport and surrounding city.***

acter's going to look right and blend in and feel like it's sitting beside Obi-Wan. So that is our overlap.

On set George is talking about the story and the scene and the shot. I can watch him with the actors and the voice actors who are going to be the voice of the digital character. At that time we can decide on how much interaction there is. I'm looking to make sure that the interaction is believable, that the audience is sitting there believing Watto or Dexter is absolutely real.

Rick McCallum When you're shooting a four-minute scene on film, after each take you've got to reload because a reel is 10 minutes—that takes 5–10 minutes.

2.92

2.93

George Lucas Every time you do that, you lose the energy of the scene. The actors go to lie down and everybody talks for a while, so you lose all of the momentum to make a really intense scene work. Any director will tell you that.

Rick McCallum With digital we didn't cut — we would keep rolling because the camcorder tapes held a 40-minute load.

George Lucas We'd finish a take, I'd run in and say, "Look, that was great. Back to the first marker. I just want it a little bit faster and more intense," and do it all over again — I would do three takes in a row. The actors

would get into the rhythm of it, and I'd get better performances.

The first shot was completed at 8:45 a.m.

Mike Blanchard When you're shooting film and you finish a camera load it has to go off to be developed. Anything can happen

2.94 *Final frame showing Anakin meeting Watto and asking what has happened to his mother Shmi. Watto sold Shmi to a moisture farmer named Lars, and heard that she was freed and they married.*

2.94

2.95

to the negative in transit between the set and developing it. Likewise in the developing and printing processes. That's a scary few days for producers.

But with digital, whenever we were finished shooting on a tape we would run it straight over to editorial, put it in the studio deck, copy it in real time to another deck to make a clone of the original, and then vault the clone in a different building — all within an hour. That meant we had two originals. That was the first time any film ever had that luxury.

We'd also do a down-conversion to standard definition so that the footage could be edited on the Avid. This meant the editor could be cutting the morning's footage that same day before you've wrapped. With film, it would be the next day or more usually a day after that, depending on where you were shooting.

Rick McCallum The difference in cost is about $1.8 million. We shot the equivalent of 1.2 million feet of film. That's the equivalent of 220 hours. When you take the cost of the negative, developing, and printing it, the transfer, the sound transfers, and the telecine it equals a serious amount of money. And if you're shooting in different countries you have that negative shipped out, processed, and shipped back. There's freight agents involved and you risk your negative being lost or destroyed. When you're shooting in the digital arena, 220 hours of hi-def tape is $16,000. And if you're simultaneously making a clone, which becomes your safety master, that's another $16,000. And then your downconversion to put it into an editor is another $16,000. So for $48,000, you're making

2.96

SCENE 89 - EXT. TATOOINE, HOMESTEAD, MOISTURE FARM - DAY

THD.040

Medium shot C3PO.

C-3PO - "Oh, oh, oh. How might I be of service? I am See..."

Anakin - "Threepio?"

C-3PO - "Um, I...the maker. Oh Master Annie, I knew you would return, I knew it. And Miss Padme, oh my."

Padme - "Hello, Threepio."

44   thd040—Tk1—Sep11

THD.060

Close shot C3PO.

C-3PO - "Bless my circuits, I am so pleased to see you both."

Anakin - "I've come to see my mother."

C-3PO - "Um...I think...I think....perhaps we'd better go indoors."

88   thd060—Tk1—Sep11

THD.080, 100

Close shot C3PO.

105   thd100—Tk1—Aug01

END - SCENE 89 - EXT. TATOOINE, HOMESTEAD, MOISTURE FARM - DAY

TOTAL SETUPS 3

2.97

2.95 *Anakin and Padmé arrive at the Lars homestead and are met by C-3PO (Anthony Daniels), who recognizes his maker.*

2.96 *In the script C-3PO remained unfinished and his casings were later added by Padmé, so the shoot featured the puppet version of the droid operated by Anthony Daniels.*

2.97 *This is the shot list for the November 4, 2001, reshoot of Anakin meeting C-3PO at the homestead. Although C-3PO is "naked" in the images, Daniels performed the shots fully dressed as C-3PO in the shoot at Ealing Studios, London.*

2.98

a movie without any of the cost of processing or transferring negative.

George Lucas Normally, watching film dailies involved spending 45 minutes to an hour every day, either at lunch, or at four o'clock in the morning, or at the end of the day, when you're exhausted and you can't even see straight. But for this shoot we watched dailies on the set in between takes. I'd be watching for the performance and everybody else would be checking costumes, props, focus, VFX, or whatever.

Mike Blanchard Typically, a producer would have to wait for the dailies to be processed and cut together before striking a set and starting the next build, but on this shoot Rick would call editorial to make sure that there were no problems with the tapes, and confirm that we had the coverage we needed so he could strike the sets that night if he needed to.

Rick McCallum We timed everything on *The Phantom Menace*. George likes to get at least 35–40 setups a day. Film is 10 minutes a reel, so reloading and checking the gate each time takes an hour to an hour and a half every day. We save a lot of that time with digital.

Fred Meyers / High Definition Supervisor It was controversial that we were going to shoot this picture in HD using digital cameras, and certainly at ILM it raised many eyebrows. I think

2.98 *On March 30, 2001, Hayden Christensen shot Anakin speeding across the Tatooine landscape. There were four takes on two cameras with the actor sitting on a blue gimbal against a blue-screen set. The only physical item that can be seen is the handlebar of the speeder.*
2.99 *Final frame of Anakin on the speeder bike as he searches for Shmi, the twin suns of Tatooine setting in the background, signaling that time is running out.*

that after the second week of shooting it finally sunk in that we were shooting digitally, and we would come back without any film. That being said, we did spend a lot of time planning for this, and put a lot of systems in place to prepare for it. So I think we were ahead of the curve in terms of having what was needed to handle it. Not only on the set and location, but also in postproduction.

Padawan Learner

Hayden Christensen In rehearsals you're breaking down the script and trying to make sense of the lines. You interpret George's direction for how you should play this character, but he never sits down with you and says this is what Anakin is thinking. He wants you to

2.99

"When Master Annie made me, he never quite found the time to give me any outer coverings. It's so humiliating. How would you like to go around with all your circuits showing?"

C-3PO

have your own influence on how your character should be portrayed because now it is my character.

Christensen started on June 28, shooting scenes with Natalie Portman in the Naboo yacht. The following day he shot with Ewan McGregor on the nightclub alley set in the scene where bounty hunter Zam Wesell is assassinated.

Hayden Christensen Anakin has grown up with no parental influences for the past 10 years of his life, so Obi-Wan has become a father figure for him. He loves him, but at the same time there is still that resistance because Anakin wants to break free of what he is doing right now, which, I guess, is a theme of all the *Star Wars* movies. So there is that conflict and animosity between the characters when Obi-Wan won't let him make his own choices.

Obi-Wan is the master and I am the Padawan learner, so there are certain things that I can pick up from Ewan because he's already been in my shoes, so to speak. I look at the way he carries himself on set and the way he relates to his surroundings. There are certain mannerisms the Jedi have because they are confident. They also stand on guard, and there is a physicality to them since they are protectors.

Scene 10, where Obi-Wan and Anakin arrive at Senator Amidala's apartment to provide protection after the attempt on her life, was shot on July 3–4 on Stage 1.

Hayden Christensen This film is mostly a love story, particularly for my character. When Anakin is introduced in the film he sees Padmé for the first time in 10 years, and what was a very childlike desire and attraction and affection turns into a much more passionate love. Maybe that frightens Padmé a little bit.

On July 5 they shot the assassination attempt on Padmé in her bedroom using poisonous kouhun creatures.

The crew moved to the Fodder Building on July 7 to shoot on the Tatooine Homestead Garage set. This was a recreation of the set in Episode IV where Luke first sees Leia's message to Obi-Wan Kenobi. There were three scenes allocated for this set, with scene 118 shot first. This is a key scene in the movie, just after Anakin, in grief over the death of his mother, kills all the Sand People, including the women and children. Padmé brings food and drink to Anakin in an attempt to console him over the loss of Shmi.

Hayden Christensen Yoda predicted that Anakin should not be trained because he has such a strong connection to his mother, and would miss his mom. So there's a fear of and longing for love, knowing that it's not going to be there. What's Yoda's line? "Fear is the path to the dark side. Fear leads to anger, anger leads to hate, hate leads to suffering."

The crucial turning point to the dark side is when his mother dies. In this scene in the garage I've just gotten back from the Tusken Raider camp, and that's my big breakdown where I confess to all the men, women, and children that I've just slaughtered in my supreme anger.

Anakin has that feeling of failure. His most prominent goal in life was to free his mom, and he failed. So even though he is destined to be the most powerful Jedi there's that longing for a greater power, which the dark side possesses. That's seductive. He wants to be able to stop people from dying. So he'll stop at nothing, to be as aggressive as he needs, to achieve that.

George Lucas Anakin's flaws, like all classic mythological heroes, are the flaws that everybody carries with them. He's struggling with the same issues that everybody struggles with, and that allows him to be human. A good Jedi overcomes those flaws.

2.100 *Padmé waits at the homestead while Anakin is searching for his mother. In the homestead garage, C-3PO reveals to Padmé that he is embarrassed about being naked, so she offers to cover him using spare parts and metal lying around. Anthony Daniels, dressed in black, is operating the C-3PO puppet from behind. The scene was not used in the final cut.*
2.101 *Iain McCaig's costume design for Padmé's desert nightgown (October 8, 1999).*

2.101

2.103

After scene 118 was completed, the same set was used for scene 102.

Anthony Daniels The scene went something like this… Discovered alone in the homestead garage by an insomniac Padmé — concerned by the sudden departure of her fledgling murderous boyfriend — she asked if Threepio was happy. He soulfully confirmed that he was not unhappy, and that indeed everyone there was very kind and considerate. He only regretted that Master Annie had been made to leave so quickly — a midi-chlorian problem as far as I remember — and had no time to finish his handiwork as maker and add the requisite coverings to his creation. It was very difficult to be like this. "This?" inquired the

2.102 *Jango Fett's Slave I closes in on Obi-Wan's starfighter during the asteroid chase sequence in an exhilarating composition created for publicity purposes.*
2.103 *Temuera Morrison and Daniel Logan as father and son in the cockpit of Slave I.*
2.104 *Ewan McGregor waits patiently in the Jedi starfighter cockpit while adjustments are made. Only a minimal set has been built — the rest of the starfighter is covered in blue cloth and will be added in postproduction.*
2.105 *Preparing the set for Obi-Wan's starfighter landing on Geonosis. The starfighter is suspended from a rig while the crew shovels sand onto the floor of the stage.*

2.104

feeling Padmé. "Naked!" replied the ashamed and sensitive droid. "Naked! It simply wasn't protocol!" For Threepio, existence is nothing without a proper structure of what is correct. Imagine the trauma of the intervening years as he wandered unclothed around the moisture vaporators — protocol generally frowns on public nudity, even on the giant beach that is Tatooine. Moved by this confession, Padmé's eyes dropped to the empty floor where she found at her feet a box of coverings. "I never noticed," said the astounded droid, while admitting that he was not very mechanically minded, in a manner of speaking — possibly an admission of total blindness would have been more accurate. Gracefully bending to rummage in this newly noticed treasure chest, the sharp-eyed ex-queen found another chest and a face and more besides.

Shooting began at 5 p.m. with Tony Daniels operating the C-3PO puppet.

Don Bies / Droid Unit Supervisor The puppet works using a Japanese style of puppeteering called Bunraku, where the puppeteer stands behind the puppet and is attached to key points. As Tony operates it, the puppet mirrors his movements. We modified the rig for Tony

by borrowing a Steadicam harness from the camera crew that distributes the weight evenly over the torso. In Episode I C-3PO's walk was allowed to be stumbly because he was newly built, but for this movie we wanted him to walk like Tony does in the suit so, with the help of the creatures department, we changed the legs to walk a little better.

The scene ends with Padmé putting the chest piece on C-3PO. They wrapped at 7 p.m. On

2.106 *As scripted and filmed Obi-Wan climbs the rock face and is confronted by a pair of massiffs — dog-sized lizards with slavering fangs — as can be seen in Ed Natividad's concept art (April 26, 2000). Obi-Wan manages to dispatch both of them. Although originally conceived to be Geonosian creatures the massiffs would eventually be seen on Tatooine fighting over a bone in the Tusken Raider camp.*
2.107 *Filming Ewan McGregor on the Geonosian rock face trail with the Sony HDW-F900 digital camera. Throughout the shoot and reshoots a running total was made of the number of Sony HD tapes recorded and the amount of 35 mm film stock exposed. The film stock remained at zero throughout.*

July 10, shooting resumed with scene 116: early the following morning C-3PO is almost fully covered and Padmé only has the face mask to put on.

Don Bies It was George's idea that C-3PO was not gold, but that he was covered in a bunch of found pieces from different robots. Also we hadn't put Tony in the suit for 13–14 years, so we had to make sure that he fit in the suit.

George Lucas C-3PO doesn't age so I can use the same voice. Tony's voice hasn't aged that much and, amazing enough, Tony hasn't aged that much either. He looks almost exactly like he did then. And he can still fit into the outfit! He's a droid, what can I tell you? (laughs)

Don Bies For the scene, Tony wore the whole costume except the front of the head, and C-3PO's eyes were over Tony's eyes. We put magnets inside the headpiece, so that when Natalie set the mask onto the eyes it locked into place. ILM will digitally insert the puppet head into that.

The scene ends with Owen admiring the new C-3PO, and then gifting the protocol droid to Padmé just before Anakin returns.

The Weirdest Job

David Tattersall A lot of the sets have blue screen elements. So you might have one or two walls, and then the rest of the set was blue screen.

Hayden Christensen Acting to things that aren't there and acting to people wearing construction hats with little cardboard cutouts of aliens pasted on the top of it is really weird. I've got so many different marks—I wave my hand here and that moves there, and he's supposed to be an alien. You've got so many more variables to play with that it's distracting, and you sometimes lose your place.

Obi-Wan investigates the death of Zam Wesell and follows the clues to the water planet Kamino, where he lands on Tipoca City, is

2.107

welcomed by Prime Minister Lama Su, and is escorted around the cloning facility. On July 11, Lucas shot Tipoca City scenes 59 and 61–65, where most of the background would be CG or model shots.

Ewan McGregor We're just walking along blue screen with a blue curtain behind us, and then that'll be turned into some big room.

Usually when you make a film you shoot the movie, you cut the movie together, and what you shoot is what you've got to make the movie. What we're shooting here is the live action bits, which is the acting, that they need to put in the film that they've already planned and made on the computer. The acting is the bit that the camera can't create yet.

For Episode I the animatics were very basic blocks and shapes and they gave you a very rough idea of where we were going. In comparison, the animatics I've seen for this movie look pretty good and some of them could pass for final.

Rob Coleman It's remarkable to watch George shoot because he shoots like no other director I've ever seen. George showed Ewan concept paintings — "Okay, you're walking down a hallway and you're looking and seeing cloning facilities" — but there's nothing for him to see on set. It's very raw and it's very

2.109

2.108 *This Ed Natividad design presents the interior of the Geonosians' tower as being carved with a high degree of control, in contrast to the organic nature of the exterior (September 15, 1999).*
2.109 *Lucas directs Ewan McGregor as Obi-Wan spies on the activities of the Separatists.*
2.110 *Ed Natividad's concept for the interior of the Geonosians' stalagmites has a complex network of pathways that are easier to negotiate if you have wings (October 27, 1999). The design also echoes the assembly lines in the droid factory.*

2.110

2.111

2.112

rough but George is getting the Obi-Wan element for the image.

Ewan McGregor It is the weirdest job you'll ever do. There's nothing quite like doing this. It's very peculiar.

Keep Focused

Hayden Christensen My favorite set was definitely the nightclub. It's just really cool—high-tech bars with high-tech drinks, and really weird people walking around. It was hard to keep focused at times.

The scene set inside the Coruscant night-club was shot on July 17. After crashing her speeder and running through the streets of Coruscant, Zam hides from Anakin and Obi-Wan inside a local bar.

Gavin Bocquet We asked George what he wanted it to be. Is it a very small bar? Jazz nightclub? Is it a rather grand, glitzy place? Is it a warehouse-type environment in the back streets? He felt it used to be a very glitzy place, but it's lost a bit of its former glory.

Peter Walpole / Set Decorator The nightclub was one of the biggest sets. It was fun. It's nice to have that scope when a lot of people think it is all digital or all blue screen. We bought a lot of stuff off the shelf like the barstools. It was nice to have a little bit going on in the background, whether it be a roulette table or some gaming machines. We found a couple of old wrecked arcade games that were just a shell, so we turned them upside down and they took on a completely different appearance. George liked everything, but wanted us just to change the center bar slightly—he wanted

2.111–112 *Two designs for a Sith by Iain McCaig (June 8 and May 12, 1999).* **2.113** *The Sith Lord was originally conceived as a female warrior with two lightsabers, as can be seen in this concept by Dermot Power (September 1, 1999).*

acrylic tubes with liquid in, which had almost a church organ effect. That worked really well, and I wish I'd thought of it first, but, hey, that's probably why he's directing. There was a little bit of neon supplied by the art directors' construction, you fill the space full of extras, and you've got yourself a nightclub.

Anthony Daniels I have been in five *Star Wars* movies, but never as a person!

Don Bies We heard about this big nightclub scene. I was joking with Tony saying, "You should be in the film without a mask. You could ask George to let you have a little cameo." He loved the idea, asked George, and he said he could do a featured extra role. Then my crew heard about it, so pretty soon the whole R2-D2 / C-3PO crew was in it as well. Fortunately, because we knew the assistant directors and bribed them profusely, they put us in key positions where you could see us on camera.

Anthony Daniels And as we came in the actor playing the bartender said, "Get these droids out of here!"

The interior scene was completed in one day, as well as the end of the speeder chase where Anakin falls from Zam's speeder as it crashes on the street.

The speeder chase, scene 22, follows the assassination attempt on Padmé in her apartment. Obi-Wan and Anakin pursue the assailant Zam Wesell through the skies of Coruscant in speeders.

George Lucas Previously, we couldn't even think about having a chase through a city because we had to do miniatures and stop motion, and now we can do things that were unthinkable before.

Shooting on scene 22 resumed on July 21 on Anakin's speeder.

Ty Teiger / Property Master We got a carcass of a speeder from construction, then Peter Walpole and the model makers made everything inside it from the wall panels to the steering columns to all the light panels, to dials, to the foot pedals, to the seats. Even

2.114 *Lucas eventually decided that Count Dooku would be an elderly former Jedi and Christopher Lee was cast in the part. This final frame shows Count Dooku persuading the Separatists to combine forces and lead an attack against the Republic. Nute Gunray (Silas Carson) is particularly keen to ensure the demise of the senator from Naboo.*

2.115 *Sculptor Mike Murnane's concept for Wat Tambor, foreman of the Techno Union, was painted in multiple colors for Lucas to decide upon the most appropriate in relation to the other characters (September 29, 2000). Murnane: "Wat Tambor has the quality of Flash Gordon and Art Deco, a character formed of simple shapes that relate to each other."*

2.114

though it doesn't take off and fly everything has to be functional, so a lot of engineering goes into it. A lot of thought. A lot of time. And it looks fantastic.

Rick McCallum We have the speeder on a gimbal surrounded by blue screen and we put huge plasma screens in front of the speeder so the actors can watch the animatics. They can understand and interact with what's going on in this surreal blue screen world that they live in.

Hayden Christensen That was my first time in a speeder. It was lots of fun to press all those buttons.

Dave Young / Special Effects Supervisor The most challenging effect has been to build a flight simulator for the speeders. The flight simulator is multipurpose. It does six different rolls. It can fly both speeders (Anakin's and Zam's), and spaceships, and we can get animal motion control out of it for the arena scene. So it has a lot of purposes and we've managed to pull the whole rig together from the design

WAT TAMBOR
MIKE MURNANE
EPII 9.29.00
0045

2.115

> *"The tendency should be to ground a concept in reality. The nomadic women of Iraq wear heavily jeweled outfits and cover their faces with veils. I replaced the veils with simple metal parts, as if they'd been scavenged."*

Dermot Power / Concept Artist

stage to the finished product in about four and a half weeks.

On July 24, 25, and 28 shooting continued on both speeders. Anakin jumps from his speeder and lands on Zam's speeder—Anakin is trying to get into the cockpit as Zam tries to shake him off.

Hayden Christensen I was being thrown around, trying to hold on to this thing and climbing all over it. I felt like a bit of an ass as I was doing it but they said it would all work out and I trust them.

Melodrama

Natalie Portman Episode I was setting up the characters and the situations for the next five films, so there wasn't a lot of story line for any of the characters beyond the action of the movie. Queen Amidala was a very mask-like character—she didn't really have any dramatic relationships with other characters—so I had to internalize everything.

Here she's found someone who changes her, and she changes from being a stoic queen figure to someone who is able to fall in love and open up and tell her life story. She can have fun and giggle and be a normal girl.

On July 19 Natalie Portman and Hayden Christensen played the love scene between Padmé and Anakin, set in the dining room of the Naboo retreat. Sitting opposite each other while eating dessert, Anakin uses the Force to take Padmé's fruit, just as she is about to spear it with a fork.

Natalie Portman He's trying to show off to her by using his Jedi tricks.

Afterward, Padmé and Anakin sit close together in an alcove.

Hayden Christensen Anakin feels passionate for Padmé but at the same time he's intent on

SAND WOMEN — POWER 4/00   dp295

2.118

2.116 *Final frame of the Tusken Raider camp with massiffs.*
2.117 *Several sets under construction on Stage 3 at Fox Studios Australia in Sydney. At the front is the Tusken Raider camp set, with one of the tents open so that it can also be used as an interior set. The tents are designed to look like bantha horns bound together and covered with a protective mud barrier. On the left is the set for the Geonosian rock face, where Obi-Wan lands and begins climbing. To the rear, rock steps, nooks, and crannies are being assembled—Obi-Wan will use these to sneak around the Geonosian structure and spy on Count Dooku and the Separatists.*
2.118 *Dermot Power's costume design for a "Sand Woman"—a female Tusken Raider (May 19, 2000). The clothes are designed to minimize the impact from sandstorms.*

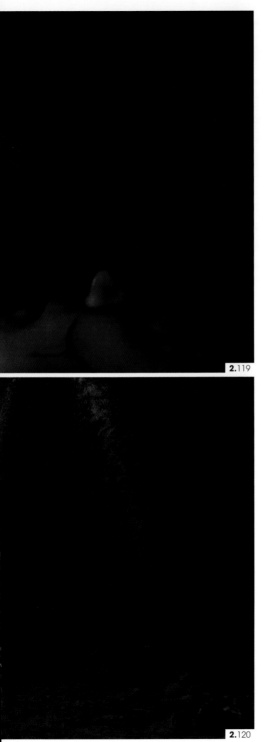

2.119

2.120

2.119 *In this final frame Anakin cradles his dead mother (Pernilla August) in his arms. Grief turns to anger.*
2.120 *Final frame showing Anakin slaughter the Tusken Raiders. No one is spared.*

> *"I…I killed them. I killed them all. They're dead, every single one of them. And not just the men…the women and children too. They're like animals, and I slaughtered them like animals…I hate them!"*
>
> Anakin Skywalker

becoming the best Jedi that he can. He understands that as a Jedi he's not supposed to fall in love in a romantic sense. Those conflicting desires root his anxiety in this film.

I think maybe that startles Padmé at first, and causes her to back off a little bit. Throughout the film they're put in these very extreme settings. They're in hiding — they spend a lot of time in a lakeside palace or in grassy fields — and it's really conducive to two people finding very passionate emotions for each other, even though they both understand that maybe they shouldn't.

Natalie Portman Padmé doesn't want to fall in love with Anakin because she has, as she says, more important things to do than fall in love. She sees a future for herself as a leader helping people and as someone who can change things for the better in a youthful, idealistic way. She doesn't really think that putting herself first and giving into her love is the right thing for her to do for her people.

Hayden Christensen Padmé is able to resist her temptations, which probably attracts Anakin that much more because she is so strong-willed. That struggle continues throughout the film until near the end where they're able to express how they really feel for the first time.

George Lucas Let's face it, their dialogue in that scene is pretty corny. It is presented very honestly, it isn't tongue in cheek at all, and it's played to the hilt. But it is consistent, not only with the rest of the movie, but with the overall *Star Wars* style. Most people don't understand the style of *Star Wars*. They don't get that there is an underlying motif that is very much like a 1930s Western or Saturday matinee serial. It's in the more romantic period of making movies and adventure films. And this film is even more of a melodrama than the others.

Cajoling

George Lucas Yoda and some of the other senior council members train young Jedi up until the age of 10, and then at 10 they are turned over to their mentor, their Master Jedi. And from then on the Master Jedi tutors them.

The scene set on the Jedi Temple veranda, where Obi-Wan interrupts Yoda's training session for the younglings to inquire about the planet missing from the archive maps, was filmed on July 20. The casting call for the younglings took place on July 7.

Ros Breden / Extras Casting The casting of the young Jedi was probably the biggest casting session that I did because we needed to find children that looked the same, identical twins if we could find them, so that we could use half of them in the four-hour morning shoot and half of them in the four-hour afternoon shoot.

The first casting session had about 60 children and we took them over the street where stunt coordinator Nick Gillard ran them through some basic Jedi moves. From that we chose 27 children.

Nick Gillard All the kids were so great it was hard to turn any of them down.

Ewan McGregor They were very good. They all stood on their spots, didn't move about. Ahmed Best helped them to keep in line and he was just fantastic with them.

Daily Production Report / July 20, 2000

Jedi children extras on four-hour calls, completed work as scheduled however required some cajoling to remove costumes.

2.121 *In this final frame Anakin admits to Padmé that he took terrible revenge upon the Tusken Raiders.*
2.122 *Hayden Christensen as Anakin returns to the moisture farm bearing the shrouded corpse of his mother, Shmi.*

Half-Built

Rick McCallum We had 12 stages in Sydney, and every single one of them had at least one set. But *Star Wars* is so plot based, we were quickly moving to another stage, sometimes

2.123 *Obi-Wan reports that the Trade Federation were behind the assassination attempt on Senator Amidala and that they are taking delivery of a droid army. Before he can complete his report, Obi-Wan is attacked and captured.*
2.124 *Count Dooku tries to persuade Obi-Wan to join him and his cause — he reveals that the Senate is corrupt, that a Sith Lord, Darth Sidious, controls hundreds of senators. Obi-Wan rejects the offer, and reluctantly Dooku thinks it may be difficult to secure the Jedi's release.*

every day. It would take six to eight weeks to build a set, we'd shoot on it maybe two or three days, then we're gone. We had to strike the set that night and start building the new one. Often we didn't have the studio space to build a set so we had to build models instead. We used models a lot and the model shop was still huge through to Episode III.
Paul Duncan Who decided whether or not to use a model?
Rick McCallum George and I — we made every decision together. We'd meet at breakfast or lunch, and I'd say, "Look, there's no way we

can strike Stage 10 and then build this in time. Is it really worth it to spend six weeks building a set for half a page of dialogue?"
Paul Duncan The Jedi Library scene was scripted at two and a half pages in length.
Rick McCallum In that case the set was half-built with a green screen backing, then a very detailed model was built over months by ILM, and they are digitally composited together. It's not that you save a lot of money building the models because we only had a limited number of artists who have the engineering capabilities and the artistic sensibility to build the models, but in this case we saved production time by not building a very complex and detailed library set.

The Jedi Temple Library scene was shot and completed on August 1.

Clean Plate

The Dex's Diner scene was shot on August 7. Obi-Wan visits his old friend Dexter Jettster to ask if he can identify the source of the dart that killed Zam.

George Lucas We always try and have the voice actor on set, doing the dialogue and playing the part. We shoot a couple of takes with the actor in the scene, and then we do a bunch of takes without the actor to give us a clean plate.

Rob Coleman I need to know if the digital character is going to hug the live-action character? If they are, we need to pay attention to what's going on. Or if they're handing a cup to them, or where they're sitting, and the timings of what's happening. When Dexter's sitting in the diner, if he slaps a table or drinks a cup of coffee, we need beats or periods of time when Ewan leans back and is watching a character that isn't there acting. Ewan has the benefit of the voice actor, and when we were shooting that sequence I would say to George that's really great, I loved that he put that into the animated character.

George Lucas I kept the positions of all the CG characters in my head while I was shooting. There was a waitress moving through the scene and sometimes, to help us keep things straight, we'd use a real waitress, even though we thought she might be replaced with a CG robot.

Swashbuckling

Natalie Portman Working in front of a blue screen is the hardest kind of acting because everything is in your imagination. On stage you can let yourself go because you've got the set, the costumes, the actors, you're working in sequence and it's very easy to feel the situation. In front of a blue screen you have to imagine the setting around you, sometimes even characters, and it's a very different skill.

The scenes set in the Geonosis Arena, where Anakin, Padmé, and Obi-Wan are to be executed, were filmed from August 10 over five days. They began on Stage 1 with Anakin and Padmé riding the reek, and then moved to Stage 3 where they are chained to the poles, and Padmé climbs on top of a pole to fight with a nexu.

Nick Gillard Natalie has to do a few stunts. She's chained to a post along with Anakin and Obi-Wan, and they let in three big monsters that are going to tear them up. Natalie makes a good account of herself.

Natalie Portman I was really excited to fight alongside the Jedi because in the first one I didn't really get much to do. I told George I don't just want to be the girl getting saved by the guys.

It's much better in this one. A lot of the stunts deal with running from and fighting with

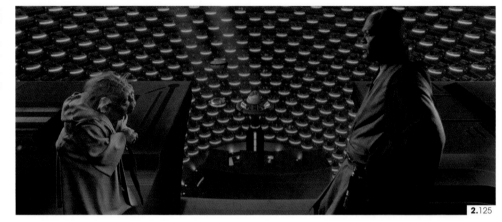

2.125

imaginary creatures, which was somewhat amusing. Everything is blue and cushiony, so when you fell it wasn't painful.

Rob Coleman I had hundreds of questions for George. Since I couldn't get more than a couple of minutes with him at any time I started feeding him questions in order of priority:

How do the arena creatures move?

Are they slow? Are they fast?

Do they stomp? Do they move around?

I would make notes of his replies and then phone or e-mail ILM.

Scenes of the Jedi fighting, as well as Mace Windu battling and decapitating Jango Fett continued on Stage 3, with August 14 seeing 71 setups completed in a single day.

George Lucas This is the golden age of the Jedi, but not all Jedi fight exactly alike.

Hayden Christensen Nick Gillard creates a unique fighting style for each of the Jedi. It reveals a certain element of their personality.

Nick Gillard If there's a similarity in the way the Jedi fight, it's that they're never exposed. They can always attack or defend. But their styles are going to vary. You know how the *dan* system works in martial arts? If you become a black belt, you become a first *dan*, second *dan*, et cetera. Once you get past fifth, you're then into your own style. And the

Jedi are a million light-years beyond that. So you'll see differences.

Ewan McGregor I didn't really notice until I was on set fighting with the others, but Obi-Wan is straight to the point, while Anakin's got more youthful vigor to him.

Nick Gillard I've always said to Ewan McGregor that if he doesn't make it in acting he can come and work for me because he has extraordinary balance and hand-eye coordination. He's only been in three or four times, but you could already shoot his fights.

Anakin's the Chosen One, so the audience will want to see that manifest itself. There

2.125 *Yoda and Mace Windu (Samuel L. Jackson) observe proceedings inside the Senate Chamber as the senators give emergency powers to Senator Palpatine. Mace decides to head to Geonosis, while Yoda declares that he will visit Kamino and see the clone army for himself.*
2.126 *Final frame of Palpatine "reluctantly" accepting absolute power in the Senate. His first act is to create a grand army of the Republic.*
2.127 *Filming the central podium within the Senate Chamber. Ian McDiarmid (as Palpatine) is flanked by Sandi Finlay (as Sly Moore, front) and David Bowers (as Mas Amedda).*

2.126

needs to be flashes of brilliance. He's more skilled than Obi-Wan. Anakin always attacks. He's better and he knows it, which means he's brash on occasion.

I've spent four weeks training with Hayden. He's fantastic. Hayden and Ewan will both be doing all of their own stunts and sword fighting.
Hayden Christensen Nick brings a story arc to the fights, so if you watch closely the fights become their own character. That's all a credit to Nick. He makes the rehearsals lots of fun, too.

Nick Gillard I started writing these lightsaber fights when I was still doing the last film. You have to start out with more than you need, and then hone it down. It's a long process and not just for the actors to get the moves, but for them to keep their character through

2.127

it. So they have as much input as anybody else does.

Samuel L. Jackson I look at these films as the swashbuckling adventures of the modern era.

Nick Gillard Mace Windu fights the bounty hunter Jango Fett. We've not seen Mace fight yet, but we know that he's second only to Yoda. I was thinking about a style for him, but it's Sam Jackson's style — he has so much style of his own there's very little that you have to do.

Samuel L. Jackson I'm a fan of Japanese samurai movies and I've watched a lot of kendo fights, so that's Mace's style of fighting. I'm doing pretty good at it but the feet have to be right so that the strikes look correct, so it's a lot like dance choreography. Since I'm supposedly the second-baddest person in the universe, I'm pretty efficient. I don't do a lot of fancy sword twirling or anything. I dispense people pretty quickly, use as little energy as possible . . .

My fight with Jango is a combination of him trying to escape and me trying to stop him. So there are a few elements, of him flying around, shooting projectiles at me, me defending myself and then going on the offensive. And once that happens he's pretty much toast.

Hayden Christensen When I was a kid I used a stick in my yard and pretended it was a lightsaber, I would make all these noises. So on the set, I was making those swooshing sounds and mouthing the noises. George finally stopped me and said, "Hayden, you can stop making those noises now. We actually have the money to put them in during postproduction."

Battle-Scarred

Christopher Lee All I know about Count Dooku's background is that he's a Jedi and, as George said to me, a battle-scarred Jedi.

He's a very inflexible character. He doesn't show emotion. He is very cold, very contained. He's very aloof, obviously completely fearless. He is extremely intelligent, perhaps more so than almost anyone else. He is very much a force unto himself, if I can use that phrase, and obviously he's not a particularly friendly character—he's not the person that you would invite to dinner, I don't think. He's obviously a man of immense power, mental power and physical power. The latter of course is shown very much in this tremendous lightsaber fight. He is the greatest swordsman in the galaxy, which he has to show during the course of this enormous contest that he has with three different characters. He fights Anakin, he fights Obi-Wan Kenobi, and he fights Yoda. And then he gets away. He gets away in the end and reports back to, as he says, "my master," the Emperor.

2.128 *Concept art by Ryan Church for the droid factory scene (May 10, 2001). This new scene was devised by Lucas to add more action at a slow point of the movie. The actors were filmed against blue screen during the March 2001 reshoot, and these shots were used as the basis for the background concept art.*
2.129 *Ryan Church's concept art depicting Padmé on the droid construction conveyor belt (May 10, 2001). The heavy machinery and molten metal enhance the danger of her situation. Church: "The droid factory is a super threatening environment, a place by robots for robots. Soft, living flesh doesn't belong here."*

But as a result of what he has done, what he has achieved, a war has begun, which is what they're aiming for—the ultimate destruction of the Jedi, and the complete imposition of their rule.

Dooku tries to flee the battle of Geonosis but is confronted by Anakin and Obi-Wan in his

2.130

2.131

2.130 *Concept art by Ryan Church showing Anakin wielding his lightsaber on the factory conveyor.*
2.131 *In this final frame Jango Fett and a number of destroyer droids have captured Anakin. With his lightsaber broken, Anakin has no means to defend himself.*

2.132 *Anakin: "I thought we decided not to fall in love. That we would be forced to live a lie. That it would destroy our lives." Aware that they are about to die, Anakin and Padmé declare their love for each other and share what may be their final kiss.*

secret hangar. The fight scene was shot from August 21 to 23.

Christopher Lee It'll look as if it's I, the actor Christopher Lee playing the part of Count Dooku, who is involved in one of the greatest fights ever seen on the screen. I hate to disillusion people but I have to be truthful about this, I'm involved personally very little. I think people realize that somebody in their 79th year is not going to be able to do this.

Nick Gillard Christopher isn't as young as he used to be, and obviously wouldn't be expected to leap around off air ramps and mini trampolines waving a sword, so Kyle Rowling will double for him. We'll also scan Christopher's face and superimpose it onto the double's face for some of the more complicated sequences.

George Lucas One of the advantages I have with Christopher is he is a great swordsman. He is very capable of and very knowledgeable in fencing. Although we use stunt doubles and digital doubles, Christopher's able to play the close-ups and some of the wider shots.

Christopher Lee This movie, in some respects, is more difficult to play because you don't know what is in front of you in the scene. But it comes down to performance, performance, performance. You have to have a very vivid imagination. If you have that as an actor any-

way, it's a help. You've got to make the audience believe what you're saying is true and what you're doing could happen. It's a terrific challenge. It's an even bigger challenge when, in a sense, they know it can't.

George Lucas I wanted to make it a different sword fight than the one that was in *The Phantom Menace* and I'm trying to evolve the sword fights so they're not all exactly the same.

Despite his power, Anakin is outmatched and overpowered by Dooku, losing his right arm.

Obi-Wan Kenobi is also no match for Dooku.

Ty Teiger It was Dermot Power's idea for Dooku to have this rapier-type lightsaber with a guard on it.

Dermot Power For the Sith's lightsaber I deliberately curved it — I wanted something exotic, almost Arabic.

Ty Teiger I've got a lightsaber standby team — four guys constantly churning out lightsabers — because we're going through 40 a day. We've got short stunt lightsabers as well as the long lightsabers. The lightsabers are aluminum rods, and even though they're durable once the actors start thrashing it out they bend within seconds. Once they bend they're no good, so you have to replace them every five minutes.

2.132

"I had eight sculptors working on the arena, so my biggest job was to keep the project unified. You need one common denominating set of eyes to say, 'Your texture is different than the guy next to you.' I was more of a conductor than a mathematician."

Michael Lynch / Model Maker

2.135

2.133

2.134

The climax of the battle pits Count Dooku against Yoda.

Rob Coleman I would say that next to the scheduling, the sequence in the movie that gives me the most concern and worry is Yoda's fight with Count Dooku. From the moment I read it I thought, "Oh my gosh, how are we going to get this to play?" We have a 2'9" digital character fighting a 6'5" 78-year-old man. It's a difficult challenge. I don't want the audience to laugh. It's a very serious moment in the film. I've tried to talk to George about it a number of times. Every once in a while I'll mention it to him, and he'll say "Yeah, yeah, I know we've got to talk about it..."

The Iconic Set

Shooting in Sydney concluded on August 25 filming scenes 42 and 44 set in Padmé's parents' house. Padmé travels incognito to Naboo, accompanied by her Jedi bodyguard,

Anakin, and stops at her parents' house in Theed where Anakin is introduced to her family, who tease her about having a "boyfriend."

The main unit then moved to Lake Como in Italy to shoot the Naboo Lake Retreat scenes for four days, beginning August 30.

Daily Production Report / August 31, 2000
Scene 50 scheduled but not shot. Long

2.133 *Ed Natividad's concept for the Geonosis execution arena (February 19, 2000). The arena's natural form casts areas of light and dark across the floor.*
2.134 *The miniature of the execution arena was 10 feet tall and 15 feet in diameter. There were eight sections, so different sections could be filmed simultaneously.*
2.135 *Final frame showing hordes of Geonosians gathering to enjoy the spectacle of the execution. This shot of the arena recalls Ed Natividad's play on light and shadow in his concept artwork.*

2.136

delays due to bad weather conditions. Rain caused delay today due to electricity malfunctioning.

George Lucas Most of the time when you're shooting in the rain you can't see it. So in this particular case, we were operating under cover—we were inside shooting out—so I could still shoot even though it was raining.

Lucas shot the wedding scene that concludes the movie—Padmé and Anakin acknowledge their love for each other and secretly marry. He also shot the scene where Anakin awakes from a nightmare and explains to

Padmé that he fears his mother is in great pain, and he must go to her. In sympathy, Padmé insists that she journey with him to Tatooine so that he will not be disobeying his mandate to protect her.

The production moved to Caserta, and on September 5 shot the scene in the Naboo Palace where Padmé reports to Queen Jamillia. Next, the unit traveled to Tozeur in Tunisia for the scenes set on Tatooine.

George Lucas I've always felt at home in the desert, so it's easy for me to work there, and I've worked there a lot. Even though it gets up to 135, 140 degrees, I'm used to it.

2.137

On September 7 Lucas shot the scenes of Anakin looking for his mother, as well as the exteriors of the Lars homestead.

George Lucas The homestead out on the lake had been run down over the last 20 years but it didn't take much to put that right. It's the iconic set of the whole series. The kids were excited because this is what they remembered Star Wars to be. For me, it was a nostalgic trip to the past. Standing out there, it was like no time had passed at all.

Lucas took advantage of the location to film the final scene for Episode III where baby Luke is handed over to Owen and Beru.

George Lucas It means I don't have to come back here. It's a long way to come and bring a crew of 60 people to rebuild the set and shoot just one shot.

Natalie Portman and other crew were delayed while traveling to the location, so the following day was declared a rest day and shooting resumed at the homestead on September 9. Anthony Daniels operated the puppet C-3PO for the arrival of Anakin and Padmé, and then donned the full suit when they are all at Shmi's grave.

2.136 *Final frame showing Poggle the Lesser (left) announcing that the executions should begin.*
2.137 *Ryan Church's concept for the execution posts in the arena (September 17, 2001). It shows the archducal box, from where the dignitaries will view the spectacle, high up in the background — an earlier concept had the box lower.*
2.138 *Anakin finally manages to gain the upper hand over the reek. He is flanked by spear-wielding picadors mounted on orrays.*

The Mos Espa scenes were shot the following day, where Watto informs Anakin that Shmi had been sold to Cliegg Lars. On September 11 the team moved to Matmata to film the scenes set in the homestead courtyard where Anakin meets Owen and Beru, and learns of the fate of Shmi.

George Lucas A lot of locations hadn't changed at all. The Sidi Driss hotel, which we use as the homestead, actually repainted it for us when they heard that we were coming back, so we had to age it back down again. They even left a lot of our props there.

2.138

After a rest day, production moved to Seville, Spain, the setting for the palace grand courtyard where Anakin, Padmé, and R2 arrive on Naboo. Four days of shooting at Elstree Studio in England (September 15, 18–20) concluded the first phase of film production with scenes set on Geonosis, including the arena battle sequence, and the Coruscant Senate building. The main unit wrapped at lunchtime on September 20, after 61 shooting days, a day and a half under schedule.

George Lucas We came in under schedule because we were able to shoot more setups a day with digital than what we were able to shoot on film, even though it was the first time we'd ever used digital cameras and the crew was learning how to make the cameras work.

Rick McCallum For weeks we shot in torrential rains on the Kamino set and in deserts that were over 130 degrees. I've always had a camera engineer on every film we've shot on rough locations. I've had to. On Episode I, which was shot on film, I had a camera engineer rebuild the cameras every night in Tunisia.

The body of the Sony HDW-F900 was based on the Digital Betacam, one of the most

2.139

EP2 SHOT STATUS (Stage Layout)

ILM Shot	X	Thumbnail	Arena Location / Shot Description	ILM Elements
GAM605	36		Arena East (medium) LOW ‹ OBI-WAN FALLS	-stage elem: arena miniature - stage elem: dust cloud / dirt chunks -cg acklay claw -fg plate -cg geonosians (crowd)
GAM610	46		Arena Northwest (hightilt, wide) /sky ACKLAY STRIKING	-stage elem: arena miniature -stage elem: dirt clots/cloud -cg acklay -fg plate -3d flying sand
GAM615	46		Arena East (medium) LOW ‹ OBI-WAN FALLS, ACKLAY STRIKES	-stage elem: arena miniature -stage elem: dirt clots/cloud -cg acklay claw -fg plate -cg geonosians (crowd) -3d flying dust?
GAM620	38		Arena Northwest (wide, hightilt) /sky ACKLAY STRIKING	-stage elem: arena miniature -stage elem: dirt clots/cloud -cg acklay -fg plate -3d flying sand
GAM687	58		No Arena BS OBI-WAN	-cg acklay -cg geopolebreak and starts to fall over -cg chains (geolink), hi-res chain sim (sim) -sand extension -cg geopoles extension -stage elem: dirt clots/cloud OR 3d flying dust -bs box removal -retime -cg nexu lying on ground at base of
GAM690	112		Arena Southeast (CU Dooku box) 2S JANGO & BOBA	-stage elem: arena miniature -cg poggle -boba looks around poggle -fg plate
GAM695	56		No Arena BS OBIWAN	-cg acklay -fg plate - cg chains (geolink) -lo-res chain sim for chain on obi's pole (td) -sand extension -cg geopoles extension -stage elem: dirt clots/cloud OR 3d flying dust -bs box removal -retime

2.140

2.139 *Ryan Church's artwork depicts shot GAM 873, Obi-Wan fleeing from the acklay (December 11, 2001).*
2.140 *Shot status sheet (dated October 25, 2001) describing each shot of the acklay battle and the ILM work required to realize it — noting both the stage and CG elements that need to be composited into the final frame.*

2.141 *Natalie Portman preparing to film atop the execution post. Her costume has been slashed and scratch makeup applied, following the attack of the vicious clawed nexu.*
2.142 *Final frame of Padmé defending herself from the nexu using her chains.*

> *"For the nexu, I was thinking of a mutated hybrid of human and feline energy, which was a very disturbing image in my mind."*
>
> Robert E. Barnes / Concept Sculptor

2.141

successful cameras that Sony has ever built. There are roughly 6,000 of them out there, so they are proven and tested. We didn't have one single problem with the HDW-F900, which I've never been able to say on any traditional film shoot.

Constant Manipulation

George Lucas Filming is interesting, but all I'm doing is gathering a lot of material so I can go in the editing room and have a good time. That's where my heart is. It's much more fun to be in the editing room creating the film.

A lot of directors come up with an idea and plot everything out, and then they very religiously follow that rigid matrix they've set up for themselves. Everything fits and you just do it. I don't do that. I like film to be organic. I like it to change. I'm very much a documentary filmmaker, in that I'm catching material, letting all kinds of funny influences come into it, and then I cut.

2.142

All of my films have been structured so that I shoot, I cut and edit the movie, I rewrite, I shoot some more, I cut it some more, rewrite in the editing process, and then shoot some more. I usually have at least two or three other shooting sessions after the main unit has finished. It's planned, it's budgeted, the cast is all clued into it, so it's all a part of the production process. The production is planned in segments rather than doing it in one piece and finishing it.

Ben Burtt After the shoot we came back to the Ranch and George sat down with me and watched what I had done. At that point he began to impose his own ideas on every shot — sometimes on every pixel of every shot.

George came into the editing room with the attitude that nothing was sacred. He was very free in throwing out anything he thought was wrong or unnecessary. He looked at it as an audience would, and was very critical of it. If a line of dialogue didn't work he threw it out. He wasn't unduly attached to anything.

George Lucas I would say that at least a third of the shots in the picture have been manipulated in some way. Sometimes I've slowed down one actor because he looks up too fast, or made other subtle changes that make the scene much better. They're the details that are so subtle it's sometimes hard to catch them on the set; you don't really notice them until you're editing. There's a constant manipulation that way. To me, it's exactly like using a word processor.

A Pre/Postproduction Facility

Doug Chiang From Episode I to III you can see the evolution of the working processes in the art department. It started off very much like how George worked with Ralph and Joe, and evolved into a digital workflow. It's happened on all levels, with editorial, with model building, with visual effects, the filmmaking. That's why the prequel trilogy is a breakthrough on many, many levels.

2.143

2.143 *Hayden Christensen, Natalie Portman, and Ewan McGregor on top of the reek gimbal waiting for shooting to commence.*
2.144 *John Knoll (center) and George Lucas (right) viewing the composition of Anakin, Padmé, and Obi-Wan astride the reek. Knoll was on set to ensure that the shots were composed in such a way as to allow the postproduction CG elements to be realized. Two digital cameras were used to capture footage from different angles and distances.*
2.145 *Final frame of Anakin, Padmé, and Obi-Wan on the reek surrounded by destroyer droids.*

Death Becomes Her (1992) was one of the first films where I created concept art digitally. However, when I started designing Episode II I made the decision to draw in black-and-white and wash, to keep it in line with what Ralph McQuarrie and Joe Johnston did. Part of it

was the challenge, but it was also because digital tools are so powerful that you can be enamored by how pretty it looks regardless of the quality of the design. By removing that, I was getting to the core of what is a good design. However, the advantage of digital tools is that in the very short, crazy schedule of film production, it gives you a lot of freedom to iterate, and it gives you a better fidelity.

Daniel Gregoire The previs department became a pre / postproduction facility. After shooting had taken place, there were still big questions to be answered. First of all, most of what had been shot was on blue or green screen, making it very difficult to cut together and especially difficult to view. Watching a 20-minute sequence on blue or green is enough to send even experienced visual effects artists to the loony bin or at least into a deep sleep. At this point, it became our responsibility to fill these plates out with digital sets and characters.

2.144

Ryan Church / Concept Design Supervisor I went up to the Ranch to be part of the animatics department. They needed somebody for a limited amount of time to quickly draw backgrounds for the animatics.

George was editing downstairs and every day he would come up into the attic and sit behind the animatics guys in that little room, eat his sandwich, and design the new shots that he wanted. The animatics guys would then go off and do hours and hours of shots.

I did one background with paint—an establishing shot of the Senate—but I knew that I had to switch over to digital right away, especially after seeing George making changes, and then iterating on those shots. I used Painter software, a Wacom tablet, and a Mac. The computers were not very fast, but Painter did

2.145

2.146 *Temuera Morrison as Jango Fett ready to battle Mace Windu.*
2.147 *The decapitation of Jango Fett. The decapitation is not bloody—the bounty hunter's empty helmet flies off (we see the shadow of the head on the ground) and the headless body falls to the floor.*
2.148 *Inside the archducal box, Samuel L. Jackson relishes his confrontation with Temuera Morrison's Jango.*

shot with Marc Gabbana's architecture. Then George would get an idea: "We're always surrounded by buildings—let's go to the industrial sector," and Erik Tiemens would come up with ideas for that.

Erik Tiemens / Concept Design Supervisor Ryan's background is in transportation design, with his love of vehicles and flying planes, while my background's in landscape painting and art history. We bring something of what we love into the film.

a good job of emulating traditional media. I approached each digital painting in the same way as I would approach a traditional one, which is to do a quick line sketch in the computer, lay down some transparent washes on it, and then bring up the lights with opaque techniques. I got very fast at that.

The art department had already done a ton of work obviously, so we were using their designs and putting them into a story context for the previs. For example, for the speeder chase, putting Doug Chiang's speeder into a

Ryan Church The job turned from helping the animatics guys out and doing backgrounds—we continued doing that—to a lot of design work, especially for the end battle.

Daniel Gregoire Not only were we putting together all digital sequences but now we were doing all the steps ILM does to complete the final shots, only we were doing them very rough and very fast. From tracking the plate, to keying out the blue, to rotoscoping, to full compositing, each artist was a full production pipeline unto himself. By completing this work in an

2.146

2.147

> *"It was great fun learning the fight choreography. Nick Gillard and I incorporated some balletic moves with very hard sword moves, which makes it look like a samurai fight."*
>
> Samuel L. Jackson

early rough form, Burtt and Lucas were able to make much better decisions about how to cut sequences of the film, and of course our work made these sequences viewable. By the time ILM started taking on the final shots, the previs department had almost the entire movie filled out with digital sets, digital characters, and digital scenes that were believable and story complete.

By the end of Episode II, the previs department had grown to about a dozen artists from four at the start of the show. Powered by Advanced Micro Devices (AMD) PC hardware and Alias's Maya with After Effects on the Macintosh we were able to take on a lot more tasks than we did at the start. The quality of our work had increased to the point where we were answering all sorts of other questions that were usually only addressed in the final stages of visual effects work. Lighting, texture, mood, feel, character animation, particle simulations, dynamic simulations were all entering the realm of previs. No longer were we only doing simple animation and 2-D cheats to get half the point of the shot across. We were not only looking to see if the shot was working, but also how we could make it visually look better. We were taking art and design direction from art directors Erik Tiemens and Ryan Church on aesthetics, mood, and feel, and trying to answer more than we had in the past. This in turn gave George a much more powerful tool in the decision-making process and helped him maintain greater control over his film.

2.149

2.150

Figure It Out

Rob Coleman After Episode I, I had the foolish mindset that there was nothing George could throw at me that I couldn't survive. Then he mentioned that Yoda has a fight scene, and later on he throws in the Clone War. Actually, I think he holds back a little purposefully because if he told us everything at once we'd have cerebral hemorrhages. He smiles when he gives us the next thing.

John Knoll / Visual Effects Supervisor There are approximately 2,000 visual effects shot in the movie. That's about three or four times what we'd normally think of as a big visual effects production. So, because of the size, we broke it down into three discrete chunks that we tackled like they were separate pictures, dividing the work along sensible stylistic boundaries, like planet or sequence, where possible.

John Knoll's team tackled the speeder chase on Coruscant, the asteroid field dogfight between Jango Fett and Obi-Wan, and the arena sequence.

Pablo Helman's team looked after sequences on Naboo, Kamino, Tatooine, Yoda's battle with Count Dooku, and the penultimate

2.149 *Final frame of the last stand of the heroic Jedi.*
2.150 *Ryan Church's concept showing the Jedi are not strong enough to defeat the droid army (January 1, 2002).*
2.151 *Obi-Wan mourns the death of one of his respected colleagues. This reflects his compassionate nature.*

shot of Palpatine surveying the clone army as it departs for battles on distant planets.

Ben Snow's team, with Dennis Muren consulting, worked on the Geonosis scenes, including the 180-shot Clone War sequence.

Rob Coleman's team of animators, responsible for supplying the CG characters that populate these scenes, the model makers, stage photography crews, and Viewpaint artists were all called upon to work for these units.

Rob Coleman There is very much a team spirit. The 400 men and women at ILM all have specializations, from modelers to lighting experts to a research and development team. And then there's a whole team of folks who figure out how to do things technologically.

Pablo Helman / Visual Effects Supervisor We may not know how to do something when George tells us about it, but it's our job to go figure it out.

Mike Blanchard The editorial process is ongoing. Periodically, we send Avid sequences to ILM, they make EDLs (edit decision lists), and digitize selects to their server. That then goes into their pipeline and they can also output directly to the TI (Texas Instruments) HD cinema projector for dailies. At this point we're strictly watching effects shots in HD off the server from the digital projector.

Michael Cooper / ILM Director of Film and Editorial Services We ended up with 14 TB in editorial alone. We kept tons of images in full HD online and accessible to our artists. Our video engineering people built an incredible database so that everybody, no matter what platform they were on, could pull up thumbnails of any shot they wanted. When someone made a request, we could pull it off the HD server and deliver it in full resolution. This allowed the visual effects supervisors to see all of their shots in sequence with surrounding shots.

Depth

George Lucas It takes longer at this point in time for them to build and finish a CG model than it does for them just to build one for real.

Pat Sweeney / Effects Director of Photography We decided to shoot practical models with digital cameras, but there wasn't an

2.151

D.CHIANG

immediate consensus that we could do it. We were trying a new format, and we were concerned. We saw the upside and downside and were a little nervous about the risks, but John Knoll said we should just go for it. Overall, it was very successful.

John Knoll All of us who do this work have gotten used to how things look on film and the level of polish you need to put into something for it to work on-screen. It's a bit different in HD. When we were working on our first miniatures, it was a bit of shock!

Carl Miller / Effects Director of Photography We quickly discovered that we had to add more detail to the models than we normally would.

We could see an effects shot immediately at full resolution on the big hi-res monitors. That allowed us to more accurately assess whether our shots were working, so we didn't have to keep tweaking them to death.

Also, rather than pulling out a light meter and reading values of exposure, you can actually look at the model you're shooting digitally and build the shot until it feels right. Unlike film, where we have to calculate the exposure and trust our intuition, with HD we can actually open or close the lens, then look at and "feel"

the image, so we can now be much more aesthetic about it.

We could also do more accurate onstage composites because the images from the HD signal were better registered and clearer, compared to the normal videotape images we're used to getting with film. If we had to add someone in a miniature shot, we could make sure his feet were tracking perfectly to the floor of the background we were shooting.

Pat Sweeney We need increased depth of field when we shoot miniatures. Typically, we like to stop the lens down a lot more than a DP

2.152 *Doug Chiang's concept art for the Republic attack gunship (May 16, 2000). The clone troopers show the scale and hence capacity of the gunships.*

2.154

does in live action. We're trying to take a very small object and make it look like a huge area. That means that everything needs to be in focus. So we are typically running the lens at an aperture of f/16 or f/22. The way we were able to achieve this previously is with cameras that are able to shoot at a slower frame rate. But the HD cameras shot, at their slowest, at 24 fps. We had to light the sets hotter than usual or shoot them in quadrants so we could shoot in different focal planes. In other words, we'd have an area in focus three different times and blend that together in post.

John Knoll As soon as we wrapped we could take a look. If it was okay, we could strike the set. It was instant gratification.

Ryan Church The model shop built part of the Geonosian Arena and it had a melted candle

finish. George wasn't happy with that — he wanted to replace it with something much more angular.

Paul Duncan Something ribbed, almost bone-like.

Ryan Church Exactly. It's a harsher look rather than a softer look. We decided to design each of those sides to look different: a window side, a crowd side, a side for Dooku's box, and a side where the creatures come out. They built that big model, which looks stunning.

Michael Lynch / Model Maker The paint job was difficult because the Geonosians are essentially the same color as the rock. The backstory about that is that the arena is built from the secretions of these creatures, and over time it erodes and they repair it.

The Knoll unit shot the arena sides (north, south, east, west) from December 10, 2000, to January 11, 2001, with further work undertaken from September 21, 2001, to January 17, 2002.

George Lucas We don't just put a model in the picture and it's done. The models are used as a starting point — then they have digital enhancements.

Rob Coleman In Episode I the Gungans and the battle droids were stacked up behind each other. What's different on this movie is

2.153 *Ryan Church's depiction of shot GCW (Geonosis Clone War) 180, where the gunships swoop down and fire upon the enemy (August 27, 2001).*
2.154 *Final frame of Yoda's gunship descending into the arena, with reinforcements behind them. This shot is from the perspective of the Jedi.*

that George has used what we call z depth, or the axis that's going away from camera. In the arena the Geonosians are the audience in the amphitheater, so you get to see them all, going up through the tiers. That makes it more complex for animation because more are seen and we have to pay closer attention to their actions to make sure there are no glitches.

The execution arena beasts were outrageous designs, but they were workable in terms of animation. I was never worried about the reek, which was big and muscular and well designed. I was a bit more worried about the nexu, because of its huge claws. In the maquette he was down very low, almost like a hunting cat, so we had to lift him up a bit to make him work. Also the walking cycle had the twisting action of a Komodo dragon, and that took some effort. The acklay had fingers coming off its six legs. I wasn't sure what to do with the fingers initially, but overall he moved a lot like a crab.

Film Is Cruel

Paul Duncan You completed the first cut in February 2001.

George Lucas It ran about three hours, so the next step was to cut out a lot of the material that seemed redundant. When you are writing a script, to make a point you make the same point three times, hoping that it will register with the audience. But when you see the film you realize that you don't need to make the same point three times — you can get away with two times or even mentioning it only once. But you can only determine that after you've seen what impression is made in the context of the whole movie.

Paul Duncan As shot and in the first cut, you show Padmé with her family, which really builds her character and background, and then later there is a conversation with Count Dooku on Geonosis that expresses her political point of view very strongly.

George Lucas Yes. They do.

2.155 *Boba Fett retrieves his fallen father's helmet. It's an iconic moment that provides backstory for Boba's appearance in later episodes. The final frame is identical to the concept art.* **2.156** *Lucas explains how he would like Daniel Logan to react to the death of Jango.*

2.155

Paul Duncan But you cut all that.

George Lucas In the end you have a time constraint for a movie. The scenes added nothing more because we already understand that she is a kind person, so the scenes had to be cut.

Paul Duncan I thought that family visit was interesting because maybe it represented Anakin's desire for a family life.

George Lucas He's got a mother, but he doesn't have any siblings. And he doesn't have a father. But that's not unusual in contemporary society.

Paul Duncan Sure. His talk in the garden with her father set him up in a family situation. So not only was he falling in love with her, going from a crush to love, but also he is enamored with the idea that he could have a family life, one that he had never experienced.

George Lucas That was part of the idea but film is cruel. It's not a book, where you can add a chapter and people will still buy the book even if it is thicker. A movie is a two- or

two-and-a-half-hour experience, and the total sum of that emotional experience is what people will remember.

Two thirds of the way through, about 90 minutes into the movie, you can see everybody getting up and going to the bathroom and wiggling around in their seats. You know that it's too long, so a lot of those decisions were made that way.

2.156

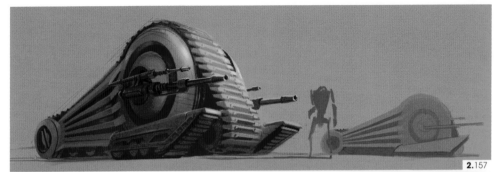

2.157

2.158

Sometimes you have to cut scenes, sometimes whole characters, and that's extremely painful. But you do it because it's for the good of the whole movie. That is what's important. Not the things that you would give your right arm for, but can't. So you weigh all these things when you're doing a movie because you really want to respect the audience, but at the same time you want to get all the pieces in that you need.

Dangerous and Lethal

George Lucas When the conversation between Padmé and Dooku was deleted, the trial that followed automatically went out too. And once I did that, the film moved in a very straight line rather than stopping along the way for these side stories. However, the droid factory had lots of potential for an exciting sequence.

Rick McCallum When Anakin and Padmé arrive on Geonosis, ostensibly to save Obi-Wan from peril, it just wasn't dramatic enough for them to walk from one place or another. So George came up with an idea of them going through this factory that is building droids.

Ryan Church George wanted a dangerous and lethal environment. So the art department went on a field trip to the NUMMI Factory, the GM and Toyota joint car assembly plant across the bay in Fremont, to get an impression of an assembly line.

Erik Tiemens We appreciated the massive scale of an operation like that, the size and power of the stamp presses, and how helpless you are as a person. We did loose sketches to come up with the concepts, like Padmé in trouble on a conveyor belt, and then we did shot compositions to inspire the animatics team.

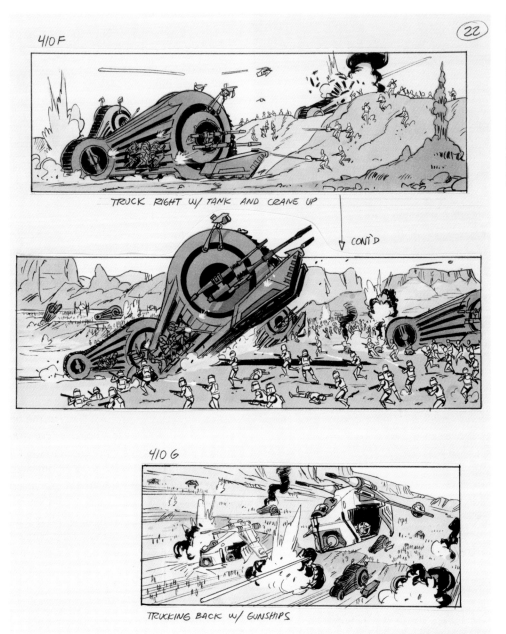

410 F

TRUCK RIGHT W/ TANK AND CRANE UP

CONT'D

410 G

TRUCKING BACK W/ GUNSHIPS

2.159

2.157–158 *Ryan Church's concepts for the Corporate Alliance tank droids (April 20, 2001). These vehicles formed the basis for the droid tanks used in* **Revenge of the Sith** *during the attack on Kashyyyk.*

2.159 *Rodolfo Damaggio's storyboards for the ground battle of Geonosis show the tanks in action.*

2.160

We took some of our painters, modelers, and R&D people out to tour the car plant. We also went to a foundry nearby. It was dirty and dark and nasty—everything I was hoping we'd get into the droid factory. We shot reference and texture material there, and I think we came up with a richer looking factory as a result of touring those facilities.

Twelve days of filming at Ealing Studios in London took place over two weeks beginning March 26, 2001, with the majority of the first five days shooting the droid factory scenes.

Natalie Portman They made me look so cool. They put me on a conveyor belt with nothing—it was all blue around me. So I basically had to run and dodge things, completely making stuff up. And then they painted stuff around me that looks like I'm jumping through things. I look so great. It was pretty exciting.

The sequence begins with scene 142A, where Padmé and Anakin explore the corridors, swing across a gaping chasm, and Anakin disposes of Geonosians as they awaken, followed by scene 142B, where Padmé and Anakin are pursued by Geonosians through the droid factory as well as avoiding the relentless machinery before being captured. Scene 142C details the parallel adventures of C-3PO and R2-D2 in the droid factory, as C-3PO's head is swapped with a battle droid head. This, in turn, required additional shots in the arena where C-3PO is decapitated and his head welded back by R2-D2.

Ben Snow / Visual Effects Supervisor We had some nice paintings of the factory from the Ranch, but we didn't have specific artwork that laid out: "Here's what each machine looks like and here's what each machine does." Doug Chiang did some line drawings of mechanical arms and we were able to extrapolate from those somewhat.

In the original script, after the speeder chase and the death of Zam Wesell, Anakin and Padmé immediately leave for Naboo. Lucas decided to add a scene where the Jedi Council instructs Anakin to take Padmé to safety. This scene was shot on April 2 with the actors against blue screen.

George Lucas I didn't want to build a new Jedi Temple interior just for that one scene, so I decided to steal one from *The Phantom Menace*. We built a number of temple interiors for *The Phantom Menace* because there were several scenes set there—a scene with Qui-Gon Jinn and Obi-Wan, and another where

2.160 *Ryan Church concept art for tri-droids. Destroyer droids are depicted to give a sense of scale.*
2.161 *Rodolfo Damaggio's storyboards show a clone use a magnetic detonator and escape on his speeder as the droid explodes.*

380 B

MAGNETIC DETONATOR ATTACHES TO SPIDER DROID

380 C

TRUCKING BACK w/ SPEEDERS GAINNING ON CAM,
SPIDER BLOWS UP IN BKGD WHILE BIKES SWERVE AROUND
BLASTED DROIDS.

CONT'D

CONT'D TRUCKING BACK - LAST
BIKER EXITS SHOT w/ SPIDER
IN FLAMES IN BKGD.

Anakin is tested. We took all the shots from one of those scenes, erased Qui-Gon and Obi-Wan and put in the new Obi-Wan and Anakin. We ended up with a filmed set in the middle of a digital movie — the only film in the movie in fact. That set had been shot on film four years ago, but it cut in just fine.

The Ealing Studios pickups were completed on April 7.

Ben Snow We brainstormed about how the droid factory would work. To figure out how one might really build a super battle droid, we took apart the CG droid model and hypothesized how each part might be made. Then we worked out each step of building a battle droid on the assembly line, drawing it up on a big foam core board: the stamping out of an ingot, the welding, the molding, et cetera. It goes by so fast in the film, I'm not sure the audience will follow it; but it was very helpful to us in understanding what was happening at each point on the assembly line and in each area of the factory.

Erik Tiemens Once the animatic incorporated the footage from London, and it's cut and in sequence, then we would paint over that to give it a lighting and mood guide for ILM to do the finished work.

The backgrounds and machines were a combination of digital and real models. The miniatures for the droid factory walls and foundry were filmed by the Muren / Snow unit between October 16 and December 13, 2001.

Ben Burtt developed the sound design for the factory equipment.

Ben Burtt The droid factory sequence required practically every bit of machinery we've ever recorded, including machines we'd recorded as far back as *The Empire Strikes Back*.

Cross-Eyed Yoda

George Lucas The secret of Yoda is to make him look like a rubber puppet.

Rob Coleman If you look at *The Empire Strikes Back*, and we took our tests from *Empire*, you

2.162

2.163

2.162 *Ryan Church's epic concept of the clones going into battle supported by clone walker tanks (January 9, 2002).*
2.163 *Concept art by Ryan Church for shot GCW 525 showing a clone walker tank firing upon the droid army, with an intimidating core ship in the background (January 14, 2002).*

can see that there were four puppets with differences between each. There's fat-lip Yoda. There's pointy-head Yoda. There's lime-green Yoda. And there's cross-eyed Yoda. So our Yoda is a hybrid. He's more of the essence or the memory of Yoda as a being.

We animated him without the rubber jiggle in the face, and it didn't look like him. You missed it, so we put it in. We also realized, from the way that Frank Oz had his fingers in the puppet—a thumb down in the bottom lip, three fingers in the top lip, and one finger up on the brow—that Yoda couldn't formulate vowel sounds. We were overarticulating. So we dialed back, and it started to fall together.

For his movement, Frank said I should be thinking about how sore he is. He said when he was puppeteering it he always was concerned about Yoda's back and his neck hurting and his feet hurting. He's this 800-year-old guy and he said that I was making him look like he was only 400.

"Someday you're going to be able to do everything you can do with models on the computer, but we're not there yet."

Dennis Muren / Visual Effects Supervisor

George Lucas He doesn't look a day over 403.

Rob Coleman Frank told me that anytime he moved the puppet anywhere, when he got to the end of its movement he would put a little breathing in, like it had been an effort for him to get there.

While animating we also have to remember who he is inside. We may even want to have a sense of this character thinking. What's the subtext of the scene? What's actually going on in his head? We need to think about who he is and why he's in that scene, and why is he in that shot.

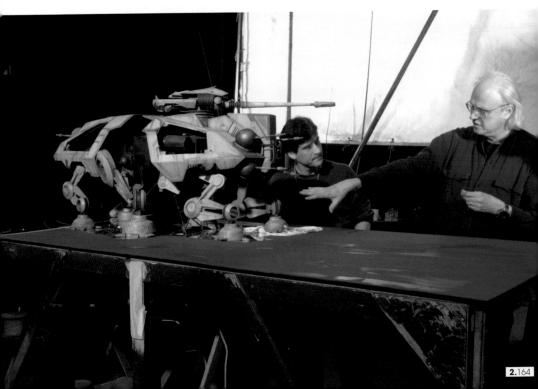

2.164

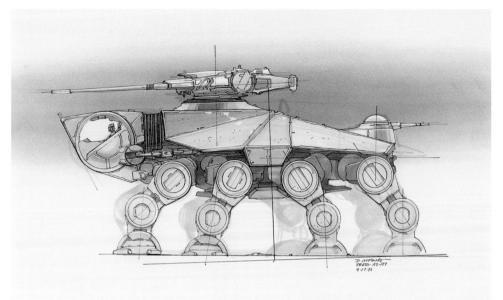

2.165

I found out about the Yoda / Dooku fight the day I received the script, June 24 of the year 2000, which was three days before we started shooting. I don't think I slept for the first three weeks after reading that. I tried to talk to George about it and I wasn't able to.

I'm already studying martial arts videos and different schools of martial arts around the world, from India and China and Japan, and trying to figure out how to apply that to a three-foot little guy, and how do you make that believable? That's my current task because we don't want people to laugh because it looks artificial. It has to be rooted in reality.

Seeing *Crouching Tiger, Hidden Dragon* (2000) helped me feel more comfortable about the fight scene. I came up with all kinds of solutions: he can hover, he can fly, he can create multiple versions of himself. And George was saying, "No, no, no." Every time we showed it to George, he said, "Amp it up! He's got to be bouncing around!" He kept saying, "He's a frog, this wicked-ass frog that's going to kick it." From what I could tell, George was asking for the Tasmanian Devil.

2.164 *Chief pyrotechnics engineer Geoff Heron and visual effects supervisor Dennis Muren discuss the best way to blow up a clone walker tank scale model.*
2.165 *Doug Chiang's concept for a clone walker tank, which he labeled a "Proto-AT-AT" (April 17, 2001). It has the same articulated leg concept as Joe Johnston's designs for the AT-AT in The Empire Strikes Back, albeit with a lower center of gravity.*

It was more about how quickly Yoda would move around Dooku, to throw him off balance or throwing him off his fight. And to me it just seemed to be such a juxtaposition—I'm trying to make this character move slowly because his bones hurt, and his head hurts and he's 800 years old, and then he turns into this little fighting machine.

I talked to George about the possibility of Yoda almost being stationary and using the Force around him to fight, moving things, or having an energy pulse come out from him. I brainstormed with Ahmed Best in Sydney for

2.166 *After the destruction of the core ship, Ryan Church's concept shows the clone troopers advancing to finish off the remaining droids (April 9, 2001).*
2.167 *Erik Tiemens's concept for shot GCW 556 shows the clone troopers going into battle. This is the attack of the clones, and a key image for George Lucas when he conceived the story. The clones advance and fire just like the battle droids, visually indicating that there is no difference between the two sides because they are both controlled by the Emperor.*

2.166

2.167

several days on how he might be able to do that — Ahmed had some great suggestions. I have all those notes and am ready to talk to George when he's ready to talk about it. It's a complex scene. It is an anxiety.

Pablo Helman We all fought it a little bit, because it didn't fit with our idea of Yoda as this aged creature who walked with a cane. But then we started to think of it as a situation where he pulls all his strength together for this fight — just like real people do when they have an adrenaline rush — we all eventually bought into that idea.

Rob Coleman After getting a general sense of the scene from George, I got together with Tim Harrington, one of my best animators, and said, "Okay, Tim, we're going to figure this out." We started moving Yoda very quickly; but as we showed that animation to George, he wanted him to move faster and jump higher. We just kept working on it, with Tim doing most of the shots himself. There was no moment of

epiphany, no moment of, "Hey, we got it!" We just gradually got there.

George Lucas If the 30 artists I had working on that character couldn't pull that off, I was dead. Yoda was the whole climax of the movie.

The Clone War

Todd Busch / First Assistant Editor The original script was vague about what occurs outside the arena. In May and June 2001, George put the art department to work, and in July the Clone War got fleshed out with animatics.

Rick McCallum They were churning out 30, 40 shots a day. After a week, you've got almost 200 shots. And it's amazing how much you can play with that.

Rob Coleman When we saw the animatic of the Clone War I had goose bumps. I rarely get that from an animatic because animatics are rough. It had everything that we as teenagers

of the late 1970s and early 1980s saw in those original movies.

Ben Snow I wanted to build a clone suit. It makes a lot of sense when we have a clone talking to an actor, for example, but George said, "This morning you showed me a CG R2-D2 that looked absolutely believable. It's fine. You'll be able to do it." He and Rick love throwing down the gauntlet like that.

The team had to animate thousands of clones for the film's climactic battle scene. Every clone on-screen was computer generated, animated using motion capture data. Character models, based on the dimensions of Temuera Morrison, were used to generate the clones' bodies.

Rob Coleman They look like stormtroopers, but they were all 100 percent CG. There were no people in suits.

On August 6, 2001, the title for Episode II was announced: Attack of the Clones.

John Williams met Lucas in September to discuss the film's score scene by scene in preparation for scoring the film.

John Williams George said, "Why don't you make a love theme like the old Hollywood movies?" It's introduced gradually when Anakin and Padmé are reunited not as lovers but as acquaintances at the beginning of the film. Five films with this huge glossary of themes but we have no love theme. So now we have . . .

2.168 *Final frame showing Count Dooku's escape to his secret hangar. In the background the pursuing clone gunship, which is without rockets, is under attack from the Geonosian starfighters.*
2.169 *Filming Christopher Lee astride his speeder bike, a wind machine swishing his cloak.*

2.170

Five days of pickups were undertaken at Ealing Studios from November 1 to 6, 2001. Some of the shots were to cover edits. For example, the scene where Padmé puts the coverings on C-3PO was cut, so the earlier scenes where C-3PO was shown uncovered were performed by Anthony Daniels in costume in front of a blue screen so that they could be composited in by ILM. Also, as scripted, Anakin is introduced when he and Obi-Wan meet Padmé in her apartment. Lucas wrote and shot an additional scene that precedes it, with Obi-Wan and Anakin in an elevator, with Anakin nervous about meeting Padmé again.

A day of pickups were shot at Elstree Studios on January 15, 2002. These were single shots and new dialogue for the end battle including Anakin asking Padmé, "You call this diplomacy?" and her reply, "No, I call it aggressive negotiations." Also shot was the scene in the gunship, after Padmé has fallen from it onto the dunes, where Obi-Wan has to persuade Anakin to join him in the fight against Dooku; the scene highlights the conflict Anakin has between following

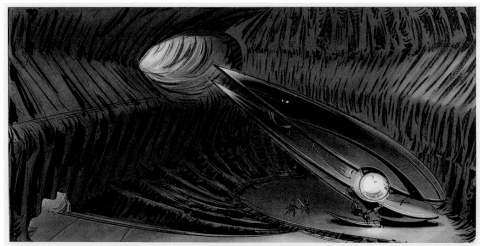

2.171

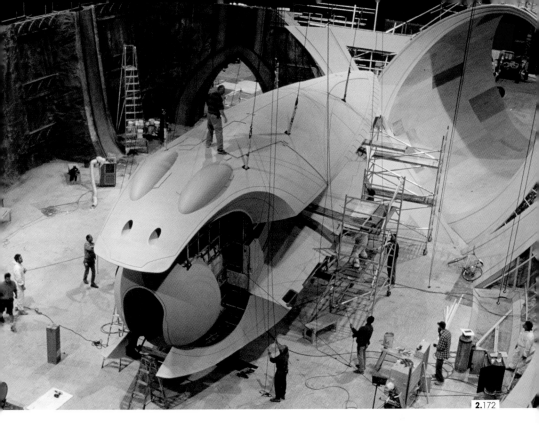

his personal desires and carrying out his duty to society.

John Williams recorded his score with the London Symphony Orchestra from January 18 over a period of 13 days, and then a final day of filming took place on February 1 at Elstree Studios. Lucas shot a scene with Dooku, Nute Gunray, and the Separatist leaders in the Geonosis command center, at the end of which Poggle the Lesser hands over the blueprints for the Death Star to Dooku.

Film-Out

David Tattersall When you looked at the image on the monitor on set it looked great. When projected digitally it was better than film, because it was a direct clone of the original, but it was not as good as we saw on the monitor because digital projection was about two years behind in terms of development. Although we shot the movie digitally, we still needed to transfer it to film for it to be projected at theaters. When you put that image through the normal film processes, the third-generation image was degraded and not that good, to be honest.

2.170 *Doug Chiang's concept for the battle with Dooku in the secret hangar that houses his solar sail ship earned a "Fabulouso" from Lucas (April 25, 2000, 5 days). It is suggested here that Dooku fights using two lightsabers.*
2.171 *Ed Natividad's set concept for the secret hangar (March 19, 2000).*
2.172 *Constructing Count Dooku's solar sail ship on Stage 2 at Fox Studios Australia in preparation for filming the first scene in the Dooku Jedi battle on August 21, 2000.*

Mike Blanchard The last piece of the puzzle to solve was how were we going to make film distribution prints from our digital original. We were all getting concerned because we couldn't get the film prints to look as good as our digital version. The quality of the prints coming back from the labs just wasn't good enough.

So, we thought, "What if we printed an entire reel from the digital file and used that as our printing negative?" Instead of doing a film-out of an original negative and going IP-IN-release print, we went from our original neg to release print, skipping those two generations.

We did the calculations of how long it would take to do this, and explained it to Rick and George. The prints looked much better, but the trouble was that a 2,000–foot reel takes 60 hours to film-out on ILM's laser recorders, and we needed seven negs of each reel—six for the US release, and one for international releases so they could put on subtitles. Each neg could produce about 1,000 prints. ILM also needed to produce 22 foreign language versions of the *Star Wars* title crawl. Seven seven-reel films are 49 reels total, and to film-out on two recorders would take just over 60 days if they ran continuously without issues.

We worked out a schedule of when George needed to finish each reel to make the deadline. We had this chart on a big magnet board in the Main House saying when each reel had to start printing. George loved it. He would say, "Guys, there are 20 shots in reel one that we don't have finals yet from ILM," and then the focus was to close out that reel so we could start to film-out.

Rick McCallum We are, in effect, going to release over 3,000 first generation prints, which has never been done in the history of cinema, ever.

Mike Blanchard Sometimes there were technical problems during the film-outs so we'd have to run it again. One time, it was a power failure. As we were finishing in post, we were getting power outages multiple days in a row. It was grim. We ended up having to hook up a generator in the parking lot at both ILM and the Ranch so that, no matter what, George's cutting room and the film recorders would be able to keep working during the power outages.

2.173 *Final frame showing Yoda preparing for battle with Count Dooku. Samuel L. Jackson: "Mace is the second-baddest man in the universe. Yoda is the baddest."* **2.174** *Count Dooku is more than a match for Anakin and severs his right arm.*

2.174

The final sound mix commenced on March 4, 2002.

Ben Burtt The final mix lasts for about a month. We go into a dark room every day and we listen to every sound and every bit of music and every bit of dialogue and we inch our way through each scene, sometimes only completing a few minutes a day.

Rick McCallum On April 8, ILM delivered the last shot and George signed off on it. On April 10, George and Ben delivered the final cut of the film complete with sound effects and John Williams's music.

Attack of the Clones was released in cinemas on May 16, 2002, making $80,027,814 on its opening weekend in America and grossed over $653 million worldwide.

Mike Blanchard There was no digital distribution channel available for Episode II, so we had to figure out how we were going to get the movie to the cinemas. Everything had to be treated like it was a one-off. We needed a team of people from THX to go to all these digital cinemas — there were about 100 or so worldwide — and load the servers. We made a file DVD, they transferred that onto the cinema's server — encrypted, of course — then that would play out to the projector.

Rick McCallum You have to be pretty brain-dead to be involved in film at this time and not realize that we are going through a very serious evolutionary step. Digital technology really gets down to one simple fact. A writer can write anything he wants to now. A director is only limited by his imagination. A producer can't say "no" anymore, because now there is a way to solve each production challenge and to do it in a cost-efficient, fiscally responsible way. It doesn't mean that by using the technology that the film is going to be any better — that's still about talent.

George Lucas Film has been around 100 years, and no matter what you do, you're always going to run celluloid through a bunch of gears. It's gotten more sophisticated over the

2.175 *Obi-Wan confers with Mace Windu and Yoda (not pictured) about the victory on Geonosis. Yoda retorts that it was not a victory but only the beginning of the Clone War.*
2.176 *In the shooting script Obi-Wan informs Mace and Yoda that Anakin is escorting Senator Amidala to Naboo and Yoda announces that this is the beginning of the Clone War. In this revision for scene 165, shot on April 2, 2001, Obi-Wan, Mace, and Yoda contemplate if it could be true that Darth Sidious controls the Senate.*

2.175

THREEPIO, with his battle droid head, blasts away at the
JEDI. Suddenly, out of nowhere, ARTOO races toward THREEPIO,
hitting him hard and knocking him over. The little astro
droid takes out his welding device and cuts the battle
droid's head off of THREEPIO's body.

ARTOO picks up Threepio's head and carries it over to the
WANDERING BODY. He replaces Threepio's head. The protocol
droid sits up in surprise.

>   C-3PO
>   (continuing)
>   Where am I...?!?

ARTOO BEEPS.

DJB Scene 161

EXT. GEONOSIS SECRET HANGAR TOWER - DAY

CLOSEUP of YODA and COUNT DOOKU sword fighting. They use the
Force to throw objects at each other. They reach a stalemate.

You have fought well my old padawan

>   YODA
>   The end for you, this is, Dooku.

>   COUNT DOOKU
>   You have fought well, my mentor,
>   but the battle is far from
>   over...this is just the beginning.
>   *Master*

COUNT DOOKU raises his hand and brings a large service arm
crashing down on OBI-WAN and ANAKIN.

JTE Scene 165

INT. JEDI TEMPLE, COUNCIL CHAMBER - SUNSET

OBI-WAN and MACE WINDU are standing in front of the window of
the **Council** Chamber.

??

>   OBI-WAN
>   *Do you* I don't believe what Dooku said
>   about Sidious controlling the
>   Senate. It doesn't feel right.

the Dark

>   MACE WINDU
>   Only time will tell. Where is
>   your apprentice?

Yoda
unreliable Dooku has
become. Jointed, The
Dark side he has.-

Become unreliable Dooku has;
Joined the dark side... lying,
deceit, part of him it is.

years, but it'll never get better than it is right now. With digital, we're at the very bottom of the medium. This is as bad as it's ever going to be. This is like 1895. In 25, 30 years, it's going to be amazing.

It's like we're the wild fanatics for wanting to change things, when this is the biggest leap forward for the business since the advent of sound films. I will never make a film with film again.

2.177 *Ryan Church's concept art showing Palpatine surveying the clone troops, in formation, preparing for the war ahead (September 26, 2001).*
2.178 *Final frame showing the assembled clone troopers ready for action.*

Reason, Love, and Compassion

Paul Duncan As you have said, this is a mystery story about who is manipulating events and who wields the power. There is a line in Padmé's discussion with Dooku — a scene that was cut — where she tells him, "What is happening here is not government that has been bought out by business... It's business becoming government."

George Lucas If you ascribe to the idea that most businesses are greedy, then it's very easy to see that they're more on the dark side than the side of light and compassion.

In business the stockholder comes first. Everything is dedicated to making more money for the stockholder.

2.178

SURVEYING THE CLONES
RYAN CHURCH

2.177

There was an article in the paper the other day that I find ironic, where the banks have decided that they need to support the towns and the cities where they're located, their customers and people in general, rather than just working for themselves and their stockholders. What a realization! I don't know whether or not they're going to do it, but they've finally realized that they're part of a symbiotic relationship.

And it's the same in politics — we're all in a big symbiotic relationship with the rest of the world. As soon as one country says, "We're the only thing that's important; they aren't important," you start pulling threads that tear the world apart. They don't realize that when you shoot yourself in the foot, it hurts. How are we going to run the country without migrants? Didn't anybody tell you that they're the ones that do all work?

Paul Duncan Corporations and states are man-made systems that seem to be more concerned about themselves rather than the people they were created to serve.

George Lucas I made that movie a while back but it's basically what's going on right now. America needs trade with China and other countries, but if we pull out, you're going to have problems with the farmers in the Midwest who depend on that trade. If you rip down the synergistic circle in the end you're going to end up with nothing. Somebody's got to put it all together again because it doesn't work.

Paul Duncan In the past, when people have been afraid, the same sort of nationalistic feelings have come to the surface and been manipulated. George Santayana wrote that "Those who cannot remember the past are condemned to repeat it." Do you think history is due to repeat itself?

George Lucas History repeats itself over and over again. There's no question about that. It's just: Which direction is it going to go?

Are we going to end up with a bunch of little wars as trade breaks down, they all get greedy and they start a fight? Eventually, after a lot of pain, whether it's a world war or just a lot of civil wars, they'll all come to the realization, "This is stupid. Let's just not do this, let's just try to help each other." We've become so globalized and the financial ecosystem is so intertwined that we feel the effects very quickly. Leaders around the world think they can do things by themselves, but they can't.

Paul Duncan What's needed are leaders, voices, ideas becoming prevalent to effect positive change.

George Lucas Life is a pendulum. We have the dark side and the light side. We're go-

2.179

2.180

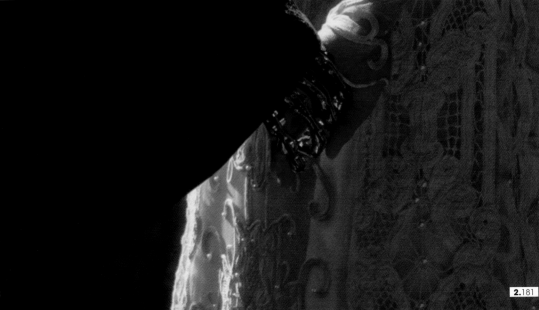

2.181

ing over to the dark side, everybody is saying "Oh my God," and we have to start pushing together to slow it down, then keep pushing it back to get to the light side. But it's human nature to not do anything, to wait until things get so bad that they are forced to do something, before pushing back.

Paul Duncan So it's part of a cycle that we have to be near destruction before we join forces to save ourselves.

George Lucas The thing is it's going to be all over for all of us in a few million years, and so we have to figure it out by then that we can't save ourselves individually. We're told that competition is good, so does this mean that a quarter of the people are going to live and the rest are going to die because they lost? No, you need all the people. You need the whole ecosystem to work together.

Paul Duncan It takes a lot of people to build the ark.

George Lucas Yeah. And it needs to be done through reason, love, and compassion, not through force.

The films are trying to stress the idea that everything is interconnected. I like to make movies that are complex, but it's not obvious to people unless they start digging into it. Most people don't realize it and can't grasp the whole entity because they're focusing on four or five pieces out of 200, and often they don't want to hear about the other pieces because it requires additional thought and ideas outside of the films.

There are cycles and circles in the story and the characters throughout all six episodes. There are cycles of the same thing being repeated over and over with different groups of people, and the outcomes change because the characters have grown or changed over the story. The repetition shows the characters' development.

It's subtle. I don't think most people realize that it's even going on, but if you look for it, you'll see it.

"I think I can safely say that I will never, ever shoot another film on film....It's inconceivable to me to go back to that method of working."
George Lucas

2.179 *In this final frame set on Naboo, Anakin and Padmé marry in secret, their only witnesses the droids C-3PO and R2-D2.*
2.180 *The kiss.*
2.181 *Lucas staged this romantic moment so that when we see the close-up of Anakin's metallic prosthetic grasping Padmé's hand it adds a premonition of dread and foreboding to the proceedings. This shot was added for the digital release of the movie.*

Revenge of the Sith

Episode III: Revenge of the Sith (2005)

Synopsis

Three years after the onset of the Clone Wars, the noble Jedi Knights have been leading a massive clone army into a galaxy-wide battle against the Separatists. When the sinister Sith unveil a thousand-year-old plot to rule the galaxy, the Republic crumbles and from its ashes rises the evil Galactic Empire. Jedi hero Anakin Skywalker is seduced by the dark side of the Force to become the Emperor's new apprentice—Darth Vader. The Jedi are decimated, as Obi-Wan Kenobi and Jedi Master Yoda are forced into hiding. The only hope for the galaxy are Anakin's own offspring—the twin children born in secrecy who will grow up to become Luke Skywalker and Princess Leia Organa.

RELEASE DATE May 19, 2005 (US)
RUNNING TIME 140 minutes

Cast
OBI-WAN KENOBI EWAN MCGREGOR
SENATOR PADMÉ AMIDALA NATALIE PORTMAN
ANAKIN SKYWALKER HAYDEN CHRISTENSEN
SUPREME CHANCELLOR PALPATINE
    IAN MCDIARMID
MACE WINDU SAMUEL L. JACKSON
SENATOR BAIL ORGANA JIMMY SMITS
YODA (VOICE) FRANK OZ
C-3PO ANTHONY DANIELS
COUNT DOOKU CHRISTOPHER LEE
QUEEN OF NABOO KEISHA CASTLE-HUGHES
KI-ADI-MUNDI / VICEROY NUTE GUNRAY
    SILAS CARSON

COMMANDER CODY TEMUERA MORRISON
JAR JAR BINKS AHMED BEST
R2-D2 KENNY BAKER
CHEWBACCA PETER MAYHEW
SIO BIBBLE OLIVER FORD DAVIES

Crew
DIRECTOR GEORGE LUCAS
PRODUCER RICK MCCALLUM
SCREENPLAY GEORGE LUCAS
EXECUTIVE PRODUCER GEORGE LUCAS
PRODUCTION DESIGNER
    GAVIN BOCQUET
DIRECTOR OF PHOTOGRAPHY
    DAVID TATTERSALL
EDITORS ROGER BARTON, BEN BURTT
COSTUME DESIGNER TRISHA BIGGAR

CONCEPT DESIGN SUPERVISORS
    RYAN CHURCH, ERIK TIEMENS
VISUAL EFFECTS SUPERVISORS JOHN KNOLL,
    ROGER GUYETT
ANIMATION DIRECTOR ROB COLEMAN
HIGH DEFINITION SUPERVISOR FRED MEYERS
SOUND DESIGNER BEN BURTT
MUSIC JOHN WILLIAMS

3.1 *Poster for* **Revenge of the Sith**
designed by Drew Struzan. It was released
on March 8, 2005.

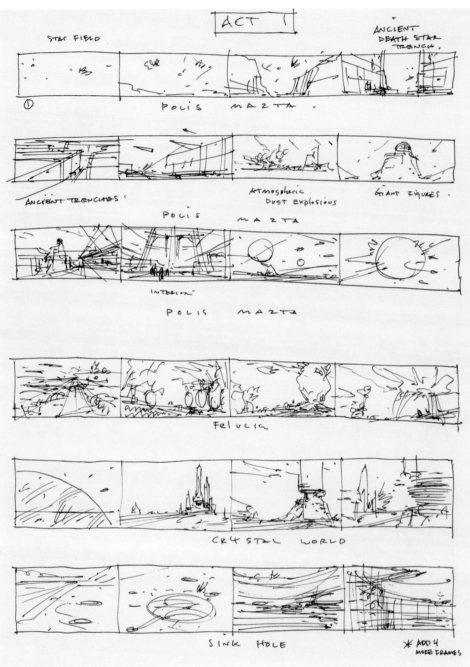

ACT 1

STAR FIELD

ANCIENT
DEATH STAR
TRENCH.

① POLIS MAZTA.

ANCIENT TRENCHES

ATMOSPHERIC
DUST EXPLOSIONS

GIANT FIGURES.

POLIS MAZTA

INTERIOR

POLIS MAZTA

Felucia

CRYSTAL WORLD

SINK HOLE

✷ ADD 4
MORE FRAMES

3.2

3.2–3 *Erik Tiemens's thumbnails showing concepts for Act 1, which was initially going to show seven battles of the Clone Wars on seven planets: Polis Mazta, Felucia, Crystal World, Sinkhole World, Bridge World, Kashyyyk, and*

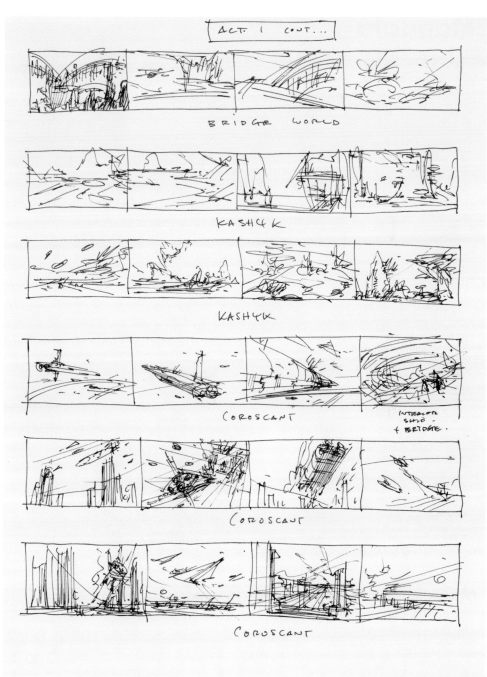

3.3

Coruscant. Palpatine is rescued above
Coruscant at the end of Act 1 and
Anakin turns to the dark side.

Mandala

By Paul Duncan and Colin Odell & Michelle Le Blanc

George Lucas I'm a movie nut and I want to make movies better, more enjoyable, and easier and cheaper to make. It's my nature to want to do the best job I can with the resources that I have available to me. I want to be proud of my work.

I don't think of myself as a pioneer. I've spent a great deal of money on research and development, and tried to push the envelope of the medium, primarily because I want to get the best possible image and the best possible way of telling my stories. I've always found myself bumping up against the celluloid ceiling — the technology that says, "You can't go here, you can't go there, you can't do that." Or the economic resources that say, "You can get there, but it's going to cost you to do it." And my feeling is that the artist needs to be free, not to have to think about how he's going to accomplish something, or if he can afford to accomplish something. He should be able to let his imagination run wild without a lot of constraints. And that's what digital is allowing us to do.

On April 20, 2002, just before Episode II was released, we had a digital conference at Skywalker Ranch with all the people who had worked in digital cinema: Jim Cameron, Robert Rodriguez, Michael Mann, me, and the Pixar guys. That was it. That was all the people

3.4

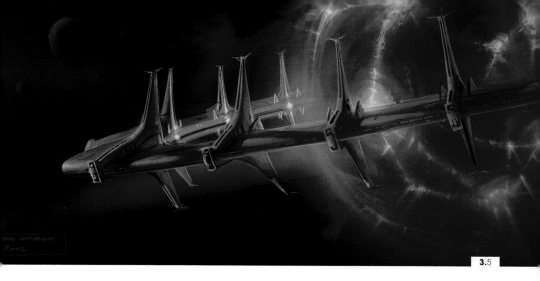

who'd had any experience with it. We invited a bunch of our friends to come, so there were maybe 25 to 30 people there. The five of us who had worked in digital cinema got up and explained what it was all about, what the problems were, what the tricks were, the advantages and disadvantages of what we were doing.

Mike Blanchard / Technical Supervisor Pixar showed how bad release prints are in comparison to digital projection.

We set up a color correction demo showing the precise control of working digitally. We explained how we shot, the workflow for dailies, and how much more efficient everything was. It was a way of saying, "Look, guys, there's all this stuff happening. We're doing it right now. And this movie is coming out next month." Then we screened *Attack of the Clones*. Some filmmakers were very skeptical, or not into it at all. We were still doing color correction on Episode II, so the minute the presentation wrapped we tore it all out, took it back to ILM, and got back to work finishing the film.

Rick McCallum / Producer The idea was to create a system where you're in a completely digital realm — not only the digital arena where you capture the images, but most importantly in the distribution pro-

3.4 *Ryan Church's concept for a ring world, a gas planet entirely surrounded by a constructed city (September 26, 2002). Originally, this planet was to be called Cato Neimoidia, and the Trade Federation Battleships of the Neimoidians can be seen flying around the structure.*
3.5 *An early version of the ring world by Church shows the planet as uninhabitable but a potential source of energy for the surrounding ring city (June 1, 2002).*

cess — so there is no loss of quality from one print to the next.

George Lucas We were investigating three possible ways to distribute the films: by satellite, via a disk, and over the phone line.

Rick McCallum For an industry that manipulates people emotionally, that is so powerful — that can change people's attitudes so quickly around the world — it is the most conservative, old-fashioned business. The technology has never changed. There isn't a single studio out there that has created any technological achievement; it has all been done by individuals. Here is a business that grosses $5 to $6 billion a year in theatrical revenue and another $15 billion in video rental, and there is nothing put back into the industry at all.

3.6

3.6 *Ryan Church's concept for Mygeeto showing interlocking hexagonal crystal* *formations on the planet's surface (June 1, 2002).*

George Lucas From the time you introduce a product to the time it gets accepted in the industry is about 10 years. The work that we did developing SoundDroid and EditDroid in the 1980s was continued by Pro Tools and Avid in the 1990s.

Rick McCallum At that time Avid were a small force in the television business, but couldn't make an impact at all in feature films. The arguments the editors made were always the same: "I need to smell it, to touch a film before I can cut it." Today, there are probably less than five out of 2,400 editors that are cutting movies on film. That is exactly what is going to happen with digital cinematography, and digital projection, and digital distribution.

Very few people understand this, but the six major studios spend between $1.2 to $1.3 billion a year in distribution costs, and yet there is nothing in place anywhere that ensures any quality whatsoever.

You could reduce that by about $1 billion per year if you could digitally distribute a perfect copy of your film to every cinema, where it could be reproduced exactly the way it was

"I'm not making these, oddly enough, to be giant, successful blockbusters. I'm making them because I'm telling a story, and I have to tell the story I intended."

George Lucas

made. It doesn't take much thinking to realize this is the way it has to happen. Yet the infrastructure is so locked in, it will take years to accomplish digital distribution.

We'll never have a huge number of digital screens until the corporate owners of the studios and the theater circuits realize that they have to get their act together. If they don't, they're going to lose their shirt because the average moviegoer can get a better

3.7 *Stephan Martiniere's concept for Mygeeto, a crystal planet (June 26, 2002).*

EPISODE 3 - CRYSTAL PLANET. IDEA1

STEPHAN MARTINIERE

3.7

experience at home with DVD than in most theaters. Nothing is as heartbreaking as going into a regular film theater and seeing your movie, even two or three days after release, with almost no relation to what you delivered. There's no possibility of quality control with the 19th-century technology in most theaters. There are more than 5,000 theaters out there, with more than 36,000 screens, and maybe 80 are equipped for digital.

The Creative Flow
Ryan Church / Concept Design Supervisor

In April 2002, about a month before Episode II opened, George casually says to us, "I want you to start thinking about seven planets—seven new planets that are completely different from each other—this is where the Clone Wars are happening. I want you to think about that." Well, this is something I've been thinking about since 1977, when I was a kid, so I said to George. "Oh, I think I've got some planets for you."

3.8 *Derek Thompson's concept for "space lemurs" (November 14, 2002). The original idea was that they were residents of the sinkhole world, Utapau. They were replaced, and then became citizens of Mygeeto, but were later not used in the film.*

SPACE LEMURS 01
DEREK THOMPSON
11·14·02
S W 3

3.8

George Lucas The first 10 minutes are going to be a huge spectacle. You're not going to know what is going on other than it's the Clone Wars. Now is the time to go way out there to be as wild as possible!

Erik Tiemens / Concept Design Supervisor I would like to underscore the sense of freedom we had to come up with ideas. George was giving us brand new ideas, we weren't doing a variation on an old theme, but new planets, new buildings, and that was neat.

George would give us a note like, "I want a new planet. Maybe there's ice on it." I would do inspirational thumbnails, to see if there was something there worth exploring. That became a crystallized iceberg planet. Then I would start painting over them to get a preview of the palette, and then line them up with the other planets and sequences to make sure they were distinct, and to see an overall mood board for the film. George said he'd like to do something more with crystals, and that became the crystal world Mygeeto.

Ryan and I did a bunch of paintings very quickly. It was a mix and match. I did a lot

3.9 Tiemens's concept for a battle raging on a sinkhole planet, later named Utapau (June 20, 2002). Tiemens: "George shared kernels of ideas that were not developed." For **Return of the Jedi** *(1983) Nilo Rodis-Jamero, Joe Johnston, and Ralph McQuarrie had drawn concepts for a crevassed planet, and then Doug Chiang developed that further in unused designs for Mos Espa in* **The Phantom Menace** *(1999).*

of early explorations on Utapau, the sinkhole environment, the battles there, and even the lagoon at the bottom of the hole,

Iain McCaig / Concept Artist George made it clear that we had to make each of the environments different from the worlds we'd seen before, and he's done a lot of planets. We would put ideas up on the board and he'd say, "That's like Geonosis," or "We saw that on Cloud City." We were trying to find a look for the sinkhole planet, which is a natural rock formation like Geonosis, and had big circular shapes like Cloud City. Finally, what helped was when he told us, "These people are not

FAMILY PORTRAIT ~ 12 · 6 ·02 ~ I·MCCAIG

3.11

3.10 *An early concept for a lagoon planet
designed by Erik Tiemens (June 20,
2002). This would evolve into Kashyyyk.*
3.11 *Iain McCaig's concept shows a
"family portrait" including Chewbacca
and a young Han Solo (December 6,
2002). Initially, Lucas had devised
a story outline where orphan Han Solo
had befriended Chewie and they were
living on Kashyyyk — Han finds part of
a transmitter droid and this helps Yoda
track General Grievous to Utapau.
Han Solo was later eliminated from
the script.*

3.10

"It's not in the script anymore, but we were told that Han Solo was on Kashyyyk and that he was being raised by Chewbacca. Han's such a persnickety guy later on — he always has to have the best of everything — so I thought it'd be great if when he was a kid, he was an absolute slob."

Iain McCaig / Concept Artist

3.12

from this planet. They're intergalactic travelers and have all kinds of high-tech stuff. They're like the Spacing Guild from *Dune*." That was the moment we knew that we could go in-side the rock itself to carve out an entire other city. The insect-like landing platforms are from one architectural period in the history of Uta-pau, and we can go inside and show that it's

3.13

been here for thousands of years with buildings in different styles. So that's how the city of Utapau evolved.

Paul Duncan In most of these concepts there are no characters.

Erik Tiemens This is because we don't always have the story, or know which characters are in the scene, or what they are doing, and if we put somebody in the image it could throw the whole painting off. So, most of these that Ryan and I were doing were environmental pieces to get a feel for the place, and then later on, after the animatics were made, we could get more specific.

Also, George is always looking for things that he might want to collage or regroup or flip or turn upside down, so that's why he has a broad approach. A lot of these ideas were also warming up to the subject matter.

Iain McCaig The biggest thrill and also the biggest hardship was that there was no script — on Episode II the script didn't come in until I'd finished the last of the costume designs. George said, "If you're clever,

3.14

3.12 *After the individual elements for Kashyyyk had been designed and approved, they were assembled into shots for the movie. This is Ryan Church's concept for shot KHA 30 (May 27, 2004). This not only depicts the forest environment, but also practical elements of the Wookiee habitation such as landing and observation platforms. The infrastructure uses natural materials, integrating with the planet's environment. In this image clones have arrived to help defend the Wookiees' planet.*
3.13 *Erik Tiemens's concept for the forested planet of Kashyyyk, home of the Wookiees, with karst-like limestone topography in the background (November 12, 2003). It clearly shows the template for the Wookiee tree that was used in the film.*
3.14 *Sang Jun Lee's concept for an athletic Wookiee warrior (November 15, 2002). He wears armor and carries a weapon as he swings from the tree.*

> *"The films follow the rules and regulations that I grew up with. They are about mythology, and show the way you should act, and the mores you should carry with you."*
>
> George Lucas

3.16

3.15

3.15 *Ryan Church concept art shows a*
battle charge on a bridge world, where
buildings hang underneath the bridge
(December 2, 2003). The foreground
battle clearly depicts the contrast between
the forces of light and dark. The creature
carrying the Jedi leading the clones into
battle bears a resemblance to the lizard
on Utapau.
3.16 *Church's concept for a space battle*
on the bridge world (August 27, 2002).
Starfighters launch from the Star
Destroyer's flight deck in the foreground
while the battle rages against the enemy
starships in the background. The bridge
world was named Cato Neimoidia for
the film.

3.17

3.17 *Church's art for the seaweed / coral environment of Felucia where the concept was that it was an underwater planet without water (July 6, 2004). Note the scale of the vehicles and creatures in the foreground, which are tiny compared with the flora and fauna.*
3.18 *The designers went into a great level of detail for each planet concept, not only*

considering its environment but also the flora and fauna. Sang Jun Lee's concept for a Felucia creature that bears a resemblance to jellyfish (December 6, 2002). A clone is shown for scale. The concept is that the creatures can absorb and digest organic matter — the armor and weapons of the victim are discarded.

3.19

you can guess what's going to happen because there's the whole six-film saga with
a little puzzle piece missing." So this time my
biggest personal fun was guessing the puzzle
pieces. I sat down with cards, and tried to
write the whole thing as if it was a script I was
working on. It was neat to draw a character,
a scene, a costume design from one of the
cards. I would stick it on the board and when
George would stamp it, I was like, "Oh! I found
that part."

Ryan Church We had a design meeting with
George every Friday afternoon.

Erik Tiemens Our meetings were fairly short.

George Lucas I would tell them about a
scene, an animal, or a character and they
would do a bunch of designs. I would okay

3.19 *Ryan Church's spiky concepts for a
thorn world (October 24, 2002). Elements
from this design would evolve into Felucia.*

some, or modify them, and we build; then
we go to the next thing. So every week, they
get more to design. Some of these guys are
designing costumes, some are designing sets,
some are designing props or cars, and I'm
writing the script.

Ryan Church After the meeting I'd drive down
to LA, where I taught a class at ArtCenter College of Design. I would sit in the car in a Red
Bull–infused fugue state, thinking about what
George had said about my artwork, and the

3.18

3.20

SPACE TROOPER (BOLIS MAZTA)

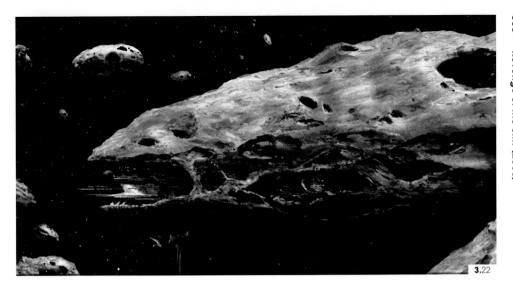

3.22

new designs he wanted, and images would come to mind.

Derek Thompson / Concept Artist On most projects, you're working from something very locked in, but we're in a situation where we're designing and working within very loose parameters. It's unique because we can thrust all of this enthusiasm and energy that we have for our respective fields of interest, and throw it out there. It may not always go well, but sometimes it will. On this show in particular it's all the things we all love.

Erik Tiemens We're always talking about things we loved as kids — toys, movies, experiences — and it never stops. Each day it's "Hey, I can pull that out of my experience bag," and bring it to the artwork.

We had an amazing researcher who helped us, David Craig. He was very eclectic. He'd bring in shells, or an old cow bone: "Look at this and see the marrow and how they dry out." I would zoom into that and get ideas. One time he brought in plastic sandwich trays and said, "Take a paper towel, get it wet, and rub the carpet." We'd put them in the sandwich trays, leave them in the closet for a week or two, pull them out, and this

3.20 *Feng Zhu's concept for Polis Massa's interiors shows a control center (November 20, 2002). Zhu: "We didn't know what Polis Massa was for, so I thought it might be where they're building the Death Star."*
3.21 *Warren Fu's concept for a space trooper on "Polis Mazta" (November 22, 2002).*
3.22 *T. J. Frame's artwork for Polis Massa, a city inside an asteroid (December 3, 2002).*

amazing fuzz was growing out of it. He was encouraging us to literally play with mud and blocks and tangible materials, to encourage the creative flow, because it's very easy to go stale.

George would sometimes reference an image from the research library downstairs, and part of my process was to go down there and bring up tons of books. I would have those open all around my desk, I'd tag images, and I'd let all of that reference and inspiration stew for a week or two, and as I was developing the sketches, they would get more informed and synthesized. After that I

felt more comfortable in conversations with George, and then he would say something unexpected and I would pursue that avenue a little bit. He would guide me in the direction that was worth pursuing.

I'd do a pencil drawing or an ink drawing, or a little gouache painting, or watercolor, scan that in, and then work on top of that using Painter software along with Photoshop.

Like a writer, an artist is exploring, fleshing things out, and the craft somehow creates more and more focus, and then you get a flow. You don't want to be constantly interrupted with meetings that maybe aren't essential. That's where Rick and George were so good—they wanted us to keep creating and not get bogged down with too many practical, logistical things. We could focus on our design and the art-making process.

Ryan Church I had gotten fast at doing these paintings in Painter. I was doing everything with my hand, but I had undo and watercolor and wash and oils all in one package. It was

the best of both worlds; and I feel very fortunate to be trained completely traditionally and work digitally.

Erik Tiemens Once we had finished, we would hand over our artwork to art department supervisor Fay David. She would name and number them correctly, then after George gave his approval, she'd distribute them to editorial, animatics, production, and ILM.

Ryan Church George was very receptive to our ideas. "That's not going in my movie but that's fun." "No, no, I would never do something like that, but that's cool." If you do a trashy, dirty, *Blade Runner*–esque dystopian planet that's moody and fun to draw, he's like, "Come on. We don't do that." But he never stopped us from trying—he always wanted to see what we had in our head.

Warren Fu / Concept Artist A lot of *Star Wars* design is about impact. Everything has to read clearly and instantly, because George is into silhouettes and how to read it right away: "Where's the front of the ship?" "Where's the back of it?" "What direction is it flying?"

3.23 *During the design process the concept artists used digital technology to copy and amend concepts. An image could be easily repainted and relit so that the basic structure of a planet could be given a very different look. For example, Church's concept of Jedi and clone troopers about to do battle on an ash planet was based on the crystal world Mygeeto (August 22, 2002). This look was eventually used in the movie.*

3.23

Ryan Church He was pushing us to go further. I had bigger ideas in my head and now they're not limited by anything. He is the best boss I ever had. He completely spoiled me.

3.24 *Church's concept for a Clone Wars battle depicts clone troopers facing an octuptarra tri-droid in a war-ravaged cathedral-like environment (August 29, 2002).*

Iconic

George Lucas Stay away from red, except for Mustafar.

In June 2002, Lucas confirmed that the climactic confrontation between Anakin and Obi-Wan would take place on the red lava planet Mustafar.

Erik Tiemens We saw that Ralph McQuarrie had made sketches of the Mustafar look for *Return of the Jedi*, and Vader's castle in lava for *The Empire Strikes Back*.

3.24

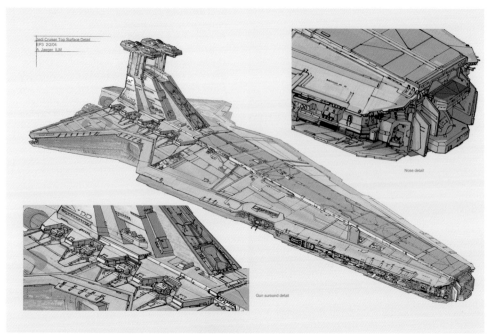

Jedi Cruiser Top Surface Detail
EP3 2/2/04
A. Jaeger ILM

Nose detail

Gun surround detail

3.25

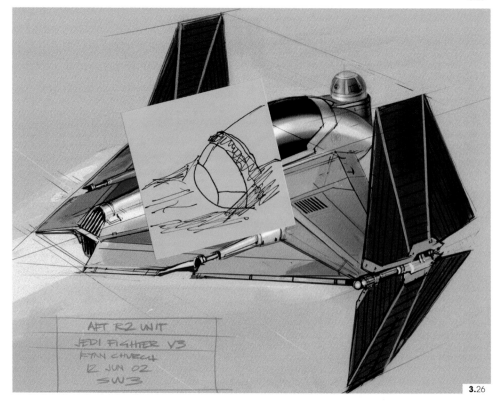

AFT R2 UNIT
JEDI FIGHTER V3
RYAN CHURCH
12 JUN 02
SW3

3.26

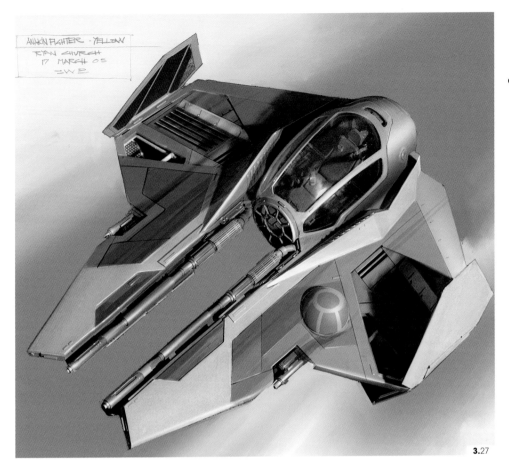

ANAKIN FIGHTER · YELLOW
RYAN CHURCH
17 MARCH 05
IW2

3.27

3.25 *In the opening shot of the film two Jedi starfighters, piloted by Anakin and Obi-Wan, skim over the Jedi cruiser. Alex Jaeger added surface detail to the Jedi cruiser (February 2, 2004).*
3.26 *George Lucas drew over Church's June 11, 2002, Jedi starfighter concept to make it look more like a TIE fighter, which signals the design evolution from the Republic to the Empire.*
3.27 *Church's modified design for Anakin's Jedi starfighter (March 17, 2003). This has a revised cockpit design with two extended laser cannons, and the R2 unit is now located on the wing, within the pilot's field of vision.*

Rick McCallum We had a very lucky break in October 2002 when we were conceiving the whole Mustafar sequence. Mount Etna exploded. So I grabbed Ron Fricke, wonderful cameraman, and we rushed off to Italy and within 24 hours we started filming for a week the extraordinary footage that we have on Mustafar of the volcano planet literally exploding in front of our eyes.

Erik Tiemens I hit Mustafar pretty hard. I spent a lot of time researching, getting books, and watching Ron Fricke's footage. I was intrigued by the theatrics of lava, especially in the evening or at night. It seemed so moody. I painted a sea of lava, which was a photo I shot of the Marin Headlands that I painted over, turning it red.

FIGHTER CONCEPT
RYAN CHURCH
1 AUG 02
SW 3

3.28 *Final frame of the opening space battle showing a vast array of ships engaged in intense combat. In the fore-ground Anakin and Obi-Wan's Jedi starfighters, supported by a squad of ARC-170 clone starfighters, head for General Grievous's ship in the background.*
3.29 *Church's fighter concept would become the ARC-170 clone starfighter (August 1, 2002).*

3.30

Ryan Church Seeing how open-minded George was, I wanted to get a breadth of talent. In August, I brought up a bunch of guys I had worked with down in LA. Feng Zhu is a good pen sketch guy. Also, T. J. Frame was an early 3-D guy who could get stuff built in 3-D very quickly, throw stuff to George, and then that went right to animatics.

T. J. Frame / Concept Artist I began using 3-D for design work on Episode III in late 2002. This was the first time the art department began incorporating digital 3-D modeling for design work on the series.

I focused on creating fast and rough concepts, beginning with bridge views of the Separatist cruiser from the opening sequence. Depicting a location or prop with drawings and paintings is obviously crucial, but by also creating a rough 3-D version of an asset designers can further resolve issues and home in on proportions and spatial relationships. A 3-D model can be quickly altered and viewed from any desired angle without having to laboriously redraw the scene by hand.

In the art department we typically used these models as an intermediate stage between a rough sketch or key painting and a finished set design or film asset. Sometimes I made models of existing sketches to ensure

3.31

the designs worked as intended before sending them to ILM. On many occasions I took sketches from multiple artists of different parts of a set and blended them together to create a cohesive set layout. These layouts were then handed off to the animatics department, ILM's modeling department, and to the set builders to serve as a reference and a starting point for further refinement.

Because these models were simple and typically untextured, we referred to them as "foam core models" in acknowledgment of the traditional models often built from paper and foam core boards. By keeping the presentation simple and straightforward, it makes it easier to focus on the overall design before materials, colors, and atmospheric effects are added.

Paul Duncan In October 2002, George changed his mind about the film's opening. Rather than begin with the wars on seven planets, and ending with the battle over Coruscant, where Palpatine is rescued by Anakin and Obi-Wan, he cut out the planets and started with the rescue.

3.30 Joe Johnston's concept for a Rebel cruiser was conceived for Episode VI.
3.31 Lucas suggested using Joe Johnston's Rebel cruiser design, and Erik Tiemens's concept became a Separatist destroyer in the battle over Coruscant (June 20, 2002).

Ryan Church I was annoyed about that at the time. The Clone War sequence got cut way down and moved, with each planet getting about four shots in the later Order 66 section, when all the Jedi are killed.

George Lucas I needed a bad guy in the movie. There has to be a bad guy in every *Star Wars* movie and Count Dooku is killed by Anakin early on in Episode III. I wanted something that was reminiscent of Darth Vader but not Darth Vader. I wanted him to be an alien that had been reconstructed into a robot.

On November 8, 2002, Lucas told the art department that the film would include a droid general as the Separatist leader against the Republic.

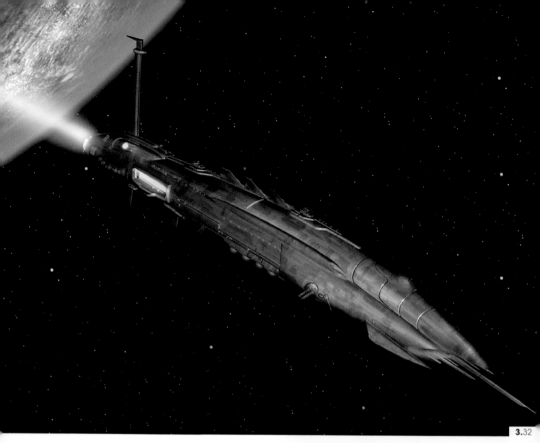

"Space battles are my favorite parts of the original trilogy, so I always carve those off for myself. The ones I supervised in the new trilogy were all different. The Episode I battle was a big swarm of fighters all around one big battleship, Episode II was in the asteroid field between two ships and a missile, and III is just total pandemonium."

John Knoll / Visual Effects Supervisor

George Lucas I won't limit it at this point to a droid. It could be an alien of some kind. I'm not sure if I want him to be human. It's got to be iconic. It's got to be evil.

Derek Thompson We all collaborated on the droid general. It was one of the most exhilarating weeks, because we all got to attack one thing.

Warren Fu I was favoring two droid designs, and then at the last minute, right before the meeting, I had one little sketch I had started but hadn't fleshed out. Darth Vader is black, so I went with pure white—in Chinese culture, white means death. So I finished marking it up, handed it over to art department assistant Ryan Mendoza, and told him, "I don't like it but can you scan it in anyway, and then we'll print it out." Ryan's like, "This is the one that George is going to pick."

George Lucas They came up with lots of different ideas and one, by Warren Fu, stood out immediately. I said, "Ooh, this is good."

Warren Fu I looked at Ryan, and Ryan was like, "Told you so!" I mentioned to George that the general might have organic eyes—George's eyes lit up and he said, "Now that's interesting."

The design was refined over several weeks, so that the general looked markedly different from the original design.

George Lucas We had two designs. I liked both of them, so I said, "Well, this guy will be the general, and these guys will be his special bodyguards, and that way I can use both of the designs." That gives me another fight level, because I needed something that was better than your average droid to fight Obi-

3.32 *T. J. Frame's concept for the Separatist cruiser (December 20, 2002). It features a hangar and high observation platform at the rear.*
3.33 *Final frame showing the chaos of the battle above Coruscant. The Separatist cruiser, General Grievous's command vessel, is in the background.*

3.33

ANAKIN - ACE
RYAN CHURCH
6 DEC 02
SW3

Wan. A laser sword can cut through anything and do anything, so I have to figure out some way to have a semi-fair fight, otherwise there's no contest and no drama. So I gave the guards electric staffs that a laser sword can't cut through.

Paul Duncan You named the villain General Grievous in early 2003.

George Lucas He was the antithesis of Vader, which is to say, Vader was mostly human and part robot, whereas this general was mostly robot with a human interior. So it was a flip of the same thing. Again, a circle.

Paul Duncan I like the fact that you gave Grievous a cough because it echoed Vader's labored breathing. Grievous foreshadows what was to come for Anakin.

George Lucas Man–machine relationships are symbiotic too, and I wanted that idea to be impregnated into this world. I did not want humans and robots to be separated because the key character is obviously a combination of the two. I wanted the idea that there are more like him.

Paul Duncan You added dialogue like "Roger, Roger" to the battle droids that give them a little bit of whimsy.

George Lucas It's funny to have robots with humanity, but I don't think it works to give robots human traits. I think it's more interesting when they are robot personalities, like Artoo, where they're funny because they don't fit. Threepio can speak many languages but he's got a big blind spot — he's dumb in the way computers are dumb, which is, "Oh, they never told me that." He's just following instructions, which leaves gaps in his intelligence.

Paul Duncan He's a translator, but he doesn't understand humans.

George Lucas No. He doesn't understand emotions.

Paul Duncan That's the irony of the character, but there's another irony in that Anakin is the one who created him.

3.37

3.34 *Church concept art of Anakin's fighter in action (December 6, 2002).*
3.35 *Filming Anakin (Hayden Christensen) inside the Jedi starfighter. A basic cockpit set was constructed for the digital camera to shoot directly inside. The background is blue screen so that the remaining elements of his ship and the background space battle can be added in postproduction.*
3.36 *Iain McCaig's costuming concept for Anakin (November 14, 2002). The cloak foreshadows Anakin's transformation into Darth Vader.*
3.37 *Anakin emerges from a volcano in McCaig's costume design (October 16, 2002). Lucas commented that Anakin is not scarred before the end of the movie.*

3.38

3.39

3.40

3.38 Church's storyboard for the buzz droids landing on Obi-Wan's starfighter (March 7, 2003).
3.39 Church's storyboard showing the Jedi flying in parallel as Obi-Wan's cockpit

glass is being attacked by a buzz droid (February 28, 2003).
3.40 Church's storyboard showing Anakin scraping the buzz droids from Obi-Wan's fighter using the tip of his

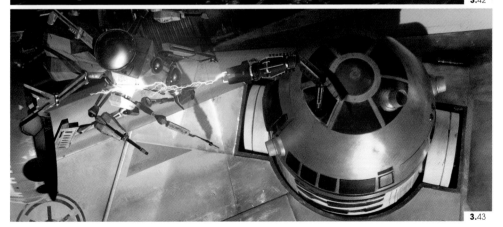

wing in a highly daring maneuver
(March 7, 2003).
3.41 *Final frame of Obi-Wan Kenobi
(Ewan McGregor) observing the buzz
droid landing on his ship.*

3.42 *The buzz droids have destroyed R4
and are working on the rest of the ship.*
3.43 *In this final frame R2-D2 defends
himself from a buzz droid attack. Obi-Wan
advises that he should hit the center eye.*

DROID GENERAL
W.FU 11/14/02
SW3

3.44

3.45

DROID GENERAL W/ WEAPONS
W.FU 12/19/02

3.46

George Lucas It is an irony, but in the end it's poetic. Anakin likes to build things, but he's just a kid. He doesn't build a super droid, but a translator droid from the junk that's lying around.

Paul Duncan Does Anakin act in a way that makes him into a machine?

George Lucas I don't think so, but he be-comes a machine. It's a metaphor as he loses his humanity through the things that he does—it's the visualization of that idea. As he goes deeper into the dark side, he becomes less and less human. That's the whole plot of the movies: "Can he be brought back from this dark place he's found himself?" It's only through the love of his son that he can do that.

Working in Clay

George Lucas I started writing the script in August 2002, and I thought this was going to be the easiest one to write. I thought I have to

3.44 George Lucas encouraged the entire design team to develop and sub-mit ideas for the droid general, the new evil character for the movie, who would eventually be named General Grievous. Lucas liked Warren Fu's initial design and used it for Grievous's bodyguards (November 14, 2002).

3.45 Erik Tiemens's design (November 12, 2002). Tiemens: "I was looking at North American Indian gurus, and maybe I went down a path I wasn't supposed to go, but I think they were worth explor-ing. There is a furnace or power source inside. I think there might be elements in tone or mood that go through to the final design."

3.46 Warren Fu quickly developed his initial concept for General Grievous and gave him a variety of weapons (Decem-ber 19, 2002).

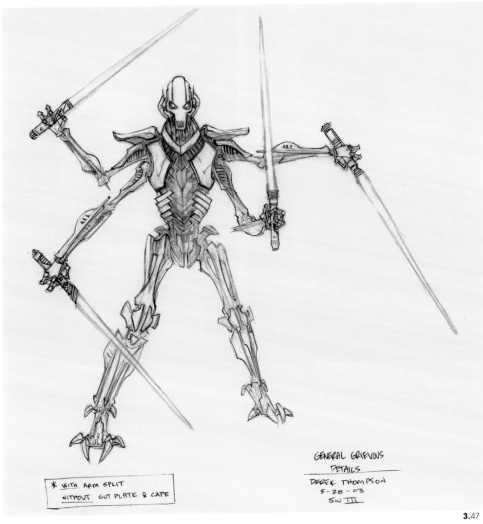

✱ WITH ARM SPLIT
WITHOUT GUT PLATE & CAPE

GENERAL GRIEVOUS
DETAILS
DEREK THOMPSON
5-28-03
SW III

3.47

3.47 *Derek Thompson's design shows details of Grievous's construction, complete with four arms that could wield multiple lightsabers (May 28, 2003). Grievous is a droid on the exterior, but he possesses organic internal organs.*
3.48–49 *Concept art by Feng Zhu detailing General Grievous's anatomy and movement (June–July, 2003). A great deal of thought was put into determining how* *he should move, the practicalities of joint articulation and head rotation. The different colors on the images represent specific elements of his construction. General Grievous, an organic-mechanical hybrid with a rasping voice, foreshadows what we know Anakin will become. The design process not only focused on physical design, but also added meaning to the characters.*

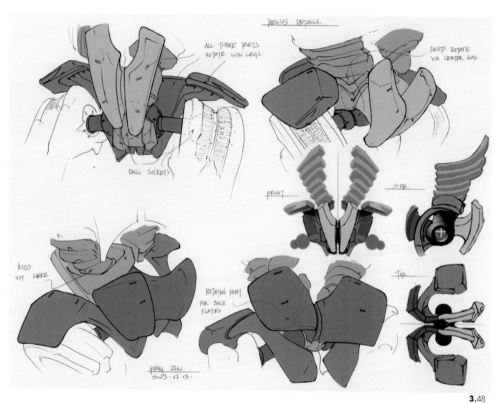

PELVIS DETAILS.

ALL THREE PARTS
ROTATE WITH LEGS.

PARTS ROTATE
VIA CENTER AXIS.

BALL SOCKETS

FRONT

SIDE

RIBS
SIT HERE

ROTATION POINT
FOR BACK
PLATES

TOP

FENG ZHU.
SW3 · 67 · 13.

3.48

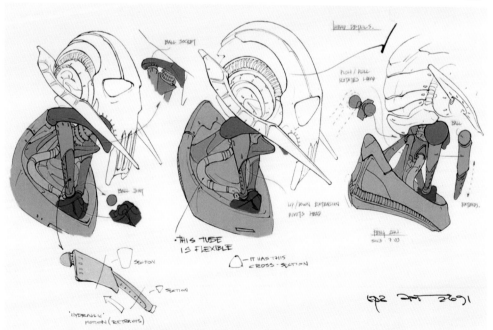

HEAD DETAILS.

BALL SOCKET

PUSH / PULL
ROTATES HEAD

BALL

BALL JOINT

UP / DOWN EXTENSION
PIVOTS HEAD

ROTATE.

FENG ZHU
SW3 · 7 · 03

· THIS TUBE
IS FLEXIBLE

— IT HAS THIS
CROSS - SECTION

SECTION

SECTION

'HYDRAULIC'
MOTION (RETRACTS)

EP2 ART 3691

3.49

draw a line from Episode II to Episode IV, but a lot of the material I had didn't fit.

The script starts to have its own life. Characters start to tell you what to do—and you end up with problems. I have characters left over from the previous films, and they're all running around yipping and yelling and saying, "What about me?" I have to solve these problems, because what I thought was going to happen isn't happening. I got far enough with the outline to realize that the bridge between Episode III and Episode IV still had them about 50 feet apart. So I had to disassemble Episode III and rethink it, to make it line up with Episode IV. This one is like a Rubik's Cube, with a lot of puzzle-solving. It has got a lot of characters, and a lot of things that have to happen. I don't want it to be a three-hour movie, and I don't want it to be boring.

On January 31, 2003, Lucas delivered the first rough draft of Star Wars: Episode III Revenge of the Sith to Rick McCallum. Running to 55 pages, it was not for general circulation but would allow the producer to plan the production in Australia.

3.50 *Derek Thompson's storyboards depicting the murder of Jedi Master Shaak Ti (June 18, 2003). Shaak Ti was protecting Palpatine when she was captured by Grievous. During their regular meetings the storyboard artists made rough sketches as Lucas described events in a scene. These would be refined and sequenced into storyboards and shown to Lucas, who would explore multiple iterations of the scene.*

3.50

The story opens with Anakin and Obi-Wan flying through the battle over Coruscant, boarding General Grievous's ship, and fighting Count Dooku to rescue Chancellor Palpatine. Grievous escapes, Anakin beheads Dooku at Palpatine's urging, and the ship crash-lands on Coruscant.

A number of scenes set up the drama: Padmé announces she is pregnant; Anakin has a nightmare that she dies; Palpatine suggests Anakin should be his representative on the Jedi Council; Yoda, on Kashyyyk, locates Grievous on Utapau thanks to the help of a 10-year-old Han Solo; and Obi-Wan is sent

3.51 *Lucas directing Orli Shoshan prior to filming Shaak Ti's demise. This scene was filmed but eventually deleted.*

with thousands of clone troopers to Utapau to capture Grievous.

Obi-Wan duels with Grievous and a chase ensues with Grievous on his wheel scooter and Obi-Wan on a lizard.

With Obi-Wan's defeat of Grievous, Mace Windu visits Palpatine so that a peace can be negotiated to bring about the end of the war. Palpatine refuses and attacks Windu with Force lightning. Again, at Palpatine's urging, Anakin cuts off Windu's sword hand and the Jedi Master dies under Palpatine's onslaught. Palpatine, now transformed into Darth Sidious, issues Order 66 to the clone troops, and the galaxy-wide execution of the Jedi commences. Yoda, forewarned by fluctuations in the Force, defeats the troopers and escapes. Obi-

> **"Making a film is an evolutionary process for George. That's the key phrase. So you have to be quick and nimble when he makes a suggestion."**
> Rick McCallum / Producer

3.52

3.53

Wan is shot off his lizard, falls to the bottom of the sinkhole, climbs out, and escapes in a starfighter. Meanwhile, Darth Sidious seduces Anakin to the dark side with the promise of power to save Padmé from death, and makes a startling revelation:

Rough Draft Script / January 31, 2003

Darth Sidious I have waited all these years for you to fulfill your destiny. I arranged for your conception. I used the power of the Force to will the midi-chlorians to start the cell division that created you.

3.52 *Following the murder of Shaak Ti, Obi-Wan and Anakin are surrounded. They use their lightsabers to cut a hole in the floor and land in a generator room filled with highly flammable fuel. Ryan Church's concept shows the room filling with fuel and droids breaking in (October 31, 2002).*

3.53 *Church's unrealized idea for a corridor battle on the Separatist cruiser, with the ship upside down and the hull ruptured (October 31, 2002).*

Anakin I don't believe you.

Darth Sidious Ahhh, but you know it's true. When you clear your mind, you will sense the truth. You could almost think of me as your father.

Yoda and Obi-Wan secretly return to the Jedi Temple on Coruscant and witness via hologram recordings both Anakin's slaughter of the Jedi younglings and his anointment as Darth Vader, Lord of the Sith, by Darth Sidious. Yoda and Bail Organa flee to Polis Massa, while Obi-Wan visits Padmé in an attempt to hunt down Anakin.

Padmé refuses to help, but journeys to Mustafar, where Anakin has killed all the Separatist leaders. When Obi-Wan reveals himself, having sneaked aboard Padmé's ship, Anakin believes his wife has betrayed him, Force-chokes her, and throws her against a wall. The former friends then duel until Obi-Wan cuts off Anakin's legs; Anakin falls down an embankment and catches fire. Obi-Wan picks up Anakin's lightsaber and takes Padmé to Polis Massa, while Darth Sidious brings Anakin to Coruscant where, because his wounds are so severe, he must be encased in mechanical armor to keep him alive.

On Polis Massa, Padmé dies while giving birth to twins. Padmé's funeral is held on Naboo. Yoda exiles himself on Dagobah. Bail Organa takes Leia, the baby girl, to Alderaan, to adopt her as his own. Obi-Wan places the baby boy, Luke, with Owen Lars on Tatooine, with the intent of watching over him from afar. Yoda tells Obi-Wan that in his solitude he is to train under Qui-Gon Jinn, who had studied with the Ancient Order of the Whills.

3.54 *Digital storyboard by Eric Carney showing Obi-Wan being dragged underwater by a super battle droid (January 23, 2004).*

Episode III

0136

fcg530 - v02
01/23/04

Artist: Eric Carney

3.55

The final scene shows the Emperor, Governor Tarkin, and Darth Vader on the bridge of a Star Destroyer, looking out at the construction of a Death Star in space.

Rick McCallum Already, the crew in Australia has enough information from George to begin construction of environments, props, and costumes. After that, George will be writing a more formal first draft, and will keep revising right up until the start of shooting.

Virtual Filmmaking

Ryan Church I told everybody — Warren, Zhu, T. J., everybody — to do something you want to see for the end fight. It's got to have lava, and it's got to have lightsabers. Over time George had let us know which Mustafar fight ideas he liked, and which were dumb, so we quickly put the "OK" sketches in the order that we thought worked best. "Let's start in a confined space in the war room, start close and go wide."

Paul Duncan From the war room, it goes out onto the balcony, then onto the pipes, and then the big collection panels.

Ryan Church Right. T. J. built this crude 3-D model of the whole complex, we showed that to George, and we sent that over to the animatics guys.

At the beginning of March 2003 the animatics team, led by Daniel Gregoire, started working on developing assets and sequences.

Daniel Gregoire / Previsualization Supervisor We take art and storyboards from the art department and mix and match them all together, along with live-action stuff. We build everything in 3-D. We texture it, we light it, we go through every step that ILM would go through, only we do it in a more fundamental manner so that it's easy, fast, and flexible.

Rick McCallum At lunch, after we'd had our concept design meetings, George would go

3.55 *Anakin and Obi-Wan enter the elevator on their way to rescue Palpatine only to find it occupied by droids, which they dispatch with great efficiency. Erik Tiemens's artwork illustrates the lighting of the scene (June 5, 2003).*
3.56 *Filming Anakin in the elevator shaft. Anakin is on top of the elevator, so when it descends he jumps over to cling to the doorway. When the elevator ascends, he jumps back onto it. Christensen is attached to a wire to ensure his safety but he is still at some height for the camera to give a sense of scale and depth. The digital camera on the Technocrane is considerably more lightweight and maneuverable than traditional film cameras.*

3.56

3.58

3.59

up with a tuna fish sandwich and spend hours with the sequences, going through all the shots that he wanted.

Daniel Gregoire When George says, "I've got this idea. I want this shot. I just thought of it," in half a day or less we can have a viable option for him to cut into the film to see if it works.

Rick McCallum It was no different than for live action in terms of production, except that George was working with four or five kids instead of sitting there with 150 to 200 crew-members. It's virtual filmmaking.

Daniel Gregoire We started earlier than Episode II and with more people on staff with the express intent of providing a lot more

3.57 Filming Anakin and Obi-Wan's battle with Count Dooku on the General's Quarters set. Lucas uses two digital cameras to shoot the same scene from different perspectives.
3.58 Unlike their previous encounter with Count Dooku, Anakin and Obi-Wan work together as a team to overcome him.
3.59 Final frame showing a surprised Dooku (Christopher Lee) realizing that Palpatine has betrayed him (Palpatine is his master Darth Sidious) and that he is about to meet his demise. This is the first time that Anakin acquires a red light-saber, red being the color of dark side blades. The image also recalls the crossed lightsabers in the final duel of Episode VI.
3.60 Filming the decapitation of Count Dooku. Anakin takes another step toward the dark side.

3.60

material to Lucas. For Episode III, the concentration has been more on shot quality and substance. We're spending more time on character animation, shot blocking, and proper cinematic techniques than we ever have before. It is important that we try to be more realistic so when it comes time to re-create shots on set or at ILM, George has confidence that they will work. This by no means hinders us creatively. In fact, it has made our work more easily edited and believable, leading to more exciting sequences.

George Lucas When the animatics guys deliver the videomatics that we're after, editor Ben Burtt starts to cut those together. After a while, I'll start working with Ben in tightening the editing on those so that around the time we start shooting the film we've got a pretty tight version of what these action sequences look like.

Daniel Gregoire We went through 23 revisions of the opening space battle in the previsualization department, and we were able to do that for a fraction of the cost of ILM.

Rick McCallum It wasn't so much about saving time, because you were putting the work in up front, but the economic savings — the cost efficiency of being able to walk onto the set on the first day with 60 to 70 minutes of film cut together that you could show the actors and the crew — made the whole system incredibly efficient.

Lockdown Mode

George Lucas Here in San Francisco I was working on the script, and I was working with the designers, and the editors, and the previsualization people. In Australia, Rick was in charge of the art department, the wardrobe department, the prop department, and the camera department to coordinate what we were developing over here with what they were doing over there.

Rick McCallum / March 14, 2003 It's hard to give you a progress report of where we are because I'm a man without a script,

⑦ HIGH ANGLE FACING DOOR (EXIT)

which is like being on a sea without a ship. But everybody's focusing on what little information we get each week. We started set construction two weeks ago, the costume department are in the middle of fabricating a number of costumes, and the creature shop will start in the next two weeks. So everything is moving. We're heading for a destination, but we're not sure where we're going to end up.

George Lucas / March 21, 2003 I've written about half of the first draft. I still have elements, like Artoo-Detoo and Threepio, which I haven't fit in everywhere. They're in one scene, but I haven't filled in their reality yet, because the film doesn't center on them.

I am very diligent about going to work at 8:30 every morning and leaving at 6:00 every night. I get it done; I write five pages a day. But left to my own reality, I would probably write a page a day. I force myself. It becomes agonizing to get those other four pages.

Ryan Church I would go to George's house twice a week and bring over a packet of artwork that we were going to discuss. His inspiration room has a little glass wall that hangs out over some trees and the other walls are

books. We would sit there talking with production designer Gavin Bocquet on the phone from Australia.

While we were waiting for the phone connection, we would talk about the books on his wall, or about the designs. Design is my whole life. It's a tiny part of his life, but he knows it as

3.61 *Ryan Church's concept art shows the space battle between mile-long Star Destroyers in the upper atmosphere of Coruscant (March 12, 2003).*
3.62 *The Separatist cruiser is damaged and turns on its side. Filming Ian McDiarmid, Hayden Christensen, and Ewan McGregor as the Jedi and Palpatine run down the elevator shaft to jump into a doorway and avoid the oncoming elevator.*
3.63 *Concept art by T.J. Frame showing Obi-Wan, Anakin, and Palpatine inside the hangar. The ship is on its side, with the top of the ship on the right. The Jedi are trying to reach the exit, shown in the distance, so must climb along the pipes. Obi-Wan is in front, followed by Anakin, with Palpatine tied to him by a line. At the same time R2-D2 flies from "A" to "B."*

3.64 *Often, multiple artists separately contributed composition, backgrounds, characters, and lighting details to the same image in the visual script. This visual script image for scene 43c shows Obi-Wan and Anakin battling General Grievous and his guards, while Palpatine and Artoo keep clear of the action on the right. The idea was filmed but cut from the scene.*

3.65 *Grievous captures Anakin and Obi-Wan, and he is ready to add their lightsabers to his collection.*

3.64

3.65

3.66

well as I do. It's very intimidating. You begin to realize that he's not like you and I. His brain moves much faster, and he's got a much denser amount of material to hold and deal with at any given time.

That's where I had some of the best discussions about the designs. I made notes and little sketches, and came back to the team and filled them in on what George wanted to see from us. Erik and I had already done the establishing shot backgrounds, and they now lived in the animatics, but now George was asking for different lighting, different colors. He'd say, "Pinker, more like *Arizona Highways*," referring to the magazine.

Gavin Bocquet was in charge of designing and constructing 72 physical sets.

Ryan Church George was in cost-cutting mode. He said to us, "We're in lockdown mode here. I'm not building an asset twice. You get to build it in CG, or you get to build it as a real thing, but choose one." He's spending his own money so it's understandable that he wants us to find out how to make the movie cheaper.

Gavin Bocquet / Production Designer For the previous two films we sent photographs of card models to give George an idea of the sets. For this film, for the first time, the preliminary concept designs get turned into 3-D

3.66 *Warren Fu's concept for the dramatic splitting of the Separatist cruiser (December 12, 2002). The ship is now within the gravitational pull of Coruscant.* **3.**67 *Ryan Church's concept of a Federation cruiser crash site outside the Jedi Temple (November 5, 2002). Church: "My thought for this was that the ship is coming in to destroy the Jedi Temple, and all the Jedi work together to somehow use the Force to push it away."*

SEPARATIST CRUISER SPLIT
W.FU 12/12/02
SW3

3.67

3.68

3.69

3.70

models and we send him a small animation for him to approve the general idea. Then we do a more sophisticated model with more detail on it, and do an animation of that. This gives George a much better feel for the whole environment that we're building. And for me too. Normally, as the sets are being constructed, there's always a slight nervousness because you're thinking about size and scale and proportions. Should the set be four feet wider or shorter or higher? The advantage of these 3-D models is that they give an extra confirmation that you've analyzed the space well. And as the sets are going up on this film I haven't been surprised about anything I've walked into.

Rick McCallum Stunt coordinator Nick Gillard started in early April.

Nick Gillard / Stunt Coordinator I get the blueprints for the set from the art department and we mark them out with tape on the floor of our rehearsal room. We have to know when we're going through doors. We have to know when we're going to turn left and right to match the set, because otherwise you're turning straight into a wall. Once we've test shot everything, I'll edit it on my computer, and it'll go to the Ranch for George to look at. Anything that he doesn't like, he can change.

Iain McCaig General Grievous is meant to be the big scary bad guy in the film, but I wasn't scared. I came up with the idea that Jedi Master Shaak Ti was protecting Palpatine, got captured, and is aboard the Separatist ship. When Anakin and Obi-Wan come into the room with General Grievous, Grievous should have her with his hand around her throat, and he should break her neck. George is considering working it into the script.

Paul Duncan During your story conference with Leigh Brackett in November 1977, you tell how Han had been orphaned on the Wookiee planet, been raised by Wookiees, and befriended Chewbacca. You resuscitated that idea for Episode III and in the rough draft script a young Han Solo helped Yoda on Kashyyyk.

George Lucas I rejected it after I read it. I said, "This is stupid." I was being a smart aleck, tying things together, and being a little too clever for my own good.

On April 13, Lucas delivered the 111-page first draft of the script, which contains many refinements and action details. Shaak Ti was added to the opening sequence on the Separatist cruiser, where she is killed by Grievous in front of Anakin and Obi-Wan. Han Solo had been removed; instead Chancellor Palpatine sends Obi-Wan to Utapau to locate General Grievous. Grievous now has two arms that separate into four arms, and he has been trained how to wield lightsabers. Palpatine no longer claims that he arranged for Anakin's conception, although he does tell the young Jedi the story of Darth Plagueis, who could stop life-forms from dying. After seeing the holograms in the Jedi Temple, Yoda insists that Obi-Wan kill Anakin, and Yoda goes to confront Palpatine. Yoda is defeated, and Bail Organa helps him escape. At the end, when Darth Vader emerges from surgery, he asks about Padmé and is told by Darth Sidious, "I'm afraid she was killed by a Jedi... she is no longer our concern."

3.68 Church's concept shows the Separatist cruiser's dramatic descent, with Coruscant fire ships attempting to extinguish the flames as it falls toward the surface of the planet (February 23, 2003).
3.69 The ship descends rapidly, accompanied by firefighting ships, but Anakin manages to steer it toward a landing strip, preventing major casualties on the ground.
3.70 Ryan Church's concept for the crashed cruiser (October 20, 2003).

> *"I studied Carrie Fisher's performance, especially in Empire. I tried to get more of the spunk and grooviness of those films into the role...and of course the lip gloss."*
>
> Natalie Portman

George Lucas As I write the next drafts there'll be a lot more cutting and pasting. Certain sequences will be right, and I'll jump through them. The last thing that will be dealt with is the dialogue because that you can change on the set or even afterward—I'm not known for my dialogue. I think of it as a sound effect, a rhythm, a vocal chorus in the overall soundtrack. Mostly, everything is visual.

On June 13, the revised second draft script was delivered. At 135 pages it was significantly more polished, with characters and motivations more defined. At the end: Padmé dies of a broken heart; Vader is told by Sidious: "I'm afraid she died...It seems in your anger, you killed her," and Vader screams out in pain; and the last shot is now on Tatooine watching the twin suns set.

Three days later George Lucas arrived at the Fox Studios in Sydney, Australia.

George Lucas Our communications are so close between the various departments that I can travel from San Francisco and end up in Sydney the next day, and I know everything that's been going on. I've seen the sets, so there're no surprises. I walk on, and it's like I've been there the whole time.

Rick McCallum He's got a very tight schedule. He starts about 6:30 a.m. and spends a couple of hours on the script. Then he does a walk-through of the sets for about an hour and a half with cinematographer David Tattersall every day.

David Tattersall / Cinematographer When we are working in the total green or blue environment, and probably with one or two small props, then the visual script is referred to much more often.

John Knoll / Visual Effects Supervisor The visual script was put together out at the Ranch. Ryan Church and Erik Tiemens did these beautiful concept pieces of what the different environments will look like. Those are extremely helpful for David Tattersall and Gavin Bocquet and George when we're shooting because, especially on sets where

3.71

3.71 Iain McCaig's costume design for Padmé with a background image of her holding a bird of prey on her arm (October 30, 2002).
3.72–73 During the reunion of Anakin and Padmé (Natalie Portman), she reveals that she is pregnant. For Anakin it is "The happiest moment of my life."

we just have the floor and a column, it's good to have a nice concept piece for the whole environment. That very much affects how David lights things, and how George likes to frame things.

David Tattersall My main interest would be to see where the windows are, what the light sources are, what time of day it is. The visual script is also useful for the actors to see.

Rick McCallum Then George usually shoots a test for a half hour: hair and makeup, and lighting tests on the set. Then he spends about an hour and a half with Nick Gillard. Then he lunches with assistant director Colin Fletcher and me. Then he rehearses with the actors

from 2:00 to 5:00. From 5:00 to 7:00 we go over any changes he's made that day. Then usually between 7:00 and 8:30 it's working through the schedule again and making adjustments on each day's shooting. Then it's home, dinner, and start all over again.

June 30, 2003

Colin Fletcher / First Assistant Director The mood of a set is always set by the director. George is so calm and knows what he's doing it makes for a quiet set. Everyone gets on with it. It's a nice environment to work in. It's great for actors as well, to come on a set

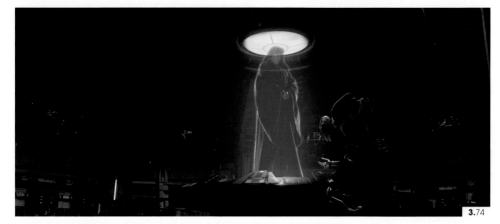

3.74

where there's no tension. That all comes from the director. And the speed of the set is also dictated by him—we have to keep up as best we can.

Shooting began on June 30, 2003. Breakfast for 140 was served before crew call at 7:00 a.m. on Stage 2. The first scenes to be shot were set in the hallway of the Separatist cruiser with the elevator doors at one end. In scene 5B, Obi-Wan and Anakin order Artoo-Detoo to stay with the ship in the hangar. In scene 23, the Jedi emerge from elevator at the General's quarters, Obi-Wan feels the presence of Count Dooku and warns Anakin, "Careful, the jaws of the trap are about to snap shut." Lunch was served for 681 cast and crew working on and off set. Lucas completed 48 setups by camera wrap at 7:10 p.m.

John Knoll The shoot for this show was remarkably similar to the shoot for Episode II, in that we were shooting in the same studio, with the same crew. Very quickly, we fell right back into the work rhythms we'd established in the last show.

Samantha Smith / Third Assistant Director The actors arrive on set and do a rehearsal. George has a clear idea of what he wants and where the actors will stand, so we'll set the shot for focus and lighting with the stand-ins. Then the actors will step in. We'll do maybe one rehearsal with them, and then Colin will call out, "Final check," for wardrobe and makeup to make sure the actors are all right for the take. Then Colin will yell out that we're rolling, and he'll say, "Bell up," which means for me to ring the bell and make sure that everybody stands still, is quiet, and knows that we're about to roll. Then he'll roll up, and then George calls his action. When we've cut, we'll ring two bells. That let's people know that they can get busy and working on whatever they're doing.

George Lucas In Episode III, not much was new, but it was more. It was completely shot digitally. We used lots of digital sets, where

3.74 *Final frame showing General Grievous, who has escaped to Utapau, seeking instruction from Darth Sidious on their future strategy.*
3.75 *Ryan Church's concept for the planet Utapau's surface resembles a sandy ocean floor (April 22, 2004). This was created after the main shoot had concluded, and refers to shot UJA 10.*
3.76 *The sinkhole planet, Utapau, used to be underwater, hence shells and fossils can be seen as part of the environment, as seen in this Tiemens concept art (January 8, 2003).*

3.75

UJA 10
RYAN CHURCH
22 APRIL '04

3.76

3.77

3.78

3.77 *On the balcony of her apartment Padmé finally gets to spend some time alone with Anakin.*

3.78 *Final frame: Anakin has woken from a nightmare in which he had a vision of Padmé dying in childbirth.*

3.79 *Anakin consults Yoda on the meaning of his dream. As a Jedi he is not allowed to marry or have children so he talks more generically about having premonitions of "pain, suffering, death." This scene is set in darkness, a concept that visually opposes what we know about the Jedi Order, in that they are perceived to be a force for good.*

before we only had a few; we had huge numbers of digital characters, where before we just had a few. Now, we're able to intermingle them more seamlessly, so it was taking the technology we developed on *The Phantom Menace* and *Attack of the Clones*, using it to tell the story, and then having the story be bigger.

John Knoll On Episode II, we used the first-generation Sony CineAlta cameras, which worked well, but we had to be careful of an overexposure characteristic. David Tattersall had worked with the cameras before we got into principal photography and tailored his shooting style a bit. We got good images, but it was because we had a good DP shooting them. When we went to III, almost every aspect of the HD experience improved considerably.

3.79

3.80

The production had four Sony HDC-F950 HD-CAMs with Fujinon E Series digital cinema-style lenses, recording to Sony SRW-5000 4:4:4 HD recorders, all of which could be moved from stage to stage in 15 to 20 minutes.

George Lucas The cameras have autofocus now, the lenses are better. A lot of the wires have been condensed down into one wire instead of many wires. Small changes, but it makes a difference.

Mike Blanchard There was a fiber connection from the cameras to the video village, so we could record directly onto HDCAM SR studio decks. Those decks have a 4:4:4 sampling rate, which is a big improvement over what we had for Episode II and part of the reason Episode III looks so stunning.

3.80 *After Anakin has visited the Jedi Temple he goes to the Senate Office Building to meet with Palpatine, who appoints him to be his personal representative on the Jedi Council. This sequence, set in the daytime, is brightly lit, another visual conflict in a scene where Palpatine begins manipulating Anakin in earnest. The Yoda and Palpatine scenes follow one another, reflecting the conflicting emotions within Anakin since he has to choose between selfless duty and selfish love.*

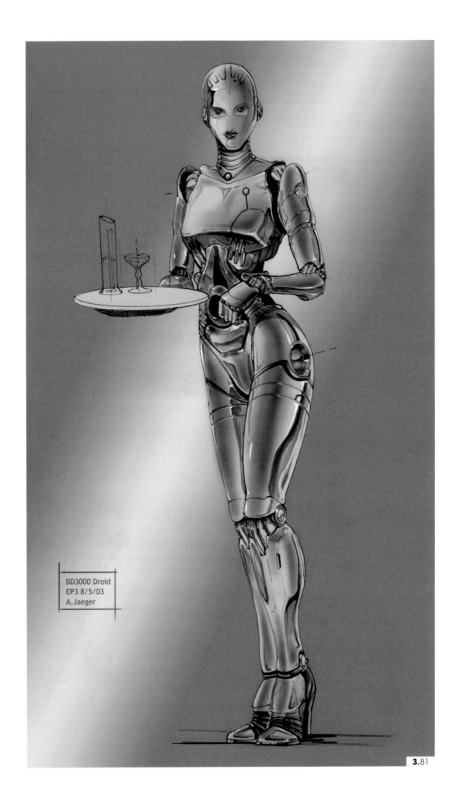

BD3000 Droid
EP3 8/5/03
A.Jaeger

3.82

John Knoll 3-D matchmove supervisor Jason Snell is getting measurements of camera positions and set measurements.

Rob Coleman / Animation Director George Lucas is like no other filmmaker I've ever worked with. He thinks of the first unit shoot as the place where he captures his elements. Most directors set up a master shot, the wide shot of a scene, and start there and go into coverage, and so does George. But George goes one further. He goes back to what he's called the control take, and the control take is the set without any actors. This will give him a clean plate of that set environment, which may only be standing here for one day of actual shooting. Later on, he will be able to shoot his actors in front of blue screen, and ILM will composite the actors into the clean plate. George will not have to come back and have the expense of building that set again, because he's got it digitally.

On July 2, the unit moved to the interior of Padmé's apartment on Stage 1, to shoot scene 69, where Obi-Wan visits Padmé to express his concern for Anakin and to ask for Padmé's help since he knows that they have feelings for each other.

Scene 71 shows Padmé, Mon Mothma, Bail Organa, and other senators discussing the Chancellor's subversion of the constitution, and how they are to challenge this with the "petition of the two thousand." Later, in scene 75, Anakin tells Padmé, "I feel... lost. I'm not the Jedi I should be. I want more but I know I shouldn't."

3.81 *Alex Jaeger's concept for the BD-3000 droid (August 5, 2003).*
3.82 *Tiemens's concept for a meeting in Bail Organa's office (June 13, 2003). Lucas wrote a scene in which various senators, including Padmé, Mon Mothma, Fang Zar, Terr Taneel, and Giddean Danu, meet in secret to discuss the Chancellor's increasing power and the ineffectiveness of the Senate. Bail and Mon Mothma have set up an organization to try to prevent Palpatine becoming a dictator. All those present realize that this is a very dangerous proposal. The scene was filmed on July 30, 2003, but was later deleted from the final print.*

George Lucas There's a bit more soap opera on this one than there has been in the past, so setting the scenes up and staging them was more complex than it usually is. Normally, we would have rehearsals at the beginning of the film. We would read through and then rehearse certain scenes that were tricky. Then we would work out the staging on the set as we were shooting each day, and do the rehearsal as we shot it.

3.83 *Concept for Jedi Master Plo Koon in battle dress and wielding a two-pronged lightsaber by Derek Thompson (December 6, 2002). Lucas has stamped it "OK" for the costume but not for the lightsaber.*
3.84 *Anakin takes his place at the Jedi Council as a personal representative of Chancellor Palpatine but is insulted that the Council refuses to promote him to Jedi Master. He is later asked by Obi-Wan to spy on Palpatine, a conflict of interest for Anakin given that he is Palpatine's representative. His loyalties to his two mentors, Obi-Wan and Palpatine, are being tested.*
3.85 *Additional Jedi designs were needed to fight the Clone Wars and for the Jedi Council. Derek Thompson suggested a Wookiee Jedi (December 6, 2002).*

3.83   OK

This one, because there was a lot more complex staging, I would take the week's work and on the previous Saturday I would spend all day rehearsing with the actors and the cameraman, and we would stage the scene and rehearse it a couple times. So for the rest of the week we would have a very clear vision of what we were doing, and we didn't have to spend time on the set trying to figure things out.

The unit moved back to Stage 2 on July 4 to shoot scene 66 on Padmé's Veranda, where Padmé and Anakin argue about politics (Padmé: "Have you ever considered that we

3.84

WOOKIE JEDI
DEREK THOMPSON
12·06·02
SW 3

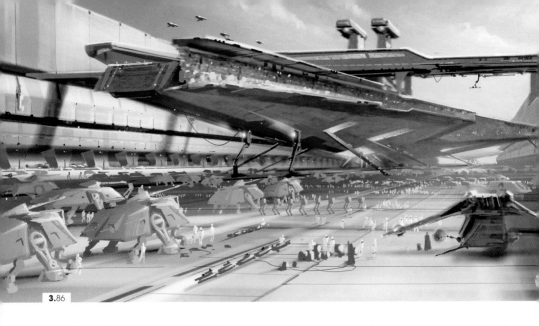

may be on the wrong side?") but eventually allow their love for each other to defer any serious differences that they might have.

Paul Duncan Right from the beginning of their relationship Padmé and Anakin argued about how to negotiate political problems. Padmé wants to explore all diplomatic avenues, while Anakin, despite being a Jedi, is often keen to pursue more "aggressive" solutions. You set up that dilemma in Episode I: the Jedi go to negotiate a peace with the Neimoidians but a war starts; then Padmé asks the Senate for help, but they will not give it; so the Naboo join with the Gungans to get their planet back.

George Lucas People are upset by the fact that the whole series started out with a blockade over a trade dispute. Well, that's how wars start. That's how they lost the Republic. The whole Republic went under because the bad guys took advantage of the fact that the Senate couldn't come together about what they were going to do. It was encouraged by the commerce guilds, which wanted to make money. That's all they wanted to do, make money.

Paul Duncan There's a cut line from Episode II where Padmé tells Dooku that businessmen are becoming the government.

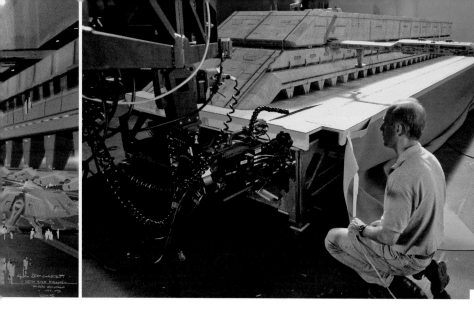

3.87

George Lucas Yeah. That's how a democracy dies. It's true.

Paul Duncan Padmé tries democratic means to curb Palpatine's power, but they fail, and she realizes that democracy is not going to work.

George Lucas That is when Mon Mothma, Bail Organa, and Padmé started the Rebellion. That's usually the way it works. You have the peasants who are rebelling around the galaxy but getting wiped out, and then the intellectuals and people in power organize a serious Rebellion. Padmé's a key player, but Mon Mothma is the one who's leading it. Of course, Padmé doesn't get to take part in the Rebellion because she goes into childbirth and dies.

Paul Duncan It's implied that she lost heart.

George Lucas Yes. Her soul has been crushed. The thing that breaks Padmé's heart in the end is that Anakin says to her: "Come and join me. I have all the power now. I can rule the universe and you can do it with me." So the idea of saving her life has become a minor issue. And that's when she says, "Wait a minute. This is not what I want, and you're not the guy I fell in love with!"

3.86 Ryan Church's art for shot CJG 200 showing the loading of the Star Destroyer on the clone landing platform (December 11, 2003).

3.87 David Owen inspects the miniature of the Coruscant clone landing platform. Even though the film was shot digitally and most of the postproduction generated in a digital environment, models and miniatures were still used where it was considered to be more efficient and cost-effective to do so. In this case, the miniature was used for two scenes.

3.88 Final frame of the gunship landing as Yoda prepares to go with clone troopers to Kashyyyk to help the Wookiees fight the Separatists.

The Rule of Two

George Lucas There was never a war between the Jedi and the Sith Lords. The Sith Lords were in control for a long time. And what happens when you have a world full of Sith Lords? They start killing each other to see who's going to be the top Sith Lord. They don't vote; they just kill. It's like a medieval feudal system.

There may have been thousands or millions of them and eventually, after 100 or 150 years, they killed everyone except for two. And the more powerful of the two decided, "You're my apprentice. I'm your master. I will pass on my knowledge to you to keep the dark side of the Force alive." But he would keep a close eye on his apprentice.

But the arrangement never worked because the apprentice was constantly trying to recruit another person so that the two of them together could be more powerful than their master—they could kill him and take over. Likewise, the master is also looking for another apprentice, so that he can keep the first apprentice in line. The rule of two ensures that if there's more than two, they'll kill each other until there are two left.

Then the Republic came to power and the Jedi brought peace to the galaxy by being ambassadors and troubleshooters. So when

3.89 Set construction of Padmé's apartment and veranda on Stage 2 of Fox Studios in Sydney, Australia.
3.90 Final frame of Anakin's return to Padmé's apartment. They sit together and Anakin puts his hand on his wife's belly to feel the baby. Amidst their personal happiness they also discuss their growing concerns about the Jedi Order and the nature of democracy within the Republic.

the Senate decides to do something, or the Jedi Council discover something that's amiss, the Jedi fix it. The Jedi don't like to fight or kill people. They're monk-warriors. They're monks first, and they try to convince people to get along. And if you don't comply, your hand comes off. They use their power to keep the governments of all the planets in line, so that they don't do terrible things.

Paul Duncan And they have the moral authority for that?

George Lucas Yeah. They are the most moral of anybody in the galaxy. They're monks.

The Sith practice the dark side and are way out of balance. The Jedi aren't as much out of balance because they're the light side of the Force. They still have the bad side of the Force in them, but they keep it in check. It's always there, so it can always erupt if you let your guard down.

The Emperor snookered the Jedi with Order 66. The nascent Rebellion and the Jedi didn't move fast enough.

Paul Duncan They're fallible.

George Lucas They're not super people.

Paul Duncan They've been as manipulated and outplayed as everybody else. Darth Sidious had ordered the clone army pre–Episode I, so it feels like they lost from the beginning.

George Lucas Nobody knows who ordered the clones. It's played as if it were somebody from the Jedi Council who foresaw there was going to be a war, so he was preparing for it, but it turns out that was somebody working for Palpatine, Sifo-Dyas. He was the apprentice before Darth Maul.

Paul Duncan And then Count Dooku took over from Maul.

George Lucas With Count Dooku I set up the idea that some of the Sith Lords were fallen Jedi who went to the dark side. The Emperor picked them up and trained them in the dark side, but they were already trained to use the Force as Jedi.

Palpatine told Dooku, "I have somebody who I think will become a great Sith Lord and I think we can get him to join us, but we need to test him. So we're going to set up a situation where you fight him. If he gets the best of you, then I'll stop the fight and he'll have passed the test. If you get the best of him, then we'll let him go, and we'll let him stew a few more years until he's ready." But behind it, obviously, is Palpatine's real intention: if Anakin is good enough, Anakin can kill Dooku and become Palpatine's apprentice. But he didn't tell Dooku that.

I have to say one thing for Palpatine. He goes through apprentices pretty quickly. That's why he wants Anakin. Because it's hard to get help and this Anakin kid is going to be good.

Paul Duncan He's a keeper.

George Lucas He's better than all these other ones. He thought, "I'll put him up against Dooku and see who wins," and Anakin won.

The rule of two is referred to in all the movies — Darth Vader wanted Luke to join him in Episode V: "Come with me, my son, and we'll

3.90

3.91

rule the galaxy together." Every time you come across a Dark Lord, he always wants somebody else to be there with him so that they could take over. It's the same when the Emperor is trying to get Luke to kill his father in Episode VI because he thinks Luke's stronger than his father.

In Episode III Anakin becomes a Sith, becomes Darth Vader, when he kills Mace. Even at the end, he says to Padmé, "I can be more powerful than the Emperor," and he wants her to join him, but she refuses.

That's greed. Greed means that you're either afraid you're not going to get what you want, or you're afraid that, when you get it, somebody's going to take it away from you. It's all fear driven. You've got to not be greedy. It puts you in a bad place, and then you're unhappy.

So, philosophically speaking, that's how the whole thing fits together, and that is what drives all the stories.

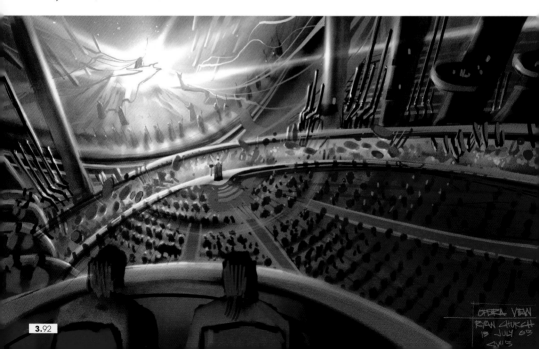

3.92

OPERA VIEW
RYAN CHURCH
13 JULY 03

3.93

Scene 99

Ian McDiarmid I got the script for Episode III, like everybody else, a few days before we were ready to shoot, and I was knocked out by the fact that George concentrated so much on the relationship between Anakin and Palpatine to the extent there were these enormous dialogue scenes. Which is great, but daunting.

At 10:00 a.m. on Saturday, July 12, George Lucas met with actors Hayden Christensen, Ian McDiarmid, and Samuel L. Jackson, as well as David Tattersall, script supervisor Jayne-Ann Tenggren, dialogue coach Christopher Neil, and Samantha Smith, on Palpatine's Office set on Stage 7 to rehearse and block scene 99, where Mace Windu tries to arrest Palpatine but the Chancellor fights back. At 10:30 a.m. Jackson left and the remainder continued with scene 67, where Palpatine tells Anakin about General Grievous in Utapau, sows dissent against the Jedi Council, and recounts the story of Darth Plagueis the wise.

George Lucas I said, "My God, this is a four-page scene—I've had five scenes in Palpatine's Office already!" So I moved it to an opera house, playing a ballet, *Squid Lake*, which worked out great.

3.91 *Final frame of Senator Chi Eekway (Katie Lucas), Baron Papanoida (George Lucas), and Senator Terr Taneel (Amanda Lucas, center) in the corridor outside the main auditorium.*
3.92 *Church's concept for the opera house interior includes the view of the opera Squid Lake from Palpatine's private box (July 15, 2003). This design follows a conventional theater configuration of the audience looking upon a stage at the rear of the theater. The final design had the opera stage located in the center of the auditorium with audience seating surrounding it to give a more immersive 360-degree experience.*
3.93 *Palpatine (Ian McDiarmid) tells Anakin the story of Darth Plagueis the Wise, who "could keep the people he cared about from dying." This is the final trigger for Anakin's seduction to the dark side.*

Since scene 67 required a new set to be prepared, it was moved back in the schedule to the end of the week. The rehearsal continued on scene 94 (in the hallway between the Chancellor's main office and anteroom, Palpatine reveals to Anakin that he is a Sith Lord) and scene 89 (in the main office, where Palpatine implies that Padmé is hiding something from Anakin) until 1:00 p.m.

KASHYYYK CITY - LOW/ WARM
RYAN CHURCH
12 NOV 05
SW'3

"Kashyyyk was a combination of all sorts of things: digital stuff, background plates that we shot in Thailand and China, and water elements that we photographed in San Francisco. It was like a giant jigsaw puzzle. You put it all together and Kashyyyk comes out the other end."

Roger Guyett / Visual Effects Supervisor

As a result of the rehearsal, script changes to scenes 67, 94, and 99 were delivered on July 14.

Scene 94 was shot on July 14. The following day scene 89 was completed and work began on scene 99, where Mace Windu enters the anteroom with three other Jedi. Anakin is with the Chancellor (this continues from scene 94), so Palpatine Force-moves Anakin's lightsaber to his hand and lunges at the Jedi; all but Mace are killed. The scene continued filming on July 16.

Gavin Bocquet It's quite a fluid process. Originally, the fight started and ended in the main room. As George saw the space evolve, he

and Nick saw that the fight might be better moved into those environments.

Rob Coleman The fight between Sidious and Mace Windu is a cool fight—it starts in Sidious's anteroom, goes down a long hallway, and into the big room.

Ian McDiarmid I imagined that the Emperor, when he achieved his horrible apotheosis,

3.94 Ryan Church's concept for the forested Wookiee planet Kashyyyk (November 12, 2003). In the foreground can be seen the Wookiee ornithopters and catamarans skimming over the lagoon.

would only have the electric lightning emanating from his fingers, because that's what he had in *Return of the Jedi*. But no, he has other skills. When I read this script he seemed to have turned into Action Man.

George Lucas You're always using stunt doubles for action set pieces. It's just a matter of whether you use them more or less. For the older actors, Christopher Lee, Ian, and Yoda, it's more difficult for them to do the highly physical types of work, so you use a combination of stuntmen and the actors to create the sword fight in a way that is realistic and looks good. The huge advantage we have now is that we don't have to hide the stunt double's face the

COMMAND CENTER

FINAL KASHYYK TREE
RYAN CHURCH
6 APRIL 04
SWD

3.95

way we used to; we can put digital faces on the stuntmen, and we can film closer to them.

Nick Gillard I was lucky enough to get Kyle Rowling again to double Count Dooku. He doubled Dooku on *Attack of the Clones*, and he brought a friend of his along, Michael Byrne, to double Palpatine.

Rick McCallum It was always our idea to use stunt doubles to do the majority of the work but George was reluctant to do that. He wanted to be close-up. He wanted to be right on Sam's face and on Ian's face. It's a fight of close-ups, a fight of the two of them sensing who has the greater strength.

George Lucas The fight has to be changed. You can't change Ian. You've got to change the fight.

Rick McCallum So on the day Ian and Sam had to learn everything. It was a testament to Nick and his ability to think on his feet and to solve the problem. We got the film back on track after 30 minutes of discussing what we needed to do.

Palpatine lunges at Mace Windu and forces him back through the hallway to the main office. During the swordplay, Mace shatters the window and disarms Palpatine.

Samuel L. Jackson I had to learn, I think, 97 moves in two to three days, and then learn to speed them up over that period. It's an elaborate sword dance: more so than a fight because your feet have to be coordinated to back up, back up, stop, turn, twist, move, jump, run, and do all this other stuff. I had learned to move at a specific speed with Michael Byrne, then we had to incorporate Ian into that sequence, and Ian didn't have that speed and dexterity yet because he wasn't expecting to do the fight.

Rob Coleman It was evident that Ian could stand and move his hand — Sidious holds his lightsaber in one hand — but moving around the room was not his strong suit. So

they changed the schedule a little bit and gave Ian a little bit more time to practice. A day after, Ian came back and could do a lot more. So Nick obviously had spent some real quality time with him, and I'm confident it will be fine.

Filming on the scene continued on July 17. Palpatine is at the mercy of Windu's lightsaber so he attacks with Force lightning, which Windu reflects back, causing Darth Sidious's face to become disfigured. This meant McDiarmid had to don the "mask of evil" as it is referred to in the script.

3.95 *Concept art for the Wookiee tree by Church (April 6, 2004). It is titled "Final Kashyyyk Tree" and shows the command center located just above the tree's main branch looking out over the water.*
3.96 *It took 13 weeks to construct and detail the 12-foot model of the Kashyyyk tree.*

3.96

3.97

3.97 *Final frame showing Chewbacca (Peter Mayhew), Yoda (Frank Oz), and Tarfful (Michael Kingma) confer with the Jedi Council via hologram to update them on the situation on Kashyyyk.*
3.98 *Church's concept art shows the Wookiee command center as the Separatist attack begins in the background (January 31, 2003).*

Ian McDiarmid For the best part of 30 years I've been switching between two different makeups on a regular basis. These makeup guys are getting good at it now, and they've got it down to an hour and three quarters. Now I think they could probably do it in their sleep. They certainly do it in mine.

Paul Duncan When Windu has Sidious at his mercy, and decides to kill him — the Chancellor has the Senate and the law courts in his pocket so will never face justice — it is set up as exactly the same dynamic as with Dooku on the starship. Yet this time, Anakin decides to save the captive.

George Lucas Anakin's rationalization is "Everybody is after power. Even the Jedi are after power. Therefore, they're all equally corrupt now. So which side am I going to be on? Do I align myself with Palpatine, who is a Sith Lord and who can possibly help me save Padmé? Or do I side with the Jedi and maybe lose Padmé?"

Paul Duncan Anakin goes to the dark side, severs Windu's hand, and Sidious forces Windu out the window to fall to his death.

KASHYYYK
- HOLOGRAM ROOM -
RYAN CHURCH

3.98

Rick McCallum Sam had to jump out of a window. We were going to put him in a harness, but Nick turned to Sam and said, "You're not going to have a harness. You're a star. You're jumping out that window and you're going to jump onto a stunt mat and that's the way we're going to do it." And Sam said, "Okay, I like that. Fantastic." And that's all they did all afternoon. Sam kept on jumping off the balcony and jumping into the mat. They have fun with it. That's what Nick is able to do with our actors.

Samuel L. Jackson I feel pretty great about that whole fight scene. I've been waiting for a scene like that my entire life, ever since I was a young man pretending to be an Errol Flynn–like swashbuckler, fighting with sticks. It's amazing!

A Solid Block of Evil

Ian McDiarmid The great thing in playing Palpatine is that it's clear in Episodes I and II that he's a hypocritical politician, so that's what you play. And then there is this dark

3.101

3.99

3.100

person in a black robe who crops up. He's a solid block of evil. No redeeming features. Except one: he has a scene set at the opera. He's obviously a patron of the arts.

On July 18 and 21, Lucas shot scene 67 at the opera house, where Palpatine continues his seduction of Anakin to the dark side.

3.99 *The shot of the Wookiees leaping through the barricade to fight the droids was directed by Rob Coleman on May 17–18, 2004. The image is comprised of multiple takes of the same group of six actors in costume, switching positions and weapons with each new shot, to give the impression of a greater number of Wookiees.*
3.100 *The actors playing the Wookiees were so tall that the crew needed stepladders to reach the topmost parts of the costume.*
3.101 *Church's art shows the Wookiees meeting the droids in battle on the water (August 30, 2002). The monopod droid tank was designed by Church for Episode II but was not used.*

Hayden Christensen Ian does such an amazing job of playing the puppet master. He pulls each string with such charming yet evil precision.

Ian McDiarmid I like Hayden very much, and he's a fine actor. You know that when you are working with somebody eyeball to eyeball over several very tightly shot scenes. He's a wonderful listener, and everything passes across his face. As Palpatine, I'm having to look very closely in those eyes and see what emotions were going on to manipulate him, and every take I would get something different from Hayden to use as raw material. It was enormously exciting to work with him. It's interesting that in the previous film not everyone understands his behavior, and his behavior isn't particularly understandable, but I think in Episode III a lot of people will look back and understand why his character behaved as he does in Episode II. He is a confused young man, to put it mildly.

Hayden Christensen Anakin's very conflicted and being pulled in different directions. Palpatine is picking up on some of his frustrations and his wants and needs.

Fourth Draft, Yellow Revisions, July 3rd, 2003   62*.

69 CONTINUED: V69A   V69B   V69C   V69D   V69E   69
    V69
Lost
                        OBI-WAN
            10.You should be a Jedi, Padmé.

                        PADMÉ
            11.You're not very good at hiding your
            12.feelings.

                        OBI-WAN
            13.It's Anakin... He's becoming moody
            14.and detached. He's been put in a
            15.difficult position as the
            16.Chancellor's representative...but
            17.I think it's more than that. I was
            18.hoping he may have talked to you.

                        PADMÉ
            19.Why would he talk to me about his
            20.work?   *
                                                                       *
OBI-WAN studies her.

                        OBI-WAN   *
            21.Neither of you is very good at   *
            22.hiding your feelings either.   *

                        PADMÉ   3/8
            23.Don't give me that look.

                        OBI-WAN
            24.I know how he feels about you.

                        PADMÉ
                        (nervous)
            25.What did he say?

                        OBI-WAN
            26.Nothing. He didn't have to.

PADMÉ is a little flustered. She stands and Obi-Wan follows. She
walks to the balcony.

                        PADMÉ
            27.I don't know what you're talking
            28.about.
                                        V69G
                        OBI-WAN   V69H
            29.I know you both too well. I can
            30.see you two are in love. Padmé,
            31.I'm worried about him.

PADMÉ looks down and doesn't answer.

                        OBI-WAN
                        (continuing)   *
            32.I fear your relationship has
            33.confused him. He's changed   *
            34.considerably since we returned...   *

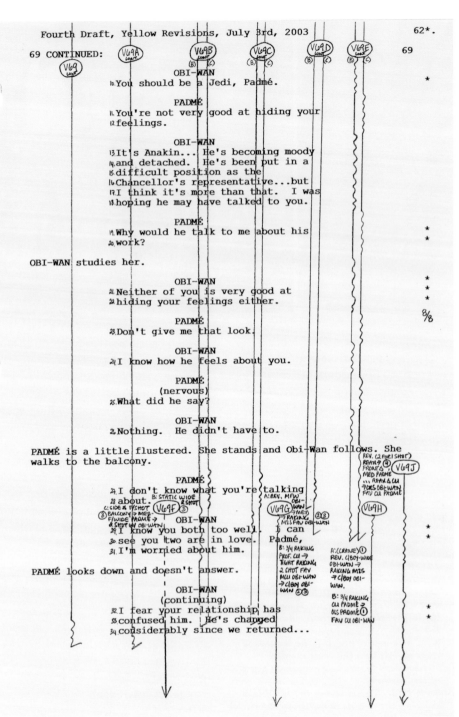

                                                                   3.102

3.103

3.102 *Lined script, a revision dated July 3, 2003, for a scene where Obi-Wan goes to meet with Padmé at her apartment. He reveals to her that he knows she and Anakin are in love. The meeting is interrupted by a call indicating that General Grievous has been located. Obi-Wan assures the senator that he will not tell the Jedi Council about Anakin and indicates that he believes himself to be a friend to both of them. This scene did not appear in the film. Instead, Obi-Wan's meeting with Padmé took place later, after the execution of Order 66.*

3.103 *Final frame: Obi-Wan is leaving for Utapau in search of General Grievous. Anakin apologizes to him for being unappreciative of his training. Obi-Wan lets Anakin know how proud he is of him. This scene's purpose is to highlight that, even though they are Master and Padawan, they have a strong brotherly love for each other.*

3.104 *Palpatine has supplied intelligence that General Grievous is on Utapau, so Obi-Wan departs Coruscant with some Star Destroyers to confront him. With Yoda and Obi-Wan, as well as other Jedi Masters like Ki-Adi-Mundi and Plo Koon, away from Coruscant, Palpatine is positioning himself to take control of the Republic.*

3.104

Sang Jun Lee
SW3. 11. 1. 02
Lizard Creature #2

3.105

3.105 *Sang Jun Lee's concept for a lizard creature, which would form the basis for the Boga lizard (November 1, 2002).*

3.106 *Obi-Wan astride the Boga lizard — his transportation as he searches for General Grievous through the complex corridors inside Utapau's sinkhole.*

Ian McDiarmid When you're playing a dialogue scene in which there are many beats, you can make different choices. Not ones that interfere with the continuity, but you're able, if you can find them in yourself, to offer George and the editor lots of different things.

Christopher Neil / Dialogue Coach Ian has been amazing to watch. He comes from that English stage background where he learns the lines, and he nails it every single time. And it's interesting to watch George sit back and go, "Ahhh."

Hayden Christensen He steals the show. I think so much of why this film works is from his performance. He makes choices I don't know that I could muster the courage to make. And he pulls it off. You can see the process in his eyes. And between scenes, you see him doing that same obsessive, constant analysis of things. He doesn't go anywhere. He stays on set, pacing back and forth.

On July 29, McDiarmid shot scene 137 in the Senate, where Palpatine (as Darth Sidious) crowns himself Emperor of the First Galactic Empire. He also completed a short hologram scene for Episode V, so that he appears in five of the six movies.

Ian McDiarmid The extraordinary thing is that I was an actor in his 40s playing someone around 110, and then to go back and be my own age and play the character at the age contemporaneous to mine is extraordinary. It's a very retrospective journey. I now have the benefit of hindsight and foresight. It's unique in the history of acting.

Level Nine

George Lucas In the dramatic scenes the actors have to understand the character and the emotional content of what's going on, and memorize the lines. For the sword fighting you have to learn hundreds of moves, and memorize them or you get hit in the head. It's a very different focus. I decided that it's better to have the actors focus on their acting for the first part of the filming, and then later on focus on their sword fighting and the action set pieces. To mix those up I think is harder for an actor to cope with.

It's also a very different way of shooting. It's tedious shooting action set pieces because it gets broken down into little pieces. It's not like setting up and staging a scene from beginning to end, having the actors run through it like a stage play, and then covering all the different angles.

There are stunts involved. It's dangerous. It's very physical, and people wear out and get

3.106

tired at the end of the day. We have one of the longest continuous sword fights that has ever been filmed, which meant we had weeks of those guys coming in at 7:00 in the morning and fighting until 7:00 at night with not very much rest. So it was very physically exhausting for them.

Nick Gillard The fighting has evolved considerably in these last three movies. George works on a system of skill levels. Yoda is a level nine. Darth Sidious is a level nine. Mace Windu is a level eight. On *Phantom Menace* Obi-Wan was level six or seven. On this film he's moved up to level eight, which affects his style of fighting. Anakin in *Attack of the Clones* was a level seven. In this film he has moved up to a level nine. He's gone past Obi-Wan, and the difference is because of the dark side. Even though Yoda is a level nine, it's controlled.

You have to go through each level to attain the next level, and if you do it too quick, you're going to get in trouble. Anakin is too young to go through the trials, so he's got to this level too soon. Anakin's downfall is going to be his

3.109

aggression. Obi-Wan is also aggressive, but he has gone through all the levels, taken the time, and learned everything he needs to learn. That's going to give him an edge.

Hayden had to be much bigger on this film, so eight weeks before shooting began he came to train and work out. He'd be in the rehearsal room four hours a day sword fighting, and then spend two or three hours in the gym on a brutal exercise routine, working on specific muscle groups. They sorted out a good diet for him and he put on a huge amount of weight.

I've been working with Ewan now for six or seven years, and Hayden for three years. Both of them are phenomenal at fighting. Brilliant memories. Ewan has over 1,000 moves to learn in this film. He has the most to learn, and he had the least time because he came from another film, so he had three weeks before we started shooting. But he's managed to do it.

Obi-Wan and Anakin should mirror each other because they're master and pupil. They both come from the same line of training — Qui-Gon, Darth Tyranus, Yoda — so they match each other perfectly. The end fight between them is incredibly long. They travel a quarter of a mile, and perform about 800 moves across five sets.

3.107 *Erik Tiemens's concept for Utapau's Level 10, where Tion Medon indicates thousands of battle droids are located (March 20, 2003). Its spherical structure recalls that of the Death Star, even suggesting a super laser concept.*
3.108 *This is Church's idea for shot UTC 170 showing Obi-Wan surrounded by a variety of menacing droids (August 2, 2004).*
3.109 *Fearing that Grievous may leave, Obi-Wan confronts him and is surrounded by Grievous and his guards.*

The fight begins in scene 145 on the Mustafar Landing Platform. After shooting Darth Vader's final scene with Padmé on August 6 and 7, the fight with Obi-Wan began filming on August 11. They continued on August 25 in the Conference Room, and spent the next six shooting days, up to September 2, on the epic duel. They finished the final part, in the Control Room, on September 9.

George Lucas The sword fight is very realistic; it's not sped up. Hayden and Ewan are both very good and obviously as actors there's a little bit of competitiveness about who's going to be the better sword fighter. So we got some very good performances out of them, trying to be better than the other guy.

> *"I wanted to make Grievous move differently, as if he's not fully in control of all his mechanical pieces, which is kind of creepy and weird."*
>
> Rob Coleman / Animation Director

Hayden Christensen Ewan and I were constantly hitting each other, and I still have scarred knuckles from the reshoots, and Ewan the same. The lightsabers become a liability, and so you have to be 100 percent present at all times when you're doing the fights.

Nick Gillard We've got two good stunt doubles for Obi-Wan and Anakin, but they rarely get to work because the boys do it pretty much themselves.

The Right Shot

Rick McCallum We had two editors: Roger Barton and Ben Burtt. Ben was in California while we were shooting in Sydney so he could continue to work on all the animatic sequences that still needed to be filmed. Roger was in Sydney the whole time. We were simultaneously cutting the picture while we were shooting.

Roger Barton / Editor George said, "Don't expect to see a lot of me while we're filming," and he's held true to that. His parting words to me were "Go ahead and cut your own *Star Wars* movie," and that's what I'm doing.

When George shoots something in the morning, generally I'm working on it that afternoon. When I think a scene is complete, I'll piece it together as best I can with what footage I have. The advantage to having me here is in the very few cases where I feel like we're missing a beat that would enhance a scene, I communicate that to George, and he can decide whether or not he wants to shoot it here, or pick it up in a reshoot.

Ben is working at the Ranch doing animatics of the big action set pieces, so when there is live-action footage for the space battle, or for the Utapau fight and chase, I send that directly to him so he can work that stuff in.

The most important part of editing for me is when I make my select rolls. I'm looking at all of the dailies that were shot, and taking pieces out of it that I am emoting to. So in building those select pieces I am able to craft the scene together. Once the scene is evolving, there are always choices that an editor has to make. What's more important? Is it what the person is saying, or is it the reaction to what the person is saying? I'm a big fan of reaction shots because what I'm telling you may not be as important as how you are responding to what I am saying. The actors are great in giving me those reactions. As an editor, I'm trying to be on the right shot at the right moment.

As fun as it is to cut the action pieces, if you don't care about the people, they don't mean a whole lot. So I hope that what I bring to the movie is a sense of character

3.110

3.110–111 *After Obi-Wan dispatches the guards, General Grievous orders his droids to stand down: "I will deal with this Jedi slime myself." Final frames of Obi-Wan battling with General Grievous, who has twice the number of arms and four times the number of lightsabers.*

3.111

DROID GENERAL ROUGHS
DEREK THOMPSON
12-20-02 SW 3

3.112

3.112 *Derek Thompson's sketchbook for General Grievous as well as additional droids and vehicles that he might use* *(December 20, 2002). Note that in these rough ideas Grievous has a gun attachment on one arm.*

development and storytelling. It's funny because so much of this is shot against the blue and green screens without the distracting backgrounds that all I have to focus on is the performances. It's allowed me to zero in on what's going on within the characters, and between them. As I told George when he asked me how cutting was going, I said, "Basically performance is motivating about all my cuts." The actors are giving me good material.

Right now my favorite scene in the movie is when Obi-Wan goes to Padmé's veranda and tells her that Anakin has turned to the dark side. The scene, right now, is like butter. It works on so many different levels. Natalie's performance is excellent. You can tell that Obi-Wan is torn because he has been asked to kill his Padawan, to kill his best friend. You can see the heartache. The scene is wonderful. Reading it on paper didn't have nearly the same effect on me as seeing the scene play out. I cut with music, so I use John Williams as often as I can. And adding music to that scene was the clincher.

I've probably got an hour and 30, 40 minutes cut. If you take into consideration the sequences that have been cut by Ben using the animatics, then we probably have well over two hours cut. Most of the heavy dialogue scenes are already shot, and what's left on the schedule are the fight and action sequences which won't take up too much screen time. So, I'm hoping the first cut will be under three hours.

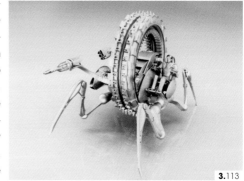

3.113

3.114

3.113–114 *3-D computer models for Grievous's vehicle designed by T. J. Frame (December 20, 2002). The original concept was that the droid was autonomous, that the wheel allowed it to move at high speed over smooth surfaces, and that the feet would allow it to crawl over uneven terrain as well as to climb rock faces. Lucas asked for it to become the general's vehicle, so this revision seats the general adjacent to the giant wheel.*

Imprisonment

B-Roll Log / June 18, 2003 Costume props supervisor Ivo Coveney says that they will be making Darth Vader's helmet to fit Hayden better. The original helmet was asymmetrical. He has made a new faceplate, and scanned it. Ivo says that their system makes things quicker, except the computer has crashed.

B-Roll Log / June 28, 2003 A prop is being cut by a computerized machine. Ivo explains that Darth Vader's faceplate was made in this machine. The rough cut took over 30 hours and the fine cut takes 19 hours. "At least this way, I will know that the face will be symmetrical. When I come in tomorrow morning, it will be done. By the end of tomorrow, we will hopefully have the other half, and

3.115

3.115 *The landscape proves hazardous in Derek Thompson's concept, which shows both Obi-Wan and Grievous, as well as their mounts, caught in the grip of tentacled creatures (March 27, 2003).*

3.116 *Erik Tiemens conceived a vast cavern with Grievous and Obi-Wan fighting top right, while figures and a beast watch from below (March 27, 2003).*

we will see how the entire face looks." Ivo shows in a book how Darth Vader's designs have changed between movies. Ivo says that Darth Vader will be on set in four weeks, "So we will probably be ready in three weeks and six days."

Ivo Coveney / Costume Props Supervisor We can't work out how the head fitted onto the shoulders. Gillian Libbert, our costume archivist, has fitted many Vader people over the years, and she's said it's never fully worked. So our biggest challenge is to make sure that the neck works beautifully with the shoulders, so that Hayden is far more comfortable.

B-Roll Log / August 5, 2003 Ivo had a fitting with Hayden last week: "We've made lots of subtle improvements and changes. We realized that from a certain angle, it looked like there was no back to the helmet, so we are adding a piece inside the back to fill it out."

B-Roll Log / August 6, 2003 Ivo has been painting the Darth Vader head black. "We have a fitting with Hayden tomorrow. Hopefully after tomorrow's fitting, we can start molding him. Costume designer Trisha Biggar will show tomorrow's photos to George. Everybody knows the image of Darth Vader, so you think it would be simple, but we have discovered that it is quite a complicated piece. Spraying it black made our perception of its size different."

Scene 174 was shot on September 1. Darth Vader rises from the operating table, entombed in a suit that is keeping him alive. Darth Sidious tells him that Padmé is dead.

3.116

"*Originally, George asked us to make some droids that can chase Obi-Wan, who's on a lizard that can climb walls. So this was meant to be a droid in and of itself. Then later he said, 'Yeah, make that into the droid general's vehicle.'*"

T.J. Frame / Concept Artist

3.117 *Grievous and Obi-Wan face off armed with a blaster and a lightsaber in this Church artwork (January 9, 2003). Grievous later carried an electrostaff.*
3.118 *Final frame of Obi-Wan jumping across from his trusty Boga onto Grievous's wheel droid as the vehicle hurtles through the Utapau landscape.*

Enraged that he is too late to save her, Vader cries out. It was the first time Christensen wore the suit on set.

Hayden Christensen It took about 20 minutes to get suited up. There's no Darth Vader underwear; I wore my own. It starts off with the pants, followed by the boots and a massive muscle suit. There's a leather jacket, then a fiberglass chest piece. Then there's a leather jock piece, which looks a little funny. Then it's the helmet and the cape. The lights on the costume don't start blinking until they plug you in on the set. As each piece comes on, layer by layer, you feel the essence of Darth Vader overcoming you.

To make adjustments for my height difference, they put huge lifts in the shoes, so it was difficult to walk. I told George I needed to practice walking around in the costume, because my movements were so rigid and I didn't feel like I was walking like the Darth Vader we knew from the original trilogy. He told me, "That's what I want. Anakin is not acclimated in this suit yet. He shouldn't be able to walk effortlessly." It was an interesting choice.

Being behind the Vader mask is almost indescribable. It's so cool. It's empowering. A beastly feeling wells up inside you — and there's a sense of imprisonment. I thought that was appropriate for what Anakin should be feeling. But it's claustrophobic in there: your vision is extremely limited, it's hot and it's awkward to move around in.

You can see what's directly in front of you and straight down because you're not seeing out through the eyes — you're looking out through the mouthpiece. There's no fighting in it — just walk, hit the mark, and say a line. That's about the extent of it. I was a little nervous because I didn't want to fall over and scratch the suit. Having George look at me, and smile ear to ear — it was one of those surreal moments that will stay with me for a very long time.

George Lucas Having Hayden finally make it into the suit completes the circle of the movies. That's the final missing piece; now they're all connected.

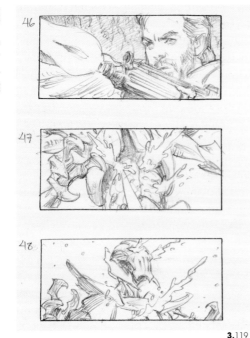

46

47

48

3.119

Shot: **USP519**   Type: **3D/A**   Frames: **59**

Printed on 10/25/2004   Page 3

USP519—Tk1—CGEP3-19886   08-26-04

34

Description   **Bid Notes**

Flames shooting from Grievous' eyes

May have spots on far side

Mandril should shake around a little
to have the flames be able to have
whip to them.

— Could introduce some spurts

3.120

Rick McCallum It was probably the most powerful moment I've ever had on set on anything I've ever done. It was a seminal moment. There were lots of films prepping at the studio, so a lot of people were around, and they all heard that Darth Vader was going to appear. There must have been about 1,500 people gathered outside the stage, so we opened it up and let everybody that we could inside and sit down on the floor.

Hayden put the mask on. It was absolute unequivocal silence. All of a sudden, you could hear a few people losing it. For most people, especially the crew, and a lot of the actors, *Star Wars* was one of the first movies they'd ever seen, and a big reason that a lot of them got into the business.

Afterwards I got 10 cases of champagne and 40 cases of beer over to the stage. Everybody went completely berserk. We opened up the stage doors and got completely drunk. I don't think people got home until midnight that day. It was a very emotional evening.

Pathetic

On the morning of September 1, Ewan McGregor and Hayden Christensen shot the scene on the lava beach where Obi-Wan defeats Darth Vader and leaves him to die. The shot was completed with VFX.

Roger Guyett / Visual Effects Supervisor
We're looking down on Obi-Wan as he slices and dices. It's a fast bit of lightsaber work seen in this overhead spiral maneuver, which was done with a digital double. Obi-Wan gets the better of Anakin and cuts off two of his legs and his left arm, so he's left as a torso with his metal right arm.

Then Anakin lands on the bank of the lava river, which was done with Hayden wearing blue over his arms and legs so we could digitally remove them, and he catches on fire because he's so close to the lava. We shot a dummy torso catching on fire, plus Hayden wearing burnt clothing and a number of different stage makeups that we're joining together with some individual fire

3.119 *In Iain McCaig's storyboard Obi-Wan uses a blaster to puncture Grievous's gutsack, and Grievous explodes. On August 21, 2003, while performing the scene Obi-Wan's dialogue was changed so that as he walks over to Grievous's carcass he looks at the blaster and throws it away saying, "So uncivilized."*
3.120 *Notes for shot USP 519, the demise of General Grievous, dated August 26, 2004, that defines the visual representation of the pyrotechnics, including "Flames shooting from Grievous's eyes" and "Could introduce some spurts."*
3.121 *Filming Obi-Wan's battle with Grievous (Kyle Rowling) against a green background with a basic model of the ship in the background. Kyle Rowling is dressed in blue to provide a physical reference for Ewan McGregor to interact with during the fight.*

elements. Then, when he's on the bank and on fire, you see the dark side manifesting itself in Anakin's face — we added an element a bit like Sidious's horribly scarred face. It is extremely horrific.

George Lucas It's important at the end that you see the physical transformation of Anakin into this burned-up crisp because that's the suffering he had to live with for the rest of his life.

Dave Elsey / Creature Shop Creative Supervisor I asked George in one of our very first meetings, "How much can we burn him?" He said, "It's going to be a bad burn, but for PG." I went away and spent about a week doing designs trying to do PG-rated burns, and eventually I went back to him and said, "I don't know what a PG burn is. I think we should try and push it as far as we can." George said, "Okay, then we'll make it a PG-13." I thought, "Wow, that was unbelievably easy." That freed us up to do a very realistic full-on burn.

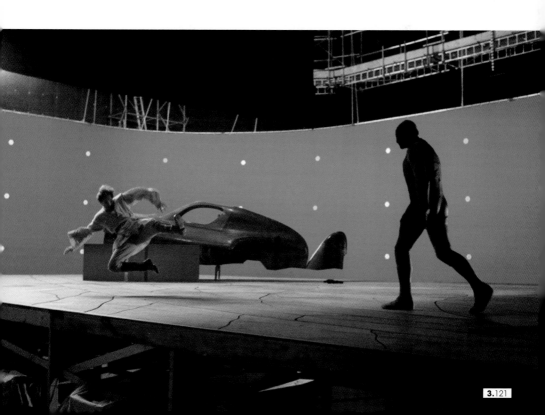

3.121

EP3 — Matchmover Plate Information Sheet

SCENE# V94R   LOCATION PALPATINES OFFICE   DATE 7/14/03

Roll# A18   CAM.Report#_____   4 Perf or 8 Perf

SHOT DESCRIPTION: MS ANIKEN + PALPATINE, TRACKING AROUND.

4 PM FILTER___ — **CAMERA & LENS Information**   T2·8 2

Camera A	Lens 12mm	Height start: 5'5" end:	Tilt start: 2·3b end:	Pan start: / end:	Dutch/Roll start: / end:	FPS 24
Filter Aspect Ratio: 1:77 ~~1.85 2.35~~	Film Stock					Focus 8'

Camera Mount: sticks / crane / (dolly) / steadicam / car
Camera Move: lock-off / pan&tilt / dutch (roll) / (dolly) / boom / crane

Take:	Lens:	Notes:
1	12mm	LONG ZOOM
2		
3		STARTED DIFFERENT POSITION
4		

3.122 *The Matchmover Plate Information Sheet, dated July 14, 2003, showing the camera tracking as Palpatine tempts Anakin toward the dark side. Anakin and Palpatine circle each other as the young Jedi realizes that his mentor is Darth Sidious.*

3.123–124 *Anakin finds out that Palpatine is the Sith Lord the Jedi have been seeking. Palpatine wonders aloud as to whether the young Jedi will kill him, and he can feel that Anakin wants to. Palpatine is confident that he can use the power of words to persuade his protégé. Indeed, the Sith Lord is so assured that he faces away from the young Jedi, even as Anakin wields his lightsaber. In the background is a frieze, requested by Lucas, depicting an ancient battle between the Jedi and the Sith, the light and the dark, as planned and sketched by Erik Tiemens and executed by model maker Richard Miller.*

On September 2, Christensen filmed all the scenes requiring him to wear the burn make-up, as Darth Vader is found on the lava beach by Sidious, taken to the Imperial rehabilitation center, and operated upon.

Hayden Christensen Filming was grueling, but afterward, when they call "cut" and you go in to have the prosthetics taken off, you feel fulfilled. It's amazing how emotionally involved you are in this film, watching the relationship between Anakin and Obi-Wan fall apart, watching them fight, and then that end result. It's tragic. As Anakin makes that final transition into Darth Vader it informs the original trilogy and changes the character. He becomes a much more pathetic figure.

Dave Elsey I took my producer, creature shop supervisor Becky Hunt, and my wife

3.123

3.124

3.125

3.125 *Final frame showing Padmé in her apartment, unsure of what the future holds. She is powerless in this situation—yet she is one of the reasons that Anakin turns to the dark side.*
3.126 *Anakin wrestles with his conscience because his loyalties are divided. Instructed to wait while Mace deals with the Chancellor, Anakin has betrayed Palpatine to the Jedi, and yet he is in agony at the thought of losing Padmé.*
3.127 *Final frame showing Saesee Tiin (Kenji Oates), Agen Kolar (Tux Akindoyeni), Mace Windu (Samuel L. Jackson), and Kit Fisto (Ben Cooke)*

draw their lightsabers as they prepare to arrest Palpatine. In the shooting script, immediately after Palpatine reveals himself to be a Sith Lord, Mace arrives to force the Chancellor to relinquish the emergency powers given him by the Senate. This meant that Anakin was present while the Jedi were being killed, but did nothing. Lucas reconfigured the action so that Anakin reports to Mace that Palpatine knows how to use the dark side of the Force, is told by Mace to stay at the Jedi Temple, and only arrives at the end of the battle, when Mace has the helpless-looking Chancellor at his mercy.

Lou to the rushes, and we watched him go through this torture, and suddenly I went, "Oh my God, what have we done?" The lights came up, and I turned to Becky and asked, "Do you think we got away with that?" She was crying. She said, "That was horrible, really horrible!" We went back to the shop thinking that there might be a phone call telling us there was no way they were going to be able to show this. I fully expected that for about a week, and then a week turned into a year, and before I know it, the movie's coming out and it's got a PG-13, and I think I know why. I know it's horrific, but it's what I wanted to see when I was 10.

Uplifting Moments

On September 3, 4, and 5, the fight scene with Count Dooku and Dooku's execution at the hands of Anakin were filmed on the General's Quarters set. The scenes were all shot with stunt double Kyle Rowling. In fact, Christopher Lee had already filmed his shots on July 31 and August 1 against blue screen and had his head scanned to be used for digital replacement.

Rob Coleman Christopher Lee is another three years older than he was in the last movie. He can still move his arms around quite well, but his legs can't do that much. So for Dooku we did head replacements on the stunt double. There were also some flips and

3.126

other moves that were too dangerous even for the body double to do; so for those shots we did a fully digital Christopher Lee. There's a lot of close-up intercutting between the real Christopher Lee and the digital double, and it's seamless.

On September 11, Ewan McGregor filmed the lightsaber fight between Obi-Wan and General Grievous on Utapau.

Nick Gillard General Grievous fights Obi-Wan a couple of times. Originally he fought with an electrified power staff, but about three weeks before we were going to shoot it George decided he would have four arms and a lightsaber in each arm. Obviously we could

handle two arms, the extra two were difficult. He's very tall so we thought of sitting people on shoulders. We thought of suspending somebody from the ceiling.

Rob Coleman They tried doing it with two stunt guys sparring with Obi-Wan at once, one standing behind the other, so they could have Obi-Wan fighting all four arms at the same time, but that didn't work very well. So they had one stunt fellow learn both the upper-arm and the lower-arm parts of the Grievous fights. Then they shot one pass with him doing the upper arms, and a second pass with him doing the lower arms. We combined those passes on my Mac on the set, so I could look at the fight with all four arms.

3.127

3.128

3.129

3.130

Nick Gillard In the end we decided to cut off two of his arms quite quickly.

On September 15, Lucas filmed the last scene of the movie, scene 180, where Obi-Wan delivers Luke to Aunt Beru (Bonnie Piesse) on Tatooine.

George Lucas Each movie has a beginning, middle, and an end. And each trilogy has a beginning, middle, and an end. The idea is to have each of the endings be inspiring. These are adventure films and comedies, not dark, deep dramas, although bad things do happen.

The ending of the first movie of a trilogy is uplifting, and the last one is uplifting, but the only one that isn't uplifting is the middle movie. Trilogies aren't constructed that way; they have tragedies.

I don't like making a down movie. In *The Empire Strikes Back*, I was worried about the father cutting his son's hand off and about how little boys would take that. But it turned out all right. Lando and Chewie fly off into what was supposed to be a sunset to go rescue Han so that the ending's not a complete downer.

Paul Duncan The end of Episode II was scripted to be the wedding with Anakin's metal hand holding Padmé's, and then Palpatine surveying the clone troopers as they go off to war. But you switched the order in the edit.

3.128 *Having quickly dispatched the other Jedi, Darth Sidious attacks Mace.*
3.129 *Once Anakin has taken sides with Sidious and cut off Mace's hand, Sidious rallies to attack with great vigor, forcing the Master Jedi out the window and to his certain death.*
3.130 *Sidious uses Force lightning to defend himself from Mace Windu, but when Windu reflects it back, it disfigures Sidious.*

"The Senate will decide your fate."
Mace Windu

"I am the Senate."
Chancellor Palpatine

George Lucas This was so that it ended, "And they lived happily ever after." But they don't. The hand shows that he's beginning to turn into the monster.

Paul Duncan The end of Episode III is the middle of the six movies.

George Lucas I had a struggle to make the last couple of shots, where Leia is with Bail Organa and his wife in Alderaan, and Luke is handed over to his aunt and uncle in Tatooine, as uplifting moments. Even though it's at sunset and it was very much like Luke's wistful moment in Episode IV, it's there to give hope.

Episodes I, II, and III are darker in tone because it's the fall of a hero. It's a bit more mythological than Episodes IV–VI, like Siegfried, where he's doomed from the start and you're watching how that happens. Maybe one of the reasons why the comic characters and the humor is a little less successful is because they work better in upbeat movies and don't work in a darker reality.

If you look at the films in order, and you don't know what's going to happen, the ending is better. You know that Darth Vader survived — he's not going to be the hero anymore, but you don't know that he's a monster. And his kids survived too.

September 17 was the final day of shooting. The last scene to be shot featured Darth Vader, the Emperor, and Governor Tarkin on the bridge of an Imperial Star Destroyer overseeing the construction of the Death Star. Dave Elsey had recommended Wayne Pygram to take on the Tarkin role, which had been played by Peter Cushing in Episode IV, noting his physical resemblance to the actor.

Dave Elsey We did a life cast and I started to sculpt on it, and the more I sculpted, the more I realized I had made the most horrific mistake and that Wayne didn't look anything like Peter Cushing!

3.131 *Anakin makes the decision to turn to the dark side and becomes the Sith Lord Darth Vader.*
3.132 *Final frame of Anakin kneeling before Sidious and learning of his new identity: Darth Vader. Sidious instructs him: "Every single Jedi, including your friend Obi-Wan Kenobi, is now an enemy of the Republic."*

Elsey eventually resculpted seven times before he was satisfied. Scene 177 was shot after lunch.

Hayden Christensen Everyone from the crew and the production office came out to bear witness and see Vader again. As I walked past people I knew and was friends with, I watched their reactions. It was phenomenal: there was awe and excitement in their eyes, but there was also a certain level of respect that needed to be paid and a tinge of fear. As I walked by, they would gasp, and then they would lower their heads and take a couple of steps back — as you would if Vader was passing.

There was a hint of sadness when I put on that costume. I was given the job of being the connective tissue from Jake Lloyd in Episode I to Darth Vader. Getting to finally don the dark helmet meant something bittersweet: my task was complete.

3.131

George Lucas called, "Cut," and principal photography was over. Lucas whispered to David Tattersall that he'd asked for an extra shot so that they made 100 setups in a day.

The shoot had taken 58 days total — five days under schedule.

Another World

Ben Burtt / Editor On one of the early episodes of *The Young Indiana Jones Chronicles* that Louise Rubacky was cutting, George wanted to move a scene, but in the new position there was a person in the background standing against the wall that shouldn't be there. George said something to the effect of, "Is there any way we can erase that person?" They used Flame VFX software to cut and paste the wall over the character and eliminated him, as George wanted. *That was a revelation moment.* I could see him thinking, "They took out the character without me having to reshoot or to pay for an expensive optical."

He didn't say anything about it, but my observation was that was the moment that we departed from analog filmmaking. If it's possible to simply erase a character for the sake of the story, and make the continuity work properly, then that opens up a big world, and that's what happened.

We experimented on *Young Indy*, where these seeds were planted. Then with *The Phantom Menace*, we begin to discover that we can manipulate a lot of things in the editing room.

In the past, the material the editor got from the director dictated the things they could do. If I were cutting a sword fight, I'd have Errol Flynn in his coverage, Basil Rathbone in his coverage, their shots together, and a shot of the stuntman doing something. You then thought, "How does it go together?" It's like a puzzle and you cut it together. You

3.133

wouldn't be thinking, "Can I make this guy go faster?" or "Can this person jump higher?" That wouldn't have been considered. But now it could be. So as an editor, you had to learn to think, "What can I do?" I can make them go faster. I can make them jump higher. I can leave one of the characters out of a shot. I can have somebody get knocked off to the side. "Would that be a good thing?" All these other dimensions were added to being an editor. George called it "three-dimensional editing."

It was no longer good enough for an editor to cut together the best of the dailies. For a dialogue scene, I could cut out take two of Padmé and take nine of Anakin, and put them together in the same scene with a split screen. George would expect it. He'd ask, "Did you look at all the dailies?"

"Yes."

"Did you try every combination?"

"Well, most, because there're 500 of them."

"Well let's see if we can find a better eyeline for this shot."

And because of that feedback loop, because we started manipulating so much in the editing room, even the dialogue scenes, he said, "It might be a lot better if we had the actors against blue all the time. Then we could cut them out and put them anywhere

we want." And so George started filming more and more blue screens on *Attack of the Clones.*

Then on *Revenge of the Sith* we said, "Let's not even build sets if we don't need to. Let's have everybody on a floor and it's blue or green. We'll fix it all in the editing room. We'll generate a background. We'll cut the actors out and key them in wherever we want." Every shot becomes a visual effect.

We had pushed nonlinear filmmaking so far that we didn't worry about a lot of things, because we could control everything. Pre-production, production, and postproduction were blurred together. The editing room becomes a way of restaging the scenes. George can include ideas as he thinks of them. "Let's run it five percent faster so there's a little pep in their step." If the actor can't make a tear, we'll add one in the eye. If the actor blinked at the wrong moment, we can take that out — freeze the eyes. "Blink" or "no blink" makes a difference. A blink is the end of a thought, or the end of a sentence, or it's a transition, and we can decide if we want that in the performance. Once you start doing that, it's another world.

Pixel for Pixel

Lucas returned to Skywalker Ranch in October for editing and postproduction.

Rick McCallum George works with Ben from 9:00 a.m. to 1:00 p.m. primarily on the action sequences. From 1:00 p.m. until 2:30 p.m. he has lunch upstairs in the animatics department, working on the visual effects shots to use as placeholders. At 3:00 p.m. George works for three or four hours with Roger, primarily on the dramatic sequences. Together, George, Ben, and Roger are creating the first rough cut so we can see the film just before Christmas.

Roger Barton After George and I cut a scene, it's sent without any backgrounds up to the animatic guys. I may have split the screen,

3.133 *Concept art by Erik Tiemens showing Padmé watching events unfold as the Jedi Temple burns (May 29, 2003). The imagery evokes memories of the then-recent 9/11 attacks.*

3.134 *The Jedi younglings have been hiding from the attack on the Jedi Temple and are relieved to see "Master Skywalker," but he slaughters them all. George Lucas: "I had to turn him into a monster. It's a tough story. You can't make a guy evil without having him do evil things."*

3.134

added people, taken people away, and done all sorts of things with what George has shot, but it's up to the guys upstairs to make a shot out of it. George works with those guys explaining to them pixel for pixel what it is he wants in his backgrounds and in his CG characters. Once we get those shots back it's a matter of, "Does the composition work?" because once you see that shot in context it may be too busy now that the background and everything else is put into it. So we may tweak it further here and, depending on how much work you do to it, we may either ship it upstairs again for a second revision, or we send it to ILM. It's invaluable on a movie like this, where so much of the frame and what the characters are relating to is missing, to have that step.

By October 31 several scenes featuring Yoda had been prepared for Rob Coleman's team to start the animation process.

Rob Coleman People assume that in computer graphics you're always on-model, but that's not true. You'd be shocked how quickly a 3-D animator can pull a creature off-model. We had basic Yoda expressions for the last movie, but we had to dial them in each time. We had 15 animators animating Yoda, and each of

3.135

3.136

them would dial in the shapes a bit differently, which made the final expression look different.

This time, we had eight key expressions loaded in ILM's Caricature software. We could hit one button and there would be "concerned" or "meditative" or "angry" or whatever. We could start animating from there.

The animatics team had to deliver the opening space battle to ILM by the end of 2003.
Rick McCallum I have so much respect for Dan Gregoire and all the animatics crew. They work under such enormous pressure because they have to make real what George dreams up every day. Often we're talking about 40 or 50 shots per day, which means 200 or 250 shots a week, of which only about 10 or 15 will be used. But they have to make the shots

for George to be able to pick them. They're working 90- to 100-hour weeks for three years. Often they spend nights. They've brought their own tents to sleep in and have alarm clocks so they can be woken up at three o'clock in the morning, after a shot's been rendered, so they can start rendering another shot. They are true filmmakers.

I have this brief period until Christmas, during which my job is to set up ILM. If you arrive on a set that has 150 people, and you're not shooting, you still pay those 150 people. In the same way, if you don't make up your mind about a visual effects shot, then you have about 350 people getting paid to do nothing. A film used to have maybe 10 to 50 effects shots; we have at least 2,000. Where you once had $1 million in effects shots, now you have 40 or 50 million dollars' worth. On *Revenge* the production crew worked for nine months, the shooting crew for three months, but the visual effects crew will work for 18 months. And as big as our sets were, we only spent about $4.5 million on all of them combined. We'll spend $10 million on our digital sets.
Daniel Gregoire We handed ILM our space battle sequence animatics on January 8, 2004.

3.135 *Although Grievous is dead, the battle still rages between the clone troopers and the droid army as illustrated in Ryan Church's concept art (September 4, 2003).* **3.**136–137 *After Commander Cody receives Order 66, Obi-Wan is attacked, and he and Boga fall to what appears to be their certain deaths.*

3.138

"The lighting on Mygeeto is very gray and diffuse because there is ash falling, as if there had been a volcanic eruption. There is a big battle in the ash with Ki-Adi-Mundi leading a bunch of troops, who turn on him."

John Knoll

3.138 *Church's concept art for an octuptarra tri-droid attack (December 6, 2002).* 3.139 *Final frame showing Ki-Adi-Mundi (Silas Carson), who has been battling on Mygeeto, executed by his former clone comrades after the implementation of Order 66.*

AnimCam

3.140

ALIEN FOREST
WALKER

3.141

3.140 *Animatic for Aayla Secura as she leads clone troops on Felucia. The clones shoot her in the back.*
3.141 *Ryan Church's concept artwork for a walker on Felucia (October 17, 2002).*
3.142 *John Knoll instructs Nina Fallon, playing Jedi Master Stass Allie, how to ride a green screen speeder.*

3.142

They got Maya files, which they could put into their pipeline and use to do the magic that they do.

John Knoll This was the most complicated space battle in any *Star Wars* movie, in terms of numbers of elements and variety of things depicted. It was also a little different. There has been a space battle of some kind in all six pictures; but for the first time, we set a space battle in the upper regions of the atmosphere — in this case, Coruscant's atmosphere. So it was almost in space, but not quite. We used that as an excuse to do smoke, fire, drag, flak bursts, and a lot of other things you can't do in space.

There is a progression in the opening space battle. We start at one place, thread through a bunch of ships, and end up at Grievous's ship at the other end. There was a big master layout done for all the shots showing where all the ships are. Then sequence supervisor Neil Herzinger wrote a tool that created default animation for each ship, which would move all the ships in a given shot along their central axis. Then we'd customize each shot from there — scoot this ship over a little bit, give this one a little more roll. We also designed a flocking tool to create background space battle action: we defined some paths and said how many of this ship and how many of that ship, and they all flew around autonomously under that tool's control. A lot of that's done to camera: "It's a little empty over here, can you throw some more flocking ships back there?"

We've seen lots of battles between fighters, but we haven't seen what happens when these mile-long ships, vessels the size of Star Destroyers, go at each other. There are dozens of them in this battle.

David Meny / Computer Graphics Supervisor We needed the laser fire to be as automated as possible so, rather than having animators decide how a weapon on a droid was aimed and what it would hit, the TDs

choreographed that, and also determined what the laser fire frequencies were and how fast they were moving. All of the ships had templates for where their guns were—on the left, top, or underneath—so the TD could say, "I'm going to be firing from the left half of this ship toward the right half of that ship." They could select those guns and auto-aim them at the other ship or series of ships. In addition, there were procedural rules that allowed the aiming to change within a shot and to vary along the length of the ship. These were all capabilities that we didn't have for Episode II. We could generate particles for explosions, and when those particles hit a proxy geometry of the high-res ship, our tools would randomly determine whether that explosion blew up the ship or left a little scorch mark. That streamlined the space battle and created the impression that there was chaos going on everywhere.

Jonathan Harb / Digital Matte Painting Supervisor The ship finally descends through the cloud cover and you see the Coruscant cityscape below. Some of those establishing shots were so complex a single artist could work on one shot for months.

Digital Doubles

Rob Coleman We use digital doubles because some of our key actors—Ian McDiarmid, for example—are not swordsmen. We do a shot with a stuntman made up to look as much like Ian as possible. We use laser technology that scans Ian's entire head and compiles a volume of images inside the computer, which our digital modelers use to create a digital version of Ian McDiarmid. Our painters and matchmovers then get involved. The first thing they do is track where the head was. The blue lines tell us whether our virtual camera—our computer camera—is locked into the real camera that George used on the day we shot. Our painters then get rid of our poor stuntman's head, painting it out frame by frame. My crew gets involved at the same time, animating a performance by using the stuntman's expressions as a guide. We move the digital face so that it is emoting. Finally, the compositors get involved and blend them together. I think that was the most successful digital double we've made yet.

Ian McDiarmid It's even more wonderful for me to see the finished film because I think, "Oh, goodness, did I do that?" And the answer is no.

3.144

Episode III

cos020 - v02
06-228-04

000200

Artist: **DORIAN BUSTAMANTE**

3.145

3.143 *Ryan Church's establishing shot for Cato Neimoidia, where the cities are suspended between the planet's rock formations.*
3.144 *Visual script art for scene 107 by Church showing the clone fighters* *firing upon Plo Koon's Jedi starfighter after receiving Order 66.*
3.145 *Dorian Bustamante's digital storyboard showing the attack on Cato Neimoidia (June 22, 2004).*

3.147

3.146 *Yoda, having felt a great distur-bance in the Force upon the deaths of so many Jedi comrades, successfully defends himself against an attack.*

3.147 *Visual script art for scene 110a by Church showing the Wookiees and clone troopers fighting the droid army on Kashyyyk.*

Gutsack

Rob Coleman Originally, General Grievous was this super-ruthless vampire, then he became this sniveling horrible creepy little sycophant, and now he's in between. George made him 7'2" then hunched him over, so he's quite a massive hulking character. For movement guides we studied the original *Nosferatu* (1922), the 1979 remake with Klaus Kinski, and Willem Dafoe in *Shadow of the Vampire* (2000). Grievous has big long cannibal fingers — more Nosferatu than Edward Scissorhands — and does that creepy finger movement when you're not expecting it. His biggest tic is this tubercular cough.

Grievous wears a skull mask, and you can see these sickly puffy creature eyes behind the sockets, as if there's a creature inside, protected behind this bony face. It's a fun acting challenge from our point of view. We have full eyeballs with nictitating membranes, and this greenish puffy skin around them, but otherwise, it's very much a white mask with dark holes for the eyes. That made it interesting to figure out how to emote with this character — no eyebrows, no mouth — and he's got a fair amount of dialogue, too. Behind these protective armor pieces are what looks like this rather disgusting bag of organs filled with beating and slithering things. George calls him the "Gutsack."

As soon as digital modeling supervisor Pamela Choy started building the Grievous model, we realized there were all kinds of issues with the design. A particular pose

3.148 *These Iain McCaig storyboards depict Obi-Wan seeing his former Master Qui-Gon Jinn as a Force ghost in the grotto chamber. When George Lucas was shown these ideas, he said: "We never see the ghost of Qui-Gon; he's not that accomplished. He's able to retain his personality, but he's not able to become a corporeal ghost."*

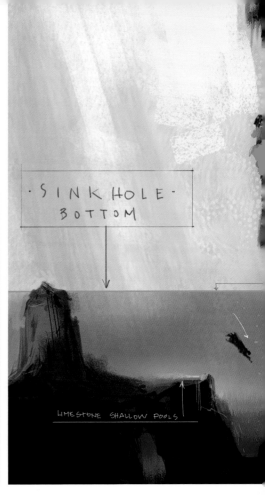

3.148

can look great in a sculpture, but when you start moving the pieces around, you can find that they crash into each other, or that the character doesn't have the range of motion he needs. Even though that design had been signed off on by George, we had to go through another design phase in 3-D. It's an inevitable part of the process, but Grievous required more modification than any character we've ever done. We did some test performances to develop the insect-like movements. Then we added in the vampire idea, and even used a temp voice track that sounded very much like Dracula. But George felt that we were going too far down that road, so we pulled back a bit.

Aaron Ferguson / Creature Supervisor Grievous constantly evolved. The animators would rig a part so it was capable of a certain range of motion, then it would have to perform new movement for which it was not designed or rigged.

Once Grievous was animation-ready, the team began crafting the walk cycles, which ultimately demanded changes to the model. Even changes in his voice necessitated alterations in his walk cycles and overall character, such as his breathing, posture, and the cadence in his step, forcing us to rework some geometrics, rest positions, or other poses.

Rob Coleman Grievous has two cool fights with Obi-Wan, and I'm pleased with how

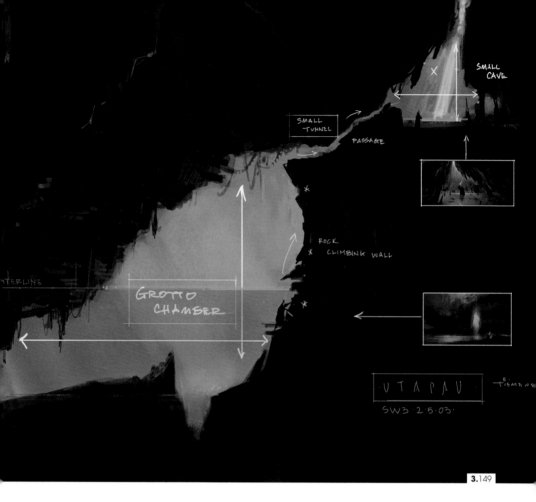

Labels on image:
SMALL CAVE
SMALL TUNNEL
PASSAGE
ROCK CLIMBING WALL
GROTTO CHAMBER
ATERLINE
U T A P A U
SW3 · 2·5·03·
TIEMENS

3.149

3.149 *Tiemens's proposal for Obi-Wan's journey back to the surface: Obi-Wan dives underwater to get into the large grotto chamber, climbs up the rock face, crawls through the small tunnel, and in the small cave grabs hanging vines to pull himself up to safety (February 5, 2003).*

the other two would hit him. Figuring out how to make that work was very difficult, but the animators came up with all kinds of justifications for knocking Grievous a bit off-balance. We had the footage of Obi-Wan's side of the fight, so we knew exactly what frames he would come in on, and we could take Grievous out of phase slightly at that moment. Even George was surprised by how well we got that to play.

they've come out, because there's a lot of interaction between the two of them—physically punching, grabbing, and throwing each other. Truth is, if Obi-Wan were fighting someone with four swords, he'd be a goner, because as soon as he blocked two of them,

The Right Track

George Lucas / March 9, 2004 The first script I wrote had stories for everybody, and I cut it down and we had a script. But when we cut

CAVE MONSTER
IAIN M'CAIG

3.150

it together, there were still problems. Finally, I said, "Okay, let's be even more hard-nosed here and take out every scene that doesn't have anything to do with Anakin." But that causes us to juxtapose certain scenes that we were never contemplating juxtaposing before. We were following Padmé and Bail Organa along with Anakin, and then most of her scenes were cut. Suddenly some of the themes grab hold of each other and strengthen themselves in ways that are poetic.

Ben Burtt / April 2, 2004 The opening action sequence in the film — the rescue of Palpatine from the Separatist cruiser by the Jedi — is an hour long. It's half a feature film, from the time they arrived in their spaceships until they get back to Coruscant. I've known for a long time that it's never going to survive as a whole, because it was out of proportion to the rest of the story. So we've cut out two-thirds of it to get the sequence down to a manageable

20 minutes or so. Shaak Ti, the Jedi taken captive by Grievous, is gone. The huge fuel generator sequence is gone. A sequence where the Jedi cross a hangar on the pipes with Palpatine, and R2-D2 rescues them, is gone. The Jedi don't meet General Grievous in the Shaak Ti scene anymore, but later when they're captured and taken to him on the bridge of the ship. There are continuity issues taking out these big chunks — we've solved that as of yesterday by bringing them together in a different way.

There are some serious story issues in the film — Anakin turning to the dark side wasn't satisfying in the last screening. George is brainstorming to fix some of that.

Roger Barton / April 4, 2004 After Palpatine reveals himself as a Sith Lord, Anakin goes to tell Mace and the Jedi Council. That was never in the original script; it was never shot. That is a scene that we came up with here, added dialogue to, and this whole sequence is intercut with Obi-Wan in Utapau. So when we come back to Anakin, Mace has already told him he doesn't trust him and he wants him to stay behind while Mace goes to arrest Palpatine. And so Anakin once again feels betrayed and untrusted. We just finished editing a scene where Anakin is reflecting on some of the things that Palpatine said to him in the opera house relating to Darth Plagueis, which was cut out of the movie, knowing that Mace is going to arrest him. Palpatine has been a mentor to him, has treated him very well, and has become a good friend. He also holds the key, most importantly, to the knowledge that will save Padmé. That's very important for us to build in this movie, and I think this sequence goes a long way in helping us get to a believable character arc to take us to the dark side.

This next screening will tell us a lot to see if we're on the right track.

3.151

3.150 *A number of ideas were proposed to add to the drama of Obi-Wan's predicament, including Obi-Wan fighting a cave monster, as per Iain McCaig's concept (January 28, 2003).*
3.151 *As scripted, Obi-Wan climbs up the side of the rock and clings close to a cave as seeker droids approach. Suddenly, a nos creature jumps out of the cave and devours one of the droids, giving Obi-Wan the opportunity to enter the cave and make his escape. Here George Lucas (foreground, left) watches on monitors as Ewan McGregor climbs up to the cave entrance. In the final cut, Obi-Wan is seen evading detection by the seeker droids.*
3.152 *Sang Jun Lee's concept for a cave monster attacking Obi-Wan (February 21, 2003).*

3.152

3.154

3.153 *Ryan Church's concept shows
Yoda being pursued by clone troopers on
Kashyyyk, the searchlight from the
Republic scout walker revealing his location (June 13, 2003).*
3.154 *As scripted, the scout walkers find
a dead Wookiee in a catamaran; a crazy
little creature covered in mud surprises
the clones, distracts them with a Jedi
mind trick, and Chewbacca dispatches
them. This is Aaron McBride's concept
for Yoda disguising himself with mud
(February 11, 2004). In the movie the
scout walkers find the abandoned catamaran and continue their search.*

KASHYYYK · CLONE SEARCH
RYAN CHURCH
13 · JUN · 0'3
JW 3

Wild

Rick McCallum Rob wants to direct and I think he would make a great director because performance is all he's concerned about. But he'd never had the experience of dealing with live action; he'd always directed within the computer. George and I gave him the opportunity to shoot Wookiees in Australia.

Rob Coleman The week before the Wookiee shoot I met with George and we went over the Wookiee hero shots.

On May 17 and 18, Rob Coleman directed the Wookiee battle scenes at Fox Studios.

Rob Coleman We shot the preparation for the battle and the battle itself. The most complicated thing about working today is we have to do multiple passes. We've got six actors in costume, but we've got to make it look like there're 50 of them. So we've got a camera in one position. We set all the lads up on one side, and we have them run over a barricade. Camera stays where it is, we move the guys across, mix around the weapons, and shoot them again. And repeat. Ultimately, these shots will take a week to put together.

They had cooled suits but they would still overheat after about 20 minutes and have to

E TIEMENS · SWS · 5 24 63 · VERANDA ·

take the heads off. To deal with that, I kept rotating them, letting a couple cool off while I shot a couple of others. We had the animatics for 40 Wookiee shots, and we shot all of that stuff. Then, in the last two hours of the last day, we shot some wild stuff — Wookiees cheering, shooting, running, et cetera.

Over the two days Coleman filmed 98 setups, including shots of Temuera Morrison as clones in cockpits for the opening space battle, and the Order 66 montage. Following the shoot, Coleman supervised the animation process at ILM.

Rob Coleman When you see the group of Wookiees jump up and cheer, the first few rows are real performers from my little group of six Wookiees, which I shot over and over again. We were on a big Technocrane, and the crane operator did a fantastic job of eye-balling that move. Then back here, Jason

Snell and his matchmove group, and Brian Cantwell and the layout group, took all of that footage and corner-pinned it so that it looked like it had been generated from one camera — when in fact it was probably eight passes, with a wild camera on a wild Technocrane.

George wanted lots of Wookiees. We had two rows of real Wookiees, so we had to create digital Wookiees, and have them all running out to battle together — we used motion capture for that. Having one of the real seven-foot-tall Wookiee performers do the motion capture work was super valuable. That extra foot makes their strides different and their weight transfer different. So we got the biggest guy from the original shoot and put him in an XXXXL motion capture suit. And because it was the same guy, everything he'd done in Sydney came across the same on the mo-cap stage.

3.155 *Erik Tiemens's concept for Padmé and Darth Vader's farewell embrace before he leaves for Mustafar (May 24, 2003). C-3PO and R2-D2 remain in the background, unwitting witnesses to the great shifts in power in the galaxy.*

3.156 *Natalie Portman and Hayden Christensen filming the scene where Darth Vader, following the orders of Darth Sidious, is about to leave for Mustafar to kill the Separatists and end the war. He tells her: "You need to distance yourself from your friends in the Senate. The Chancellor said that they will be dealt with when this conflict is over."*
3.157 *Final frame showing Padmé and Darth Vader's embrace. Like a Greek chorus the droids reflect what the audience are thinking and feeling; at the end C-3PO says, "I feel so helpless."*

Ben Burtt / Sound Design We brought out some recordings I'd done of bears at zoos for *The Star Wars Holiday Special* (1978), which had a Wookiee family. We blended those with a lot of dogs, coyotes, and a few large cats yelping and barking to create high and low voices, screaming, and crying. That way, we could make hundreds, thousands of Wookiees charging camera, like in *Braveheart*, all barking and yelping as they come.

On July 28 and 29, Peter Mayhew (Chewbacca) and Michael Kingma (Tarfful) were filmed against a green screen at ILM for their scenes with Yoda.

Peter Mayhew I think the mere fact that not many characters from the original trilogy have come back and me being one of them is a remarkable situation. I haven't worn the costume for 14 years. Get in, put it on, Chewie becomes a character again.

Dave Elsey You are hard pushed to fault what Stuart Freeborn did on the original movies with Chewbacca. It's one of the most convincing creatures ever — he's in the movie so much and you never question it. But when the head is at rest and Peter Mayhew isn't moving his face around, nothing moves, because Peter needed to open and close his jaw to operate Chewie's face. I thought perhaps we should put an override system in there whereby we can put some very subtle servo movements into the lips to keep it alive on screen.

George Lucas Peter Mayhew *is* Chewbacca. It's very unique the way he has created the character. The way he walks, and the way he tilts his head, the way he looks, the way he uses his eyes. You know it's Peter.

Unpleasant and Dangerous

Roger Guyett was appointed visual effects supervisor on August 3, 2004, to help complete ILM's work on schedule and was given responsibility for the Kashyyyk and Mustafar sequences.

Roger Guyett Our unit got approximately 650 shots. John Knoll handed what information he had about the sequences to me when I joined the show. Obviously, that's a fairly daunting moment because you think, "My God, what have you got yourself into?"

Greg Hyman / Visual Effects Editor Mustafar is a combination of matte paintings, miniature work, CG lava, digital doubles — it has all sorts of things going on. But a lot of the environment was created using some miniatures, and we put those together digitally.

Roger Guyett The whole mountainous environment is basically three 25-foot miniatures which take you down Mustafar's main volcanic river (upper river and waterfall models), plus there's

3.158

3.159

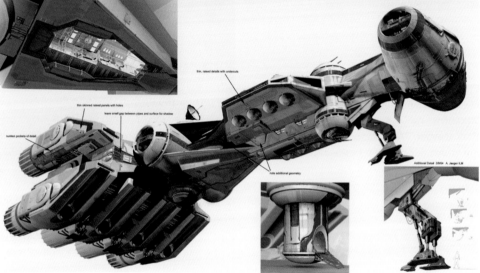

3.160

3.158 *Yoda, Obi-Wan, and Bail Organa (Jimmy Smits) meet aboard the Blockade Runner in this final frame. They decide that they should return to the Jedi Temple to switch off the coded signal luring all Jedi back to Coruscant and to their death, and to learn more about the recent horrific events. The interior of the ship is a recreation of the corridor designed by Ralph McQuarrie in 1975 and seen in the opening scene of Episode IV.*
3.159 *Ryan Church's concept art for scene CSL 270, where Bail Organa boards his*

ship, the Alderaan cruiser, also known as the Blockade Runner, at the Senate underground landing platform and leaves Coruscant with a Jedi homing beacon (June 28, 2004). The scene was cut.
3.160 *Alex Jaeger added detailing to the Alderaan cruiser (March 9, 2004). Top left shows the hangar bay doors opening, bottom center shows the personnel entry / exit pod that lowers, and bottom right shows how the front landing leg folds into the ship when in flight.*

3.161 *Erik Tiemens's concept for a Republic assault ship attacking the volcano planet Mustafar during the Clone Wars, before any details of events on Mustafar had been fleshed out (June 17, 2002).*

a larger-scale beach miniature that Obi-Wan and Anakin end up fighting on. We've added a lot of CG stuff but the miniatures did a lot of the work for us.

Shooting commenced on the Mustafar lava river model on August 16.

Willi Geiger / Digital Sequence Supervisor Brian Gernand and his team made a beautiful 1:132-scale model of the lava river valley on Mustafar.

Roger Guyett We used methocel, a food additive, for the lava river, colored it, and lit it from underneath the Perspex base, because lava emits light.

Willi Geiger They poured the gloopy methocel into the top of the model, sprinkled burnt cork on as they poured, and if they got it just right with the lighting underneath, it looked like a flowing river of lava. That was the starting point for pretty much every shot.

Brian Gernand / Practical Model Supervisor In real life, cooling lava is a bright orange, while hotter lava is bright yellow. We designed our sets so that the lava would flow at different depths. When the methocel moved into the deeper areas, it magically turned a burnt orange because of the volume. When it was out in the edges, where it was more shallow, it was thinner and bright yellow. We learned that the crust was the most important thing in making the lava look realistic. We added a binder to it to make crust pieces clump together at the bottom of the set, bunching up around pinnacles and into corners—just as it does on real lava as the movement slows.

Roger Guyett I'm looking at this sequence thinking, "How do I make that background plate feel unpleasant and dangerous?" Volcanoes have fireballs and molten lava exploding on the surface—that's our arsenal that makes that world exciting. The complex, all the mechanics with its moving arms that dip into the lava, was entirely CG. We also did a lot of simulations, hitting these structures with big forces inside the computer so the gantries they're fighting on are moving around.

Willi Geiger There were around 20 CG elements in a typical shot. We populated the shots with glops and spurts to add detail and give the environment scale, but we mainly used the CG for stuff we couldn't get from the model.

3.161

Patrick Tubach / Digital Compositing Supervisor And we put in a ton of actual volcano events shot by Ron Fricke at Mount Etna in Italy.

Unlimited Power

Lucas filmed reshoots over 11 days from August 23 to September 3, 2004, at Shepperton Studios in London. The majority of the first day was spent on reshooting much of scene 94 in the Chancellor's Office.

Scene 89 has been deleted, so Anakin arrives to give the Chancellor the news that Obi-Wan has engaged in battle with General Grievous. Palpatine continues his seduction of Anakin, continues sowing distrust in the mo-

tives of the Jedi, and leads into the revelation that he is a Sith Lord.

On August 24, Natalie Portman and Hayden Christensen film a new scene, 53A, at Padmé's apartment, before Anakin has his prescient nightmare that his wife will die. This short, sweet, loving scene is the last time that the couple will laugh together.

On August 26, Obi-Wan and Vader are on Mustafar at the volcano's edge, filming the denouement of their battle, when Obi-Wan says: "It's over, Anakin, I have the high ground. Don't try it."

On August 27 and 28, Lucas shot a revised version of scene 99 — the confrontation between Mace Windu and Palpatine, and

Anakin deciding to stop Mace from killing Palpatine.

George Lucas The fight itself was fine. The problem was that the final confrontation between Mace and Palpatine wasn't specific enough in terms of Anakin so we're working to make his conflict sharper. The audience knows Anakin is going to turn to the dark side, but the things that he's struggling with are so subtle that it may be hard for people to understand why his obsession to hold on to Padmé is so strong.

The scene begins with Mace demanding that the Chancellor end the war and relinquish his emergency powers. Anakin enters at the end of the fight. When Mace decides to kill Sidious, echoing Anakin's decision to kill Dooku at the beginning of the movie, Anakin stops Mace for the chance of saving Padmé. The dialogue and staging makes the reason for his actions explicit. Sidious then kills Mace, exclaiming, "Unlimited power!"

A new scene, 85C, was shot on August 30, set in the Jedi landing platform. This is where Anakin reports to Mace that Palpatine knows how to use the dark side of the Force and is probably the Sith Lord they have been looking for.

On September 1 and 2, the end of scene 99, where Anakin Skywalker becomes Darth Vader, was reshot. In total, 469 setups were made over the 11 days.

John Knoll We were shooting lots of little bits and pieces. There were almost no meaty scenes. It was "I need you to walk out, stop, look to your left and right, and then walk forward." I commented about that to George and he said, "This is one of my favorite parts because I'm getting all these pieces that fill the holes. I've been looking at these scenes for a year now, and it's like driving down a road with these big potholes and you get to fill them in, and now it's nice and smooth."

A Good Intention

Natalie Portman Some people think bad people were always bad. They had this tendency toward aggression and control and power from the beginning. I think the most interesting thing about George's theory of morality is that evil comes out of a good intention from a good person.

George Lucas Anakin wants to have a family. He wants to be married to Padmé and have children. When he sees in his dreams that Padmé is going to die, he doesn't know how, but it's preordained. He's in love with her. He doesn't want her to die. He wants to possess her, to control that. He keeps getting himself deeper and deeper into this pickle.

He wants a family but at the same time he knows he can't have one. Now the greed has taken over and the fear of losing his wife and baby. The whole point is you can't possess somebody because they are their own person. You can't dominate and make them do everything you want them to do.

Paul Duncan He had dreams about his mother as well, and he could not save her.

George Lucas Right. He's walking into a death trap. And there's no way out.

Paul Duncan Palpatine has been grooming him by saying how powerful he is.

George Lucas And also saying that "My mentor told me that there was a way that you could stop death." Which was a lie. They

*"**Mustafar's been around a long time. I've always had this set piece: the end between Obi-Wan and Anakin. I knew that's where this movie was going to end up. It's all this volcanic lava shooting up. So it's almost monochromatic in its red-and-blackness. I've had that image with me for a long time.**"*
George Lucas

3.162 *Church's concept for the lava mine installation is one of many that explore the industrialization of the planet (June 1, 2002). The buildings hanging down from the ceiling give a sense of scale to the cavernous mining chamber.*
3.163 *Aaron McBride's concept for the Mustafar landing platform and mining installation (May 27, 2004).*

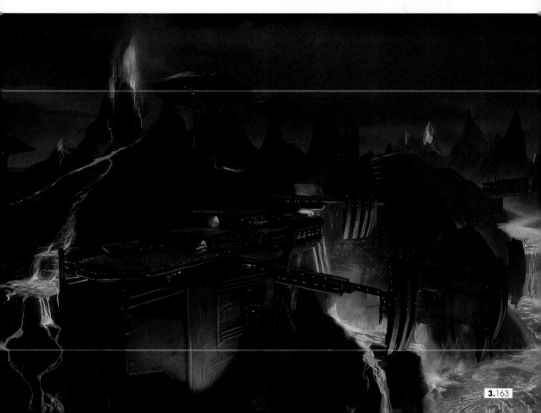

3.164

3.164–165 *The Mustafar Lava Set (Upper River) model was 18 feet wide, 33 feet long, seven feet high, and built at a cost of almost $172,000. Model-shop Bid Form (June 4, 2004): "Bid for construction of high detail lava flow set. Lava will be methocel flow, bottom lit for color, with particle dressing on surface to achieve molten lava look. Lava flow will also be plumbed with air lines to achieve bubbling lava. Set will be built with the ability to change the angle, and control the flow rate. This bid does not include methocel, nor does it include delivery and recovery system."*

can't. Anakin got sold a bill of goods because he wanted it so bad that he'd believe anything anybody would sell him.

Paul Duncan Palpatine's a snake oil salesman.

George Lucas It's a scam. Anakin's made a pact with the Devil: "I want the power to save somebody from death. I want to be able to stop them from going to the river Styx, and I need to go to a god for that, but the gods won't do it, so I'm going to go down to Hades and get the dark lord to allow me to have this power that will allow me to save the person I want to hang on to."

Ultimately, it's about power. He's traded his soul for power. It's *Faust*. The more power he wants, and the more power he gets, the more he loses. The Devil says, "You can become more powerful but you must pass this first test. The first test is you must kill your mother. The second test: you have to kill your wife. And the third test: you have to kill your best friend." In the end you have all this power but you have nobody to share it with, except some wizened old man who's even more evil than you are.

If you're going to sell your soul to save somebody you love, that's, as we say in the film, unnatural. You have to accept the natural course of life. Death is obviously the biggest of them all. Not only death for yourself but death for the things you care about.

Paul Duncan After the suit has been put on, Vader emerges and starts crushing everything around him. Why does he not revolt against Darth Sidious?

George Lucas He hears that Padmé died. He got put on the operating table before he got a chance to save her, and she died. So it's more railing at the gods or the fates that "Given another month, I could've saved her."

3.166

He thinks he was powerful enough on the landing platform before Obi-Wan intervened, so he looks at it as bad luck or fate that he couldn't get the thing accomplished in time to save his wife.

And now it's over. She's dead.

Vader was going to be extremely powerful, but he ended up losing his arms and legs and became partly a robot. So a lot of his ability to use the Force, a lot of his powers, are curbed at this point because, as a living form, there's not that much of him left. So his ability to be twice as good as the Emperor disappeared, and now he's maybe 20 percent less than the Emperor. That isn't what the Emperor had in mind. He wanted this super guy, but that got derailed by Obi-Wan. With Luke, he can get a more primo version if he can turn Luke to the dark side. Luke is faced with the same issues and practically the same scenes that Anakin is faced with. Anakin says yes, and Luke says no.

Paul Duncan So why is Vader now subservient to Darth Sidious afterwards, if he cannot save Padmé?

George Lucas What else is he going to do? It's hard for somebody like that to get a job, you know.

Paul Duncan I've got a vision now of Darth Vader picking up his local newspaper, looking through the job ads.

George Lucas "Wanted: Thug."

Paul Duncan "Must be over six foot three."

George Lucas Right. But he's all vengeance, hate, frustration. It's all the dark side anger. He's steeped in that now. He's going off on his revenge life to take it out on everybody. He's got a job.

Sidious says, "You're going to be my special right-hand guy." Nobody else in the Empire thinks that much of him. He's not this see-all, know-all, powerful, evil guy — he's mostly a beat up tin can. But he's powerful in a way that only the Emperor knows, which is with the Force. Nobody else believes in the Force. I mean, the Jedi had the Force and it didn't help them much — they all got killed. So, he's a regular guy, in a bad situation, doing bad things.

Lamentations

John Williams / Composer I think the greatest opportunity we have in film music is to create an emotional element in a scene that may be already there, but perhaps we can enhance it. And if it isn't there, we might suggest it. If there's a scene between two very animated and opposed people who are actually lovers, the music may be telling there's something else, a kind of undertext about what their mental state may be. It can also support action. If a horse race accelerates toward the end of the event, the music may want to be in sync with that, push it along, and accelerate with it. If the music gets too fast, it may make the action seem a little bit slow. And vice versa. Another important part of music for films is the opportunity for a composer to create a melodic identification for a particular character or a place, so that when you see that person, or that person is mentioned, or suggested even by someone's thought, that theme can be played and it's an aural identification for the listener. So in terms of atmosphere, identification of melody, action, choreographic timing elements in the music, it's part of the corpus, the body of what a film is.

On October 13, 2004, John Williams visited the Ranch for a music spotting session.

"We had eight months on the Mustafar miniatures. I believe it was the longest single miniature shoot in ILM's history. There was every sort of setup, and they were all immensely complicated."
Roger Guyett

3.166 *Darth Vader kills the Separatists, as instructed by his new master, to end the Clone War. Here we can see his eyes have turned yellow, showing that he is drawing upon the dark side of the Force.*
3.167 *The Mustafar war room interior set with the actors playing the Separatists costumed and ready to shoot.*

3.167

3.168

3.169

3.168 *Visual script art by Ryan Church and others for scene 133 showing Yoda and Obi-Wan discovering the slaughter of the younglings at the Jedi Temple. In the background much of the structure of the Jedi Temple has been destroyed.*
3.169 *Obi-Wan learns the awful truth that his former Padawan and friend has pledged allegiance to Palpatine and has become Darth Vader.*
3.170 *Erik Tiemens's concept art showing Obi-Wan switching off the false signal requesting that Jedi return to the temple. The visual representation of the room was inspired by the image of stacked DVDs.*

John Williams I have to confess it's always a little bit daunting when I first see these things. My first impression is usually, "My God, so much? I'm not going to be able to write all that." I may ask George something like, "How many weeks did you say we've got to do this in?" and he'll tell me, and we laugh. I was very impressed with this film, particularly the last third of it. I had some very positive and very strong reactions to seeing the film, along with my usual first shock.

I typically work backwards. I have to think about where the music is going to be at the end of the film and decompose it. So if it's something you're going to hear in the late part of the film, you'll have suggestions of that early on in the film. So I need to study the film,

> *"Twisted by the dark side, young Skywalker has become. The boy you trained, gone he is...consumed by Darth Vader."*
>
> Yoda

and get to work on sequences that have to do with the denouement of the story.

I usually look at the film and say, "Where do I know I can start? What am I reasonably sure about? What can I handle at this particular moment without knowing more about the music?" It's probably like a sculptor who will look at a stone and think, "Where do you want to risk injuring the stone?" So I'll usually start with something straightforward to give me a sense of security. I write a few measures, or even more than a few measures, and pretty soon the information begins to suggest itself as one works it out. You keep chipping away at the stone, and weeks later it's got the beginnings of a face on it.

Most of this work is intuitive. People say, "How do you know when you're on the right track?" and, I guess, my answer is maybe we never know that. What's important in the work that I do is one finds a rhythm. In any human endeavor, it's not so much the work we do but the quality of the sustained work that we perform that will get us some distance to where we want to go. We always fall, I think, a little bit short of what we might want to achieve.

There are three or four pieces of new material. A couple of them have to do with what I call lamentations—they accompany Anakin's turn from the light to the dark. There's also a fun piece, a lot of percussion for Grievous. But in this film, more than any of the other five, there are references to earlier scenes, which seem to me, and to George, to be part of the way we want to tell the story musically. There's a reference to the "Force Theme"—the positive side of the Force—which is referred to more and more in this film. There are even references to Princess Leia's forthcoming arrival. There are quotations of "The Imperial March (Darth Vader's Theme)." And as Anakin is going through his process of change and becoming Darth Vader, we have more and more need to refer to earlier melodic references. And so it's a combination of new material and old material. It's quite a musical tapestry.

3.171

3.171 *Final frame showing Padmé at the Senate to hear Palpatine's speech. She is hopeful that democracy can be restored but is horrified at the outcome. Note that her headpiece is similar to the starbird logo of the Rebel Alliance.*
3.172 *Jimmy Smits (center) and Natalie Portman (right) inside the Senate Pod set.*
3.173 *Obi-Wan implores, "Padmé, I must find him."*

We're going to a new choral piece, "Battle of the Heroes," which does contain some references to "Duel of the Fates," but most of it is entirely new. And again it's Sanskrit, and it's a translation of a very simple line, which is "Grievous are the crimes of the Empire." We don't need to know what the Sanskrit words mean, but from the sound we understand what the emotional intention of it is.

3.172

3.173

The *Star Wars* saga is tragic in many ways, but there's also a new birth, plural in this case, in this film. It has the contour of the great human stories, that people do terrible things and accomplish glowing, illustrious, and wondrous things also. So I think while it has its tragic aspect and that's part of our musical role, it's also very positive.

Totally Cool

On November 2, Lucas and his daughter Katie made a cameo in a scene set in the opera hallway. Lucas plays Baron Papanoida and Katie took the role of Senator Chi Eekway. Both wore blue face makeup.

George Lucas My daughters insisted that I be in it, and so I did it.

ILM continued work on Darth Vader's construction in the Imperial rehabilitation center with real and digital shots.

Roger Guyett The operating table was a practical and they built part of the floor, but then we tricked it out with a lot more stuff going on around Hayden. Basically, the whole rehabilitation center environment is a 3-D digital matte painting. We had this bright light shining down on the operating theater. It's got that ER look, but with a slightly more ominous feel to it

> **"So this is how liberty dies,**
> **with thunderous applause."**
> Senator Amidala

than your local hospital has — or I hope it does anyway.

We shot different pieces for it, including Hayden on the operating table wearing burn makeup and a blue screen suit, so we could track various CG elements to his movements as the droids add on the remainder of the two legs and the arm. We've done combinations of elements of the Vader suit, elements of somebody inside the suit, but you don't see Anakin getting dressed. You see him at the beginning of the process where he's looking in a real bad way, then, after he's been reconstructed, the table is rotated into a vertical position, hence the shot that was seen in the film's trailer — which we later changed. Of course, the moment most people are waiting for is to see the mask going on. First the main face mask goes on, then the helmet comes down over the top of that. We used some live-action pieces of the helmet, but in the wide shots we're using a CG helmet because it was easier to deal with.

George had done an animatic of the mask coming down, but when we were photographing it, I said, "We should definitely shoot

this over length," because I thought the interesting thing would be for the audience to be Vader for a couple of seconds. When George saw the test, he was like, "Yeah! Now I've got to figure a way to make it all cut together." For the interior of the helmet, we thought it would be easier to use a practical helmet since we had it.

Don Bies / Droid Unit Supervisor Ryan Church's direction was that the mask's supposed to look

painful; it goes on easy but it doesn't come off easy. I used the readers from computer hard drives in there—which made it look like if you slipped this thing on your face, it would cut into your cheeks.

Roger Guyett We then added the "Vader vision." We stuck with what was built by the model guys, and added all the electronics—moving screens and that sort of stuff. We went with a sort of night vision but in red and

3.176

some graphic overlays over that. One of the guys working on it said to me, "I've waited 25 years for this moment!" Well, it is a huge moment and it's totally cool.

3.174 Yoda cannot be defeated so easily. The Jedi Master ignites his lightsaber and the Emperor instantly draws his own weapon. The battle between Jedi and Sith begins.

3.175 Lucas directing Ian McDiarmid. The Emperor believes that he has dispatched Yoda using his Force lightning and is delighted that victory is his. Lucas is clearly enjoying the moment as well.

3.176 Visual script art by Church and others for scene 144b showing the battle between Yoda and the Emperor in the Chancellor's holding office beneath the Senate.

Twenty-Eight Years

On January 31, 2005, a final day of filming with Hayden Christensen and Natalie Portman was undertaken at Elstree Studios to complete scenes set in Padmé's spaceship, Palpatine's office, the Federation cruiser general's quarters, and the Mustafar lava river, where Anakin runs up the collection arm as it is about to topple over into the falls. The nine setups were finished by midday.

George Lucas Cut. Last shot. Finished. Rick, it's all over. Twenty-eight years.

On February 2, 2005, John Williams and the London Symphony Orchestra, who had worked together on all six movies, began recording the score at Abbey Road Studios in London. The recording was planned for nine days.

John Williams George Lucas's *Star Wars* films probably demand more music than any other film, in terms of quantity, because the orchestra plays almost exclusively along with the action through the two hours plus of the film. It's a tremendous amount of music, and so one

3.177

3.178

needs to be unencumbered by the insecurity that would not allow us to write so many bars of music a day.

I write the short score, then the eight or so lines that I have written — one each for flutes, oboes, trumpets, trombones, first, second, third violin, et cetera — need to be expanded onto a 32-line score where every instrument is assigned. A copyist extracts the flute part, and the flutist only sees that. And the same is true of the other parts. It's from those parts that the players play. The conductor's job is to bring it all together, coordinate that, and balance it. The balancing issues are addressed maybe 80 percent in the writing of the music, and maybe as much as 20 percent would be addressed on the stage with the orchestra.

When the orchestra comes, they will not have seen the music. The sight-reading in relation to the *Star Wars* orchestra recording sessions is phenomenal. It makes my job in rehearsing, working it up, and getting it ready to record a lot easier than it used to be. And though it begins with sight-reading, it goes so far beyond that. There's a whole area of comprehension that comes with it.

The conductor is responsible for the synchronization of the musical activity with the film; it's a big part of the job. And in many ways it's the most impossible and the most enjoyable part of the job because it's the moment where the music gets up off paper, where it's an abstraction, and becomes a live human thing.

3.177 *Visual script art for scene 145 showing Padmé and Darth Vader embracing as she tries to comprehend what has happened to him.*
3.178 *Obi-Wan reveals himself. He and Vader face off, with Padmé unconscious on the landing platform.*
3.179 *Portman and Christensen playing the final tragic scene between Padmé and Darth Vader. Darth Vader: "Together you and I can rule the galaxy, make things the way we want them to be." Padmé: "I don't know you anymore. Anakin, you're breaking my heart. You're going down a path I can't follow."*
3.180 *Darth Vader is furious, believing that Obi-Wan has turned Padmé against him. His former mentor cannot reason with him and a battle is inevitable. Vader: "You will not take her from me." Obi-Wan: "Your anger, and your lust for power, have already done that. You have allowed this Dark Lord to twist your mind until you have become the very thing you swore to destroy."*

3.179

We may perform the music of a scene four or five times to get it done perfectly. And in my mind, and also the mind of George Lucas, who has been sitting with me for years looking and listening, the second take may be much more impressive than the first or the third, or even the fifth one. Every performance is a different experience because of the conducting, the playing, the temperature, the atmosphere, the time of day, all of it. How people feel.

On days when the orchestra is not recording, ADR dubbing sessions were held with the

3.180

3.181

actors, supervised by Matthew Wood. Frank Oz recorded Yoda's dialogue on February 5.

Rob Coleman Frank slid right into Yoda, no problem. They would record it 10 times with different intonations, and George would say, "I like that one and I like that one." Matt would take a minute and then you could watch the movie with the lines cut right in. So George was able to make sure the reading worked for the length of the shot, and for any body or hand actions. I was afraid Frank wouldn't be able to sustain his voice hour after hour after hour. He must have drunk two gallons of water, but he kept going for five hours.

Anthony Daniels, who has the last line of Episode III and the first line of Episode IV, also recorded his dialogue the same day.

Ben Burtt For Grievous's voice I tried experiments like Vader's breathing, with different

3.181 *Visual script art by Derek Thompson for scene 147 showing the Emperor's battle with Yoda inside the Senate Chamber.*
3.182 *Final frame showing Yoda and the Emperor dueling atop the Senate's central podium.*

electronic tones and different sounds associated with him, but George said he didn't want to confuse Grievous with Vader and the idea was dropped. In the end the voice was executed by supervising sound editor Matthew Wood. He tried out for the part—anonymously—and won it.

A Different Story

George Lucas Most people would never hire a sound editor at the beginning of the process. Every time you make a change in a movie, you have to change all the tracks, and it costs a lot of money to be constantly changing things.

I've always had a very strong belief that sound is 50 percent of the psychological experience of watching a film. I have always hired the sound editor the same day I hired the picture editor. I've always had the sound editor working alongside the picture editor so that when we're looking at cuts, we're looking at things with proper sound, so we don't look

at it in isolation. We can incorporate sound editing into the picture editing work and look at the cuts with those ideas intact so we can say, "that works." So when you get down to the end and you have a fine cut of the picture, you usually have your soundtrack cut. You still have to do some of the ADR and Foley and fix some things, but basically it's finished.

Ben Burtt worked as editor, sound designer, and supervising sound editor on the movie, working with Avid Film Composer, Pro Tools LE, and a 7,000-effect Star Wars *sound effects library on a FireWire drive.*

Ben Burtt George and I have always wanted to have one integrated system for all editing and mixing, including picture. What we would love to be able to do is edit the film on some platform, add the soundtrack to it, and have it behave as if it were Pro Tools, with all of the voices, processing, and 5.1 mixing capabilities right there in the hands of the picture editor. You can do a picture change at any moment and ripple that change through

3.182

3.183–184 *Ewan McGregor and Hayden Christensen filming the duel inside the war room on Mustafar. The set was used as part of the fight choreography.*
3.185 *The fight progresses to the conference room. Darth Vader gets the upper hand using his artificial arm to choke his former mentor.*

all the soundtracks. A lot of the inspiration to mix in Pro Tools came from the idea, "Well, look, we can't combine picture editing quite successfully with Pro Tools and the mix, but we can now blend the sound editing, premixing, and final mixing into one system." And so we decided to commit to that goal on Episode III.

The full trailer for Revenge of the Sith *was released on March 10. It was broadcast with the teen drama TV series* The O.C., *then released online and in cinemas the next day. Episode III was the first* Star Wars *film to be rated PG-13 by the Motion Picture Association of America.*

George Lucas I don't mind a PG-13. This one is a little tougher, and I think children, young children especially, should be warned that this is not your average *Star Wars*. There's a lot more scary stuff in it. It's brutal in places, and they should be aware of that. People think *Star Wars* is extremely innocent, although we do cut a lot of people in half and cut a lot of arms.

Early screenings for Episode III: Revenge of the Sith *took place on May 12, 2005, across a number of cities in the US to raise funds for children's charities. The film went on gen-*

3.184

eral release worldwide on May 19, 2005, and made a worldwide gross of $848,754,768.

George Lucas I am happy with how it turned out, and I'm happy that I now have a 12-hour saga. It is important to me that you can see the whole story, from start to finish. I pretty much got everything I wanted. I'd say they are 96 percent of what I wanted. Even on the first films, I went back and fixed what I didn't like — that was the whole point of the special editions — so now I'm happy with those films, too. I'm not at all frustrated the way I was before.

Paul Duncan You talked before about circles within circles and a bigger structure. The films

3.185

often have mirrored events, so Episode I is like Episode VI, Episode II is like Episode V, and Episode III is like Episode IV. For example, the Gungans fighting the droids is like the Ewoks fighting the stormtroopers, only the Ewoks win; Obi-Wan holding Qui-Gon as he dies echoes Luke holding Darth Vader; the love story of Anakin and Padmé mirrors Leia and Han; the Clone War on Geonosis is like the battle on Hoth; and the rescue of Palpatine in III is like the rescue of Leia in IV.

There are also recurring events: Dooku cuts off Anakin's hand and then Anakin cuts off Luke's hand; the transferal of one father figure to another—Anakin from Obi-Wan to Palpatine in Episode III, and Luke from Lars to Obi-Wan in IV. I could go on. There's a long list.

George Lucas You're right. It's like a mandala. As you write you're doodling, but there are certain themes that keep repeating themselves in different forms. When I did the first film, I planned to do three, so there were pieces in there that I expected to pay off later. That's

"It was exhausting because you have to be at a fever pitch for every take. In II, I wasn't very good at the fighting. I didn't give it my all, really. Whereas in this, I really went for it."

Ewan McGregor

why I put back the Jabba the Hutt scene in *A New Hope* Special Edition, because he was the bad guy for VI.

Paul Duncan Were you conscious of those specifics as you were writing it, or was it an intuitive process?

George Lucas Some of it is intuitive. But after IV I intentionally thought, "Okay, we're showing you an idea, but now I'm going to turn it inside out and show it to you again. Then I'm going to show it to you again in a different way."

And then with the prequels, it became about comparing this is what Anakin did, and

3.187

this is what Luke did. Playing those ideas back and forth was fascinating to me because I was able to intertwine their actions. We have the scene where Anakin decides to save Palpatine and join him, so they could learn how to save Padmé. The equivalent scene in VI is where the Emperor's trying to get Luke to kill his dad so he can save his sister.

If you watch the films in order from I through to VI you'll see a different story from the one you remember. A big scene like the "I'm your father" speech has a completely different feeling when you already know Darth's his father and you're waiting for Luke to find out. Dramatically, I don't think it hurts anything to have some of the answers before you get the question. The films become more about the progression of the characters.

You learn that Darth Vader isn't this monster. He's a pathetic individual who made a pact with the Devil and lost. And he's trapped. He's a sad, pathetic character, not an evil big monster. I mean, he's a monster in that he's turned to the dark side, and he's serving a bad master, and he's into power, and he's lost a lot of his humanity. In that way, he's a monster. But beneath that, as Luke says in *Return of the Jedi* to Leia, "There is good in him. I've felt it." Only through the love of his children

*3.*186 **The fight continues outside the building and onto pipes that lead to the lava collection panels. Aaron McBride's concept art for shot MCB 270 shows the former friends balancing precariously on the pipes.** *3.*187 **Final frame of the fight on the pipes in the intense heat of the volcanic planet.**

and the compassion of his children, who believe in him even though he's a monster, does he redeem himself.

The Real Hurdle

George Lucas On April 30, 2005, we had another digital conference; the only new person joining us was Bob Zemeckis. So, we'd gone from five people to six people in three years. Out of the 6,000 people making movies, there were six of us doing it digitally.

When I did *The Phantom Menace*, I was in four digital theaters. We pioneered that. Then, for *Attack of the Clones* we got into about 120 digital theaters. But for Episode III we were back down to about 80.

Paul Duncan And there were over 36,000 screens in the US.

George Lucas But the problem was a business problem, not a technical problem. Technically, we had it all worked out. It was perfect in every way. The problem we had was who's going to pay for all this?

Paul Duncan What were the economics of film print distribution at that time?

Rick McCallum A print is made in the lab. A teamster has to go pick up that print, take it to the airport. There's another teamster, at the airport in Kansas City or wherever, and he takes it to the theater. Afterwards, by law that print has to be destroyed because it's chemical waste. A teamster has to pick it up, take it back to the airport, another teamster picks it up at the other end, and so on. So a print that might cost $1,500 ends up costing $3–$3,500. If you have 20,000 prints, you've got $60 million in prints.

George Lucas We told the studios, "If you have 15 big movies a year, you could save a billion dollars a year distributing it digitally." But they said, "We don't want to do this."

Rick McCallum It was insane. They were afraid of the unions, the theater owners... You have to remember that if a studio had a movie that didn't make money, and they've got another movie coming on in three weeks, they need that theater owner.

George Lucas And the theater owners and the distributors were always fighting over how much of the box office they would

3.188 *Filming the lava collection panel sequence with stunt doubles. A minimal set was constructed for the panel arm, which was on a rig that could be pulled up to a vertical position. Another part of the set is on the right foreground, so that the cast and crew can quickly set up other shots on the same stage.*
3.189 *Final frame showing Obi-Wan and Darth Vader continue their struggle as they ascend the lava collection panel arm after it has fallen into the lava river.*

get for each movie, and for how long it had to run, and there would be a bidding war between different theaters. So they didn't trust each other.

The theater owners said, "Well, if you're going to save $1,500 per print, who gets that money?" And the other question was "Who's going to pay for these digital projectors?"

Rick McCallum Which cost $150,000 each. You have to remember, the theaters have to keep the film projector right next to the digital projector, because most studios were releasing their movies on film.

Paul Duncan The major Hollywood studios formed Digital Cinema Initiatives in 2002, and it took them three years to issue industry standards for digital projection — in July 2005, after Episode III was released — and then they introduced the virtual print fee in November of that year.

George Lucas For that, the studios take the money, $1,500 a film print, which is about a billion dollars a year, and put that into an account. The theater owners essentially borrow from this fund to buy the projectors, and then they pay back each time they play a movie. The distributors agreed to this because they didn't have to pay all the transport costs, and they didn't want to keep making both film prints and digital prints.

If you look at the figures, the number of digital screens in the US goes from 300 in 2005 to 16,000 in 2010, and to 36,000 in 2014. Pixar and Jim Cameron were key players in all this because they made films like *Up* (2009) and *Avatar* (2009) in 3-D, and people paid more money to see 3-D movies. But the real hurdle was the business part of it, not the technical part.

3.190

Life

Paul Duncan One of the nice things about doing these books over the past few years is that I see that the people working for you now, and those who worked for you in the past, have a great deal of love and loyalty for you and your work. They've had tough but brilliant times.

George Lucas We've been through a war together — there is no other way to describe it. It's intense. We got through it and had the good times, and the bad times, and the pressure, and all the other stuff that goes on through that. They're a good group of people.

Paul Duncan Doug Chiang, Ryan Church, and others described to me how much free-

3.190 *Lucas explains how Hayden Christensen should claw himself up the bank of the lava river. Christensen is in burn makeup with both arms covered in blue; Vader's left arm has been severed, and his mechanical right arm will be added in postproduction.*
3.191 *Obi-Wan Kenobi: "You were the Chosen One! It was said that you would destroy the Sith, not join them!"*
3.192 *In the movie, Darth Vader leaps from the lava river, trying to go over Obi-Wan, but Obi-Wan severs his legs at the knees and cuts off his left arm. Obi-Wan anticipates Vader's move because he had successfully carried out the same maneuver on Darth Maul in Episode I.*

dom you gave them and allowed them to do the best work of their lives. The whole environment that you've created — Lucasfilm, the Ranch, ILM, Skywalker Sound — has been inspirational, so I wonder why you passed control of Lucasfilm on to Disney in 2012?

George Lucas At that time I was starting the next trilogy; I talked to the actors and I was starting to gear up. I was also about to have a daughter with my wife. It takes 10 years to make a trilogy — Episodes I to III took from 1995 to 2005.

Paul Duncan So if you started 2012, you'd finish 2022.

George Lucas I'd still be working on Episode IX! In 2012 I was 69. So the question was am I going to keep doing this the rest of my life? Do I want to go through this again? Finally, I decided I'd rather raise my daughter and enjoy life for a while.

I could have not sold Lucasfilm and gotten somebody to run the productions, but that isn't retiring. On *The Empire Strikes Back* and *Return of the Jedi* I tried to stay out of the way, but I couldn't. I was there every day. Even though the people were friends of mine and they did great work, it wasn't the same as me doing it; it was like being once removed. I knew that probably wouldn't work again, that I'd be frustrated.

I'm one of those micromanager guys, and I can't help it. So I figured I would forgo that, enjoy what I had, and I was looking forward to raising my daughter. Also, I wanted to build a museum, which I'd always wanted to do, so I was thinking, "If I don't do this now, I'll never get that done."

I've spent my life creating *Star Wars* — 40 years — and giving it up was very, very painful. But it was the right thing to do. I thought I was going to have a little bit more to say about the next three because I'd already started them, but they decided they wanted to do something else.

3.191

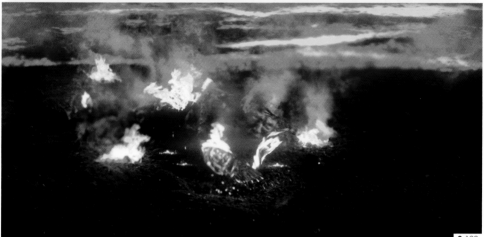

3.192

Things don't always work out the way you want it. Life is like that.

The Chosen One

George Lucas When writing the movies, I tried to make sure that aliens and droids got killed, but not people.

Paul Duncan A lot of stormtroopers died.

George Lucas That's right, but you didn't know they were people. We did kill three humans and that was unfortunate. I was always bothered by it.

Paul Duncan When was that?

George Lucas On the Death Star, when Han and Luke go into the prison with Chewie to rescue Leia, they shoot three Imperial guys. The guards drew their guns and fired first, but it's still a shame.

Paul Duncan Really?

George Lucas Yeah. We very consciously didn't kill very many humans in those movies.

Paul Duncan What about the stormtroopers? They look robotic, but they're not.

George Lucas How do you know *what* they are?

Paul Duncan Did you have a different idea of what they were?

POLIS MAZTA

George Lucas Yeah. They started out as clones. Once all the clones were killed, the Empire picked up recruits, like militia.

They fought, but they weren't very good at what they did.

Paul Duncan That's why they kept missing.

George Lucas That's why they kept missing. Then after the Rebels won, there were no more stormtroopers in my version of the third trilogy.

I had planned for the first trilogy to be about the father, the second trilogy to be about the son, and the third trilogy to be about the daughter and the grandchildren.

Episodes VII, VIII, and IX would take ideas from what happened after the Iraq War. "Okay, you fought the war, you killed everybody, now what are you going to do?" Rebuilding afterwards is harder than starting a rebellion or fighting the war. When you win the war and you disband the opposing army, what do they do? The stormtroopers would be like Saddam Hussein's Ba'athist fighters that joined ISIS and kept on fighting. The stormtroopers refuse to give up when the Republic win.

They want to be stormtroopers forever, so they go to a far corner of the galaxy, start their own country, and their own rebellion.

There's a power vacuum so gangsters, like the Hutts, are taking advantage of the situation, and there is chaos. The key person is Darth Maul, who had been resurrected in *The Clone Wars* cartoons — he brings all the gangs together.

Paul Duncan Was Darth Maul the main villain?

George Lucas Yeah, but he's very old, and we have two versions of him. One is with a set of cybernetic legs like a spider, and then later on he has metal legs and he was a lit-

3.193 *Erik Tiemens's concept for the asteroid Polis Massa (November 7, 2002).* Tiemens: *"This is an homage to early science fiction films and to Life magazine illustrations by Chesley Bonestell of astronauts visiting the moon. There is a shield to protect the base from asteroids."* **3.**194 *Tiemens's concept artwork for the conference room on Polis Massa (January 17, 2003).*

3.193

tle bit bigger, more of a superhero. We did all this in the animated series; he was in a bunch of episodes.

Darth Maul trained a girl, Darth Talon, who was in the comic books, as his apprentice. She was the new Darth Vader, and most of the action was with her. So these were the two main villains of the trilogy. Maul eventually becomes the godfather of crime in the universe because, as the Empire falls, he takes over.

3.194

3.195

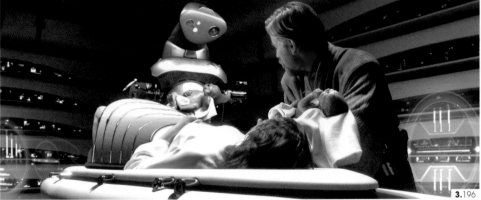

3.196

3.195 *Ryan Church's concept for the Polis Massa medical room where Padmé is being looked after (February 13, 2003).*
3.196 *A midwife droid delivers Padmé's twins; Padmé names them Luke and Leia. Padmé's last thoughts before she dies are of Vader, "Obi-Wan, there's good in him. I know there's still..."*

The movies are about how Leia—I mean, who else is going to be the leader?—is trying to build the Republic. They still have the apparatus of the Republic but they have to get it under control from the gangsters. That was the main story.

It starts out a few years after *Return of the Jedi* and we establish pretty quickly that there's this underworld, there are these offshoot stormtroopers who started their own planets, and that Luke is trying to restart the Jedi. He puts the word out, so out of 100,000 Jedi, maybe 50 or 100 are left. The Jedi have to grow again from scratch, so Luke has to find two- and three-year-olds, and train them.

3.197

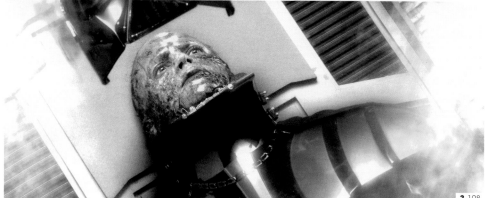

3.198

It'll be 20 years before you have a new generation of Jedi.

By the end of the trilogy Luke would have rebuilt much of the Jedi, and we would have the renewal of the New Republic, with Leia, Senator Organa, becoming the Supreme Chancellor in charge of everything. So *she* ended up being the Chosen One.

Hope and Faith

George Lucas The midi-chlorians started the birth process in Anakin's mother. The Whills communicated the command to the midi-chlorians, which activated the DNA

3.197 *Yannick Dusseault's concept for scene 170, where the critically wounded Darth Vader is fitted with a lifesaving suit (November 7, 2003). There is a clear contrast between the respective medical facilities for Padmé and Vader — the light and warmth of Padmé's medical room contrasts with the foreboding darkness and clinical robotic reconstruction of Vader.*
3.198 *In this final frame, Darth Vader is imprisoned as the headpiece descends upon his disfigured face. We will not see this face again until the end of Episode VI, when his features are revealed to Luke.*

that germinated the egg. That's why Anakin doesn't have a father. He was, in a bizarre and metaphorical way, touched by God, but in this case they happened to be one-celled animals.

Paul Duncan It reminds me of Perseus and Heracles and other heroes of mythology, who receive their powers from the gods, usually because Zeus fathered them. Zeus is an absent father. The theme of fatherhood, or lack of it, runs through the saga. Qui-Gon doesn't quite become a father figure for Anakin, I don't think, but he's certainly somebody in authority who he then loses. Then Obi-Wan becomes a father figure, and later Palpatine. The theme continues with Luke, and even Jango Fett—the Kaminoans are making all these clones of him yet he asks for one to be unaltered so that he can raise him.

George Lucas Jango was a father to thousands, but he wanted a son that was not altered to be obedient. He wanted him to have his own personality and his ability to be self-sufficient.

Paul Duncan Do the other characters, Qui-Gon, Obi-Wan, Palpatine, have that fatherly feeling also?

George Lucas I think so. I think ultimately they want to mentor someone, to pass on their knowledge and training to someone else—that's a part of fatherhood. I don't know whether you'd call it fathering, but it comes very close. Mentor and father are pretty much the same issue.

Paul Duncan Palpatine acts in a fatherly fashion.

George Lucas He's acting as a father, but what he's trying to do is recruit Anakin to be his trainee, his apprentice. And he's doing that because he knows that he has a high midi-chlorian count, so he could be a powerful Sith Lord, even more powerful than he is.

It's like he's trying to build a better spaceship or a better gun, more than it is he's a father. He sees him as a weapon for the dark side.

Paul Duncan So he's a false father, wanting to control him. Obi-Wan becomes more of an elder brother.

George Lucas He's like the reluctant elder brother saying, "You're not leaving him with me. I don't want to babysit anymore. I want to go out and do something good."

Paul Duncan Almost like a Han Solo.

George Lucas Except Obi-Wan has character and takes responsibility. Han Solo would've left him out on a desert planet somewhere.

Paul Duncan When I first saw the films, I under-valued Obi-Wan because I followed Anakin's story, but Obi-Wan became more important to me the more I rewatch the movies.

3.199

George Lucas He changed the course of history because if he hadn't done battle with Anakin, Anakin would have become very powerful and would probably have gone on to be the Emperor of the universe.

Paul Duncan At the end of their duel, Obi-Wan is so personally attached to Anakin that he couldn't kill him. He couldn't bear to see him die.

George Lucas He's human. The Jedi are not superheroes. They're regular people like the rest of us. We all have midi-chlorians. We all have the Force within us. We can all do what the Jedi can do, but we're not trained. And the secret is training. You need somebody to train you because it won't come by its own. You don't say, "Oh gee, I think I can see the future now."

It's a fallacy that you can get something for nothing. If you have the talent and you work

3.199 *Darth Vader's transformation is complete. George Lucas: "When watching the films in the right order, you get the thrill of finding out that Anakin becomes Darth Vader, so it's a big surprise."*
3.200 *Preparing to shoot a close-up of Christensen receiving the helmet as Lucas (bottom left) oversees proceedings. Note that the set's flooring is the logo of the Galactic Empire.*

"I wanted to hint that the mask was painful to wear, with lots of pointy things that poke Vader as it interfaces with him."
Ryan Church / Concept Design Supervisor

3.201

hard, then you'll achieve something. But if you have the talent and you don't work hard, you won't.

Paul Duncan The landing platform scene when Obi-Wan says how proud he is of Anakin echoes the scene in *Return of the Jedi*, which is also on the landing platform, where Luke says, well, "I know there is good in you." He has faith in his father.

George Lucas There is a strain of faith running through the whole thing. When you're in this position as a mentor, whether you're an actual father or not, this person is your charge, but you have no control over how they're going to use that knowledge.

Paul Duncan There is faith and hope and charity in that whole exchange.

George Lucas Nothing is set in stone, especially with the next generation. You hope they'll turn out okay, you hope they do the right things, you hope you raised them right, and all that stuff. But there's no guarantee

3.202

3.201 *Erik Tiemens's concept for the funeral entourage returning Padmé's body to Naboo (February 6, 2003). Tiemens: "I had some conceptual dialogue with Iain McCaig, who had some 19th-century reference of a ship going to an island. George wanted me to cool down the colors to more of a dawn."*
3.202 *Iain McCaig's concept for Padmé's burial dress, which earned a "Fabulouso" from Lucas (May 5, 2003).*
3.203 *Final frame of the two Sith Lords.*
3.204 *Ryan Church's concept artwork for the construction of the Death Star shows spherical building ships (June 13, 2003). Church: "George didn't buy the building ships for scale reasons, so they were revised."*

3.203

of anything. You never know what's going to happen. That's the challenge. And that's the drama, which has gone through history. It's all about what are they going to turn into.

Paul Duncan Even if you don't know how it's going to turn out, you still carry on mentoring because you have to live with hope.

George Lucas Hope and faith. I have faith that it's going to turn out all right. I hope it'll turn out all right. But either way, it's the same.

"Nobody thinks of themselves as bad, not even the worst people, and they rationalize their behavior to say that we are doing good by killing all these people."
George Lucas

3.204

3.205

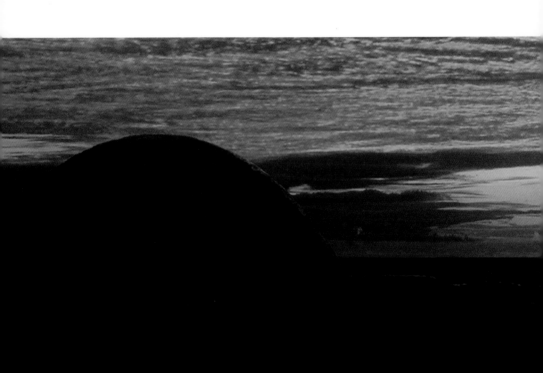

"Star Wars *is not a simple morality play; it has to do with the powers of life as they are either fulfilled or broken and suppressed through the action of man.*"

Joseph Campbell

3.205 *Final frame showing Leia's adoption by Bail Organa and his wife Breha (Rebecca Jackson Mendoza). Bail pledged that "she will be loved by us." John Knoll: "We see a couple of wide vistas of the Alderaan cruiser approaching the city and landing. Then we see Bail Organa bringing in Leia. That entire Alderaan set was about eight feet of bench — that was it."*
3.206 *Final frame showing Uncle Owen Lars (Joel Edgerton) and Aunt Beru Lars (Bonnie Piesse) cradling baby Luke in their arms as the twin suns set over Tatooine. Erik Tiemens: "The movies become autobiographical in certain respects. I went on honeymoon to Tahiti with my wife and there was this spectacular sunset. I shot a panoramic and they ended up using the clouds for the digimatte with the twin suns."*

3.206

Acknowledgments

Thanks to publisher Benedikt Taschen, who has allowed me to delve once more into the archives to find the light, and to everyone at TASCHEN, who have worked tirelessly to make this book the best that it can be: Josh Baker and Jessica Sappenfield in design; Kathrin Murr and Pimploy Phongsirivech in editorial; Stefan Klatte in production; proofreaders Aaron Bogart and Thea Miklowski; and typesetter Marcus Steinwasser. Thanks also to Colin Odell and Michelle Le Blanc for all their scrupulous help organizing the quotes and preparing preliminary draft chapters.

When I started writing, I had very little understanding about the technical aspects of digital cinema. Michael Rubin has minutely documented the early age of digital at Lucasfilm in his book *Droidmaker*, and three books by Thomas G. Smith, Mark Cotta Vaz, and Pamela Glintenkamp cover digital at ILM.

We have been aided by a large number of people around the world, who I would like to thank: Larry Cuba, Tom McMahon (formerly of Triple-I), Thomas Martin, and Aaron McBride for their help with information and with sourcing images.

At Disney Worldwide Publishing Daniel Saeva, Angela M. Ontiveros, Stephanie L. Everett, and Ashley W. Leonard guided us through the approval process.

As ever, it was tremendous fun to visit Lucasfilm at the Presidio in San Francisco to look through all the original photography with the help of the Asset Management team — Nicole LaCoursiere, Jackey Cabrera, Gabrielle Levenson, and Kelly Jensen — although they did keep me locked up in a room monitored by Gamorrean guards. Michael Siglain, Robert Simpson, Troy Alders, and Samantha Holland at Lucasfilm Publishing made me most welcome and made sure the project ran smoothly. At the approval stage it was all hands on deck at Lucasfilm with everybody lending their expertise and knowledge to make sure it was as error-free as possible, and for that I'd also like to thank Chris Argyropoulos, Mike Blanchard, Leland Chee, Lynne Hale, Pablo Hidalgo, Kate Izquierdo, Lucas Seastrom, J. Schulte, Kelsey Sharpe, Phil Szostak, and Peter Vilmur.

The original concept art, storyboards, and production documents are housed on the Skywalker Ranch in the wilds of Marin County. Kimberley Mathis, Aileen Sweeney, and MacKenzie O'Brien made me feel very welcome at the Inn. Liz Stanley, Katharine Allen, and Annie Bukowski at the Lucasfilm Archives kept me locked up in cold storage to go through the production documents and occasionally allowed me to run free with the wild turkeys. Laela French, Alina Campbell, Kathy Smeaton, Adele Barbato, Jordan Wong, and Karissa Huerzeler at the Lucas Museum gave me the time and space to go through all the concept art and storyboards, while Miki Bulos at the Lucas Research Library kept me underground with filing cabinets and boxes full of documents and clippings (with the occasional visit by a curious lizard).

Since this book deals specifically with the development of digital cinema, George Lucas thought it would be a good idea for me to talk to some of the pioneers who made it happen, so I would like to thank Mike Blanchard, Ben Burtt, Doug Chiang, Ryan Church, John Knoll, Rick McCallum, Fred Meyers, Dennis Muren, David Tattersall, and Erik Tiemens for taking the time to tell me their fascinating stories for this book.

Over the course of the past two years, Connie Wethington and Kristine Kolton in George Lucas's office have made sure that I had full access to everything I needed on the Ranch.

The structure of the book follows George Lucas's struggle to develop and then push digital cinema into the mainstream, but it also traces his battle to integrate his underlying philosophy into the prequel trilogy. Once again I am indebted to George for kindly allowing me additional time with him so that he could explain once more the "why" of *Star Wars*, and these conversations form the nucleus of the book.

This book is dedicated to the memory of F. X. Feeney, the sweetest guy, a great writer, and my best friend.

Image Credits

Lucasfilm hired unit photographers to take stills on set, as well as "special photographers" to do shoots for magazine, posters, and formal portraits. ILM staff also made a visual record of their work. I'm happy to credit them here:

Episode I: *The Phantom Menace* (1999): Keith Hamshere (1st Unit), Jonathan Fisher, Bill Kaye, Giles Keyte, Jay Maidment, ILM: Sean Casey, Alex Ivanov, David Owen.

Episode II: *Attack of the Clones* (2003): Lisa Tomasetti (1st Unit), Sue Adler (1st Unit), Keith Hamshere (Special), Barry Clack, Evelyn Rose, Paul Tiller, Giles Wesley, Ianna White.

Episode III: *Revenge of the Sith* (2005): Merrick Morton (1st Unit), Ralph Nelson Jr. (1st Unit), Keith Hamshere (Special), Frank Ockenfels (Special), Frankie Malhotra, Paul Tiller.

All *Star Wars* images in the book are copyright Lucasfilm Ltd., and all *Star Wars* images and production documents were sourced from Lucasfilm Ltd., Lucas Museum of Narrative Art, and Lucas Research Library. Used under authorization. All rights reserved.

**A.1 The Phantom Menace *(1999)*
George Lucas directing Jake Lloyd
in Tunisia.**

Imprint

EACH AND EVERY TASCHEN BOOK PLANTS A SEED!
TASCHEN is a carbon neutral publisher. Each year, we offset our annual carbon emissions with carbon credits at the Instituto Terra, a reforestation program in Minas Gerais, Brazil, founded by Lélia and Sebastião Salgado. To find out more about this ecological partnership, please check: www.taschen.com/zerocarbon
Inspiration: unlimited. Carbon footprint: zero.

To stay informed about TASCHEN and our upcoming titles, please subscribe to our free magazine at www.taschen.com/magazine, follow us on Instagram and Facebook, or e-mail your questions to contact@taschen.com.

© 2022 TASCHEN GmbH
Hohenzollernring 53, D-50672 Köln
www.taschen.com

Editor Paul Duncan/Wordsmith Solutions

Printed in Bosnia-Herzegovina
ISBN 978-3-8365-9327-4

A.1